Short Histories are authoritative and elegantly written introductory texts which offer fresh perspectives on the way history is taught and understood in the twenty-first century. Designed to have strong appeal to university students and their teachers, as well as to general readers and history enthusiasts, *Short Histories* comprise novel attempts to bring informed interpretation, as well as factual reportage, to historical debates. Addressing key subjects and topics in the fields of history, the history of ideas, religion, classical studies, politics, philosophy and Middle East studies, these texts move beyond the bland, neutral 'introductions' that so often serve as the primary undergraduate teaching tool. While always providing students and generalists with the core facts that they need to get to grips with, *Short Histories* go further. They offer new insights into how a topic has been understood in the past, and what different social and cultural factors might have been at work. They bring original perspectives to bear on current interpretations. They raise questions and – with extensive bibliographies – point the reader to further study, even as they suggest answers. Each text addresses a variety of subjects in a greater degree of depth than is often found in comparable series, yet at the same time in a concise and compact handbook form. *Short Histories* aim to be 'introductions with an edge'. In combining questioning and searching analysis with informed historical writing, they bring history up-to-date for an increasingly complex and globalized digital age.

For more information about titles and authors in the series, please visit: https://www.bloomsbury.com/series/short-histories/

A Short History of ...

the American Civil War	Paul Anderson (Clemson University)
the American Revolutionary War	Stephen Conway (University College London)
Ancient China	Edward L Shaughnessy (University of Chicago)
Ancient Greece	P J Rhodes, FBA (Durham University)
the Anglo-Saxons	Henrietta Leyser (University of Oxford)
Babylon	Karen Radner (University of Munich)
the Byzantine Empire	Dionysios Stathakopoulos (King's College London)
Christian Spirituality	Edward Howells (Heythrop College, University of London)
Communism	Kevin Morgan (University of Manchester)
the Crimean War	Trudi Tate (University of Cambridge)
English Renaissance Drama	Helen Hackett (University College London)
the English Revolution and the Civil Wars	David J Appleby (University of Nottingham)
the Etruscans	Corinna Riva (University College London)
Florence and the Florentine Republic	Brian Jeffrey Maxson (East Tennessee State University)
the Hundred Years War	Michael Prestwich (Durham University)
Irish Independence	J J Lee (New York University)
the Italian Renaissance	Virginia Cox (New York University)
the Korean War	Allan R Millett (University of New Orleans)
Medieval Christianity	G R Evans (University of Cambridge)
Medieval English Mysticism	Vincent Gillespie (University of Oxford)
the Minoans	John Bennet (University of Sheffield)

the Mongols	George Lane (SOAS, University of London)

the Mughal Empire	Michael H Fisher (Oberlin College)

Muslim Spain	Amira K Bennison (University of Cambridge)

New Kingdom Egypt	Robert Morkot (University of Exeter)

the New Testament	Halvor Moxnes (University of Oslo)

Nineteenth-Century Philosophy	Joel Rasmussen (University of Oxford)

the Normans	Leonie V Hicks (Canterbury Christ Church University)

the Ottoman Empire	Baki Tezcan (University of California, Davis)

the Phoenicians	Mark Woolmer (Durham University)

the Reformation	Helen L Parish (University of Reading)

the Renaissance in Northern Europe	Malcolm Vale (University of Oxford)

Revolutionary Cuba	Antoni Kapcia (University of Nottingham)

the Risorgimento	Nick Carter (Australian Catholic University, Sydney)

the Russian Revolution	Geoffrey Swain (University of Glasgow)

the Spanish Civil War	Julián Casanova (University of Zaragoza)

the Spanish Empire	Felipe Fernández-Armesto (University of Notre Dame) and José Juan López-Portillo (University of Oxford)

Transatlantic Slavery	Kenneth Morgan (Brunel University London)

the Tudors	Richard Rex (University of Cambridge)

Venice and the Venetian Empire	Maria Fusaro (University of Exeter)

the Vikings	Clare Downham (University of Liverpool)

the Wars of the Roses	David Grummitt (University of Kent)

the Weimar Republic	Colin Storer (University of Nottingham)

A SHORT HISTORY OF THE RENAISSANCE IN NORTHERN EUROPE

Malcolm Vale

BLOOMSBURY ACADEMIC

LONDON · NEW YORK · OXFORD · NEW DELHI · SYDNEY

BLOOMSBURY ACADEMIC
Bloomsbury Publishing Plc
50 Bedford Square, London, WC1B 3DP, UK
1385 Broadway, New York, NY 10018, USA

BLOOMSBURY, BLOOMSBURY ACADEMIC and the Diana logo are
trademarks of Bloomsbury Publishing Plc

First published in Great Britain 2020

A catalogue record for this book is available from the British Library.

A catalog record for this book is available from the Library of Congress.

ISBN: HB: 978-1-7807-6384-2
PB: 978-1-7807-6385-9
ePDF: 978-1-3501-4563-4
eBook: 978-1-3501-4561-0

Series: Short Histories

Typeset by Deanta Global Publishing Services, Chennai, India
Printed and bound in Great Britain

To find out more about our authors and books visit www.bloomsbury.com
and sign up for our newsletters.

For Anne

Contents

Figures

Acknowledgements

My thanks are first of all owed to Alex Wright for inviting me, more years ago than I care to remember, to write this book. His patience, which must have been sorely tried at times, was exemplary, and the encouragement that he has given has kept me at work on a task that has proved far more difficult than I had anticipated. The aim of a series of this kind not to produce a 'bland neutral introduction' is a challenge to any writer. I hope that this book will ask – and attempt to answer – searching questions from less conventional standpoints than those often adopted when considering a period's art, literature and thought as a whole rather than as separate entities. I am also indebted to many friends, colleagues and former students for their help and advice. In particular, a seminar course which I ran in Oxford with Gervase Rosser on 'Flanders and Italy in the fifteenth century' helped to stimulate and test some of the ideas behind the book. Hannah Skoda has read sections of the book in draft and offered some very helpful comments. Cristina Dondi kindly read the chapter on printing. I have had productive conversations on the subject with Patrick Lantschner. My college, St John's, has enabled me to continue researching and writing in retirement by generously electing me to an Emeritus Research Fellowship. My thanks also go to the staffs of the Bodleian Library, the Library of St John's College, Oxford, and the Special Collections of the John Rylands Library, University of Manchester, for their unfailing help. Anne Wheeler has read much of the book in draft, and has been a patient listener, as well as an admirably constructive and objective critic. My thanks are also owed to Joanna Godfrey, Olivia Dellow, Rennie Alphonsa and the production team at Bloomsbury. All views expressed, and any errors and omissions which may remain, are entirely my responsibility.

Malcolm Vale
Oxford, July 2019

Timeline

1384 Philip the Bold, Duke of Burgundy, succeeds to the counties of Flanders and Artois.

1395 Claus Sluter begins construction of the Moses fountain at the Charterhouse of Champmol.

1406 Death of Claus Sluter.

1416 Limburg brothers complete the illumination of the *Tres Riches Heures* of Jean, Duke of Berry.

1419 Duke Philip the Good succeeds to the Burgundian dominions.

1427 Thomas Kempis's *Imitation of Christ* completed.

1432 *Ghent Altarpiece* completed by the Van Eycks.

1434 *Arnolfini* double portrait painted by Jan van Eyck.
Cosimo de Medici becomes ruler of Florence.
Brunelleschi completes the Dome of Florence cathedral.

1435 Leon Battista Alberti's treatise *On Painting*.
Rolin altarpiece painted by Jan van Eyck.

1441 Death of Jan van Eyck.

1444 Death of Robert Campin.

1450 Rogier van der Weyden completes the Last Judgement altarpiece in the Hotel-Dieu at Beaune.

1455 Gutenberg prints the Bible at Mainz.

1461 Death of Charles VII of France and accession of Louis XI.

1464 Death of Rogier van der Weyden.
Death of Cosimo de Medici.

1467 Death of Philip the Good. Charles the Bold succeeds to the Burgundian dominions.

1471 Death of Thomas Kempis.

1474 Death of the composer Guillaume Dufay.

1478 Hugo van der Goes completes the *Portinari Altarpiece*.
1475 William Caxton produces the first book printed in English.
      Death of Dieric Bouts.
1477 Death of Charles the Bold, Duke of Burgundy, at the Battle of
      Nancy.
      The Habsburg Archduke Maximilian of Austria marries Mary
      of Burgundy.
1479 Memling's *Two St John's Altarpiece* completed at Bruges.
1481 Death of Jean Fouquet.
1482 Death of Mary of Burgundy.
      Philip the Fair, son of Maximilian and Mary of Burgundy,
      inherits the Burgundian lands.
      Death of Hugo van der Goes.
1486 Maximilian, Archduke of Austria, succeeds as king of the Romans.
1490 Aldus Manutius founds the Aldine Press at Venice.
1491 Death of Martin Schongauer.
1492 Christopher Columbus sails to the New World.
1493 Maximilian succeeds to Holy Roman Empire as Maximilian I.
1494 Death of Hans Memling at Bruges.
      Sebastian Brant's *Ship of Fools* published.
      Charles VIII of France invades Italy.
1498 Philip the Fair marries Joanna of Castile.
1506 Philip the Fair succeeds to the throne of Castile.
1507 Margaret of Austria appointed governor of the Netherlands.
1509 Erasmus's *Praise of Folly* first published.
1516 Erasmus's Latin translation of the New Testament published at
      Basel.
      Death of Hieronymus Bosch.
1517 Martin Luther's *Ninety-five Theses* published at Wittenberg.
1519 Death of Maximilian I and accession of Charles V to the Holy
      Roman Empire.
1521 Death of Sebastian Brant.
1522 Luther's German translation of the New Testament published at
      Wittenberg.
1523 Death of Gerard David.
1526 William Tyndale's English translation of the New Testament
      published at Worms.
1528 Death of Mathias Grunewald.
      Death of Albrecht Durer.
1531 Henry VIII becomes supreme head of the Church in England.

1533   Death of Lucas van Leyden.
1536   Death of Erasmus.
         Dissolution of the monasteries in England.
1538   Death of Albrecht Altdorfer.
1543   Death of Hans Holbein the Younger.
1553   Death of Lucas Cranach the Elder.
1558   Death of the Emperor Charles V.

Introduction

The 'Renaissance in Northern Europe' may, for some, prove a puzzling title. The concept of a 'Renaissance' in the arts, in thought and in more general culture north of the Alps often evokes the idea of a cultural transplant which was not indigenous to, nor rooted in, the society from which it emerged. Classic definitions of the European 'Renaissance' during the fourteenth, fifteenth and sixteenth centuries have seen it as what was, in effect, an Italian import into the Gothic North. The present book, however, adopts some rather different approaches. First of all, it is written from the point of view of a later medieval historian, rather than a specifically Renaissance or early modern specialist. Second, it is *not* a history of the impact and influence of the Italian Renaissance on the world which lay on the other side of the Alps. Many studies and textbooks have dealt with that important theme. The approach adopted here does not therefore give pride of place to the reception and adaptation of ideas and practices originally born in Renaissance Italy as they manifested themselves in later medieval and early modern Northern Europe. It is to that extent, perhaps, not what many readers might expect from its title. The 'Renaissance in Northern Europe', I argue, was not simply a result of the introduction, transfer or transplant of Italian humanism, artistic influence and its offshoots into the North. While, quite justifiably, historians have looked to classical antiquity as the inspiration for so much of what we associate with the *Italian* Renaissance, this book – while in no way ignoring or diminishing the importance of the Hellenic and Roman legacy – seeks other sources, and different uses of classical antiquity, for a rather different kind of 'Renaissance', if such it was, in the North. The very concept of a Renaissance, especially if applied outside its traditional birthplace and cradle, namely Italy and the city of Florence, demands some explanation and the use of the term some justification. Chapter 1 attempts to do this. One purpose of this series of Short Histories is to offer 'new insights into how a topic has been understood in the past, and what different social and cultural factors might have been at work' (see p. i). Hence a concentration on the historiography of the Renaissance concept and its changing nature over the centuries is a marked feature of the book. I make no apology for setting out and assessing the approaches taken by past cultural historians of great stature, such as Burckhardt or Huizinga, as a vital element in, and starting point for, all subsequent work on the subject. Such is the fragmented nature and highly specialized approach of much current interpretation of the period, especially in the field of art history and the history of the book, that it is regrettably difficult to include references to as many of its more recent products as one might wish in a general survey of this kind. One contention of this book is that the arts are a product not simply of the creativity of individuals, working within certain defined media, producing objects and artefacts with what might be seen as having a free-standing history and purpose of their own. It is argued here that artistic creations are not only historical documents but also products of the cultures and societies in which they were conceived. The autonomy of a certain kind of art history, in which visual and material objects seem to live an existence almost independent of historical contexts and developments, is therefore not endorsed in this book. Of course the work of art is not a mere 'illustration', or even a kind of photograph, of certain features of a given historical period. But it can be seen as part of the evidence which, if properly interpreted, forms a vital source for the historian and itself becomes an expression, even an embodiment, of the ideas, beliefs, illusions, fantasies and aspirations of those who inhabited the later medieval and early Renaissance worlds.

The present chapter will therefore attempt to briefly set the scene and offer a scenario for the cultural and other developments with which we shall be concerned. It is important, as always, to establish a context, or contexts, for the intellectual, religious, artistic, literary, musical and other more broadly cultural movements which took place within a given civilization. The social, political, economic and material infrastructure of Northern Europe at this period is therefore not irrelevant to the aims and purposes of the cultural historian.

To explain such cultural phenomena as 'Renaissances', historians have not only employed metaphors about 'rebirths', 'dawns', 'flowerings', 'awakenings' and so forth but also tended to set up antitheses, opposites and polarities. They can, after all, be useful interpretative tools. To be 'reborn' (Renaissance: 'rebirth') instantly gives rise to comparison and contrast, because what has gone before a regeneration can be as significant as what follows. What *is* it that is reborn and how does it differ from the immediate – and less immediate – past? This antithesis has left an indelible mark on the study of later medieval and Renaissance culture. Its study has often tended – quite justifiably – to be determined by the drawing of contrasts, the setting up of dichotomies and the making of comparisons, not least between Southern and Northern Europe. Above all, those artificial constructs of historians, critics and connoisseurs – 'late medieval' and 'early modern', 'Gothic' and 'Renaissance', 'courtly' and 'civic' – have been applied to the study of both aristocratic and urban societies in Europe between the later fourteenth and early to mid-sixteenth centuries. We have to consider the contexts, economic, political, religious, social, urban and courtly, in which this culture developed. A major determinant of much artistic expression, in both princely courts and in cities was, it is argued, the devotional, liturgical and pastoral practices of the Church: I outline, in Chapters 2 and 4, the main currents of devotional sentiment and practice, and assess the extent to which they affected the arts. From 1378 until 1417 the Western Church was in a state of schism, and the period from then on until the first stirrings, in the early 1520s, of the Protestant Reformation in the North was one in which papal authority was very slowly, but only partially, restored, while the ideas of reformers and critics, both radical and moderate, found expression in much of the literature, and some of the art, of the age. A major theme of any survey of Northern European culture at this time must also address the question of humanism, its nature, origins and the manner in which thinkers accepted or rejected its tenets and beliefs. This is considered in Chapter 3. The so-called communications revolution or information technology revolution produced by the advent of new techniques, above all that of printing with movable type, from the mid-fifteenth century onwards, and the wider dissemination of both written texts and images which it enabled are addressed in Chapter 5. An increasing tendency to express religious and many other ideas in vernacular languages, as well as in the Latin of the Church and the humanists, was apparent at this time, to which printing contributed, and this is also considered in Chapter 5. Finally, Chapter 6, 'Wisdom, Folly and the Darker Vision', introduces themes which were of profound concern to contemporaries and which produced both satirical and didactic writings, often accompanied by images exemplified by the art of, among others, Hieronymus Bosch. The Conclusion attempts to draw the main strands together and argue for a type of Renaissance in Northern Europe which, while certainly sharing some characteristics with Italian developments, had distinct qualities and attributes of its own. A Timeline (pp. xiv–xvi) has also been included, to give a chronological outline to the period, listing events in Northern Europe, but also in Italy and elsewhere for purposes of contrast and comparison.

A brief overview of the period may help to orientate the reader and set some of the themes referred to above into perspective. This book tends to challenge a traditional periodization of the Northern Renaissance which places it between the late fifteenth and early seventeenth centuries. The relatively recently founded *The Journal of the Northern Renaissance* (2009), for instance, still concentrates largely on that period, extending it well into the seventeenth century.

The present book's chronological range adopts a different time span, running from *c.* 1380 to *c.* 1540, although such divisions of historical time can, especially in the case of art history and cultural history, only be very approximate.[1] We are often told that this was an 'age of transition' from the later medieval to the early modern world. But the very terms 'later medieval' and 'early modern' or 'Renaissance' immediately set up polarities: the former ('later medieval'), for some, has conjured up a world of outmoded feudalism, decadent chivalry, an institutionalized, moralizing, devotional religion, a collapse of older, universal authorities such as the Holy Roman Empire or the papacy, and the early burgeoning of warring, competitive monarchical nation states. The latter ('Renaissance'), for others, has conveyed a vision of a kind of golden age, that of Dante (1265–1321), Giotto (1266–1337), Petrarch (1304–74), Masaccio (1401–28), Botticelli (*c.* 1445–1510) and Leonardo da Vinci (1452–1519), an increasingly secularized world picture, an intellectual humanism replete with allusions to the classical past and a thriving city-state culture, giving way to the rise of princely despotisms and the splendour of the Renaissance court. That picture was derived largely from the study of the city of Florence. In the popular mind, guided today largely by the media, the Gothic North has tended, with a few exceptions, to be placed firmly in a 'later medieval', not a 'Renaissance' context. Not, that is, until the effects of Italian-derived and Italian-influenced artistic styles were fully felt in the North after *c.* 1490. The great German artist Albrecht Durer's visits to Italy (1494–5, 1505–7) are both significant and symbolic in this respect, but their influence may have been exaggerated. Yet this view has not gone entirely unchallenged, even outside the world of specialist scholarship. A press review of a 1992 exhibition of the art of Andrea Mantegna (1431–1506), court painter to the Gonzaga of Mantua, at the Royal Academy, London, implicitly attacked what the reviewer regarded as a false dichotomy. He observed: 'One of the chief lessons of this show lies in its demonstration of how clumsy and falsifying such generic terms as "Gothic" and "Renaissance" really are.'[2] The point was made even more strongly in the catalogue of an exhibition held in 2001 of the work of the Italian painter and medallist Antonio Pisanello (*c.* 1394–1455). Pisanello's essentially aristocratic, chivalrically inspired yet also classically influenced, works prompted the view that

> we have been taught to view Italian Renaissance art through Florentine-tinted glasses, as monumental, 'realistic', reviving classical forms and focused on the human figure. Pisanello introduces us to an alternative, imaginative, more inclusive, Renaissance.[3]

That alternative Renaissance has now begun to command more attention, seeking to set both Northern and Southern European art into a more convincing context and interpretative scheme. Yet there were certainly differences, divergences and dichotomies between North and South which have to be addressed. This book argues for a Northern Renaissance which, while cognizant of Italian developments, displayed strong continuities with the indigenous cultures of Northern Europe. But it also contributed novelties and innovations which often tended to stem from, and build upon, those continuities. The material, economic and social underpinning of that cultural phenomenon now requires a brief survey.

THE URBAN CONTEXT

Although the great majority of the European population during this period lived and worked in the countryside, urban growth had been a feature of the Western economy since at least the later twelfth century. Demographic increase came to an end in the fourteenth century, with the onset of plague and famine, especially after the eruption of the Black Death in 1348. Despite these shocks and setbacks, a number of sizeable cities are thought to have become independent, to varying degrees, of external political control. And it was from the towns that much of the cultural life of this period stemmed. Between 1300 and 1500, it is argued, a marked contrast could be observed between city life and culture and that of the surrounding regions, dominated as they were by both ecclesiastical and secular feudal lords. Politically, the dominant form of government was monarchy and princely rule, often contested by nobles who could rival, and who were sometimes powerful enough to overthrow, monarchical rule. In the densely urbanized areas of both Northern Italy and the Low Countries, a constant state of tension between 'trade and territory, cities and monarchs' has been identified. The dichotomy is complete: on the one hand, we have the independent, self-governing city, with its own values and culture; on the other, the prince with, it is argued, his predominantly rural power base, his apparatus of government, itinerant court, administration and taxation, his 'chivalric' culture and authoritarian image vigilantly (but sometimes unsuccessfully) upholding his rights against the claims of feudal franchise and urban liberty. Now this picture is, of course, overdrawn. Alliances and mutual agreements between princes and – at least – the upper classes or patriciates of the cities and towns of their dominions were common. But the sturdy burghers of Ghent, Bruges, Bern, Lubeck, Augsburg and Nuremberg were seen fulfilling a similar role to the citizens of the surviving Italian republics of Florence, Venice and Genoa. To some nineteenth-century historians, the towns upheld the defence of liberty and independence against feudal and ecclesiastical oppression and foreign domination – French, Spanish or Austrian. Historians such as Sismondi in Italy and Pirenne in Belgium concurred in tracing the origins of liberty, unity and democracy to the thirteenth- and fourteenth-century towns in their respective countries.

Other, more recent, approaches – for example, to the economic history of the period – also tend to emphasize the fundamental importance of towns. A shift in the economic centre of gravity within Europe favoured certain towns at the expense of others. From the mid-to-later fifteenth century onwards, the rise of Antwerp, Amsterdam, Augsburg or Nuremberg, while Florence and other Italian cities tended to decline, meant that the economic centre was moving northwards. The Fuggers of Augsburg, flourishing from the 1480s onwards, supplanted the Medici of Florence as the greatest bankers and moneylenders to the ruling houses of Europe – especially to the emperors Maximilian I and Charles V. Within the North, regional changes were also taking place, as Bruges declined and other centres, in Flanders, Brabant and Holland, took its place. In both Northern and Southern Europe, moreover, a decline in the costs of foodstuffs after the mid-fourteenth-century epidemics gave rise to a shift of emphasis towards manufactured goods in the Western European economy. These goods were often produced for export and longer-distance trade, as well as for inter-regional commerce. This inevitably benefited the towns, rather than the countryside, as centres of production and distribution. Exceptions must of course be made for rural industries (especially in the manufacture of cloth and in mining of minerals, precious metals, etc.). Newly discovered and exploited silver mines, for instance, before the advent of silver from the New World, played an important part in increasing monetary circulation at this time. But voyages of exploration to both Africa and the Far East, and the setting up of trading posts and settlements there, had already begun to widen the base of the European economy by 1500.

The attempts of rulers to exert greater degrees of control over the more densely urbanized areas of Europe suggest that the greatest concentrations of wealth, and hence the wherewithal and resources with which to patronize arts, crafts and letters, now lay in the towns. This was one of the many consequences of what has been called the 'long thirteenth century', dated by economic and monetary historians from the 1160s to the 1330s. One result of this process was that both rulers and nobles were increasingly freed from the necessity of living in the countryside. They were progressively less dependent on direct consumption of produce from their rural estates and demesnes, received more or less on the spot, thereby determining their itineraries. They no longer had to eat their way from one rural estate to the next. When the amount of yield from their landholdings which they received in money rents, taxes and cash returns substantially began to increase, it was easier for them to gravitate towards the towns, where so much was for sale. The town could also serve as a collecting and distributing point for produce from a ruler's rural estates. The picture should not be overdrawn, because many rulers still relied upon 'purveyances' in kind as well as monetary receipts. Yet this gradual process of liberation from the necessity of residing in the countryside enabled both rulers and those who surrounded them, and made up their courts, to spend at least some of the year in cities and towns, occupying town houses or urban fortresses close to the prince's residence. This was as much a characteristic of Italy and Spain as it was of Northern Europe. Greater liquidity, expressed by accelerations in the flow of silver and consequent monetary circulation, meant that princes and nobles could spend more lavishly on luxury goods and pursuits, within an urban setting, and the rise of credit facilities in the course of the thirteenth century (mainly, but not exclusively, after the expulsion of the Jews in many countries, the preserve of Italian merchants, bankers and financiers) simply furthered this 'urbanization' of life in many areas. The town, in the words of Jacques Le Goff, became an even more vital 'agent of civilization' in the later Middle Ages than it had been at earlier periods.

But when we refer to 'urbanization' during this period, what do we really mean and what were its cultural consequences? The citation of raw estimates of population can be of some help but does not tell the whole story. For example, demographic increase did not necessarily produce cultural hegemony: both Ghent and Genoa (neither selected by historians as in the first league of leading sources of cultural patronage) had large populations. Ghent's estimated population in *c.* 1350 was 60,000, while Genoa's total agglomeration housed about 120,000 in the fifteenth century.[4] Bruges, on the other hand, had a mere 35,000 in *c.* 1340; Siena an estimated 30,000 before the Black Death. The middle-sized and smaller towns therefore had an important part to play in the growth of urban-centred artistic production over this period. But, this said, we can form some impression of *degrees* of urbanization, or the extent to which people actually lived in towns. It is believed that, in 1500, 154 European towns had at least 10,000 inhabitants. The highest 'urban potential' value of all (in terms of size and spread of the city, the proximity of other large towns, and the ease of travelling between them) was held by Venice. After that, according to the economic historian Jan de Vries, the areas of highest urban potential lay in Northern Italy (Milan, Genoa, Florence and Venice as major centres); the Northern and Southern Netherlands (Antwerp, Bruges, Ghent, Brussels, Amsterdam and Rotterdam as centres, with Lille, Tournai, Leiden and Dordrecht on the periphery); and the city of Naples with its immediate surroundings. Below these three privileged regions came (at some distance) the Paris area, the Rhineland, Northern France, Southeast England and the Rome-Naples-Palermo axis. The lowest ratings were scored by Portugal, Castile, Scandinavia, Celtic Britain and Eastern Europe. This was the picture in 1500 and, despite the ravages of plague in the mid-fourteenth century, the position had not perhaps been so very different (in terms of orders of magnitude) in 1300.

So the map of urbanization in the later Middle Ages has certain correspondences with the map of cultural development and artistic production. Towns exerted a magnetic attraction. It was felt not only by those immigrant labourers who made up some of the workforces for the Flemish and Florentine cloth and silk looms but also by nobles, clergy (after all, many of these towns were the seat of bishoprics) and, above all – in view of its evident cultural effects – by princes. If political power was becoming more urbanized, artistic and cultural developments increasingly took place in an urban context. The monastery, often set in the countryside, which had in the early Middle Ages been a major centre for literary and artistic production, was becoming at least partially eclipsed by secular, urban-based sources. The history of manuscript production and illumination admirably demonstrated this tendency. As we shall see, the princely court was also of vital importance to cultural developments. By gravitating towards the towns of a ruler's dominions, it served to link (or at least juxtapose) the power centre of princely rule with the cities and towns. Of course there were many tensions between courts and cities, perhaps increasingly so over this period. But there were also contacts, influences and mutual exchanges which make too sharp a polarity between 'court' culture and 'city' culture essentially misleading. This artificial distinction has to some extent been perpetuated by some recent work in art history, which sees 'merchant' or 'bourgeois' artistic patronage and production as distinct from its 'courtly' equivalents. This is perhaps to misunderstand the social and political composition of many patrician- and oligarchy-dominated cities and towns in Northern Europe. Within many a burgher a nobleman was often trying (and succeeding) to get out. Nobility, depending upon the given region, its social and legal structures and traditions, could in effect be for sale. Any analysis of art patronage and market demand based on inappropriate forms of social classification can therefore be profoundly misleading. The cities of Ghent and Bruges alone, with their noble-burgher families such as the Vijd or Gruuthuse, or Nuremberg and Augsburg, with their patrician dynasties, immediately give the lie to assumptions about the class-based nature of patronage and its effects on artistic production. And very few, if any, artists and craftsmen worked exclusively for courtiers, on the one hand, or burghers on the other. Rogier van der Weyden, at Brussels, would be a prime example. Perhaps there was no such thing as 'court' art, as there was no such thing as 'bourgeois' art? If the meaning of those concepts are so unclear, then it is no less the case for the idea of the court itself.

THE COURTLY CONTEXT

First, we have to establish what the princely court actually was. Sir Geoffrey Elton, writing of the Tudors, asserted that 'the only definition of the court which makes sense … is that it comprised all those who at any given time were within "his grace's house"; and all those with a right to be there were courtiers'. So the court was, at its most basic level, the extended household of the ruler. But it was, or could be, more – or less – than that.

It could be an occasion, convened as a plenary assembly at certain times of the year, corresponding to the liturgical feasts of the Christian year or significant events in the life of a ruling house. It was also simply the space around the ruler, entry to which gave access to the prince's person, thereby potentially conveying political influence and power. It was also a place of residence: the German *Residenzstadt* was the seat of a court and this remained the case for centuries. But there were many members of a prince's household who were certainly not members of a court – especially that tribe of servants and menials who serviced the daily needs of the ruler and his entourage. Nor did all those who had access to the prince's person necessarily have a place in his household: although this was a tendency which became more marked during this period. The court was essentially defined by the presence or absence of the ruler. Its character was in part dictated by that fact. The personal styles of rulers could shape and determine the nature of their courts: the court of Philip the Good, Duke of Burgundy (1419–67), for example, was unlike – if only in its scale – that of Federigo da Montefeltro, Duke of Urbino (1444–82), although they shared some common features. The court of Louis XI of France (1461–83) was unlike that of his exact contemporary Edward IV of England (1461–83), and this was very much the result of differences in personal style. But, behind every medieval and Renaissance court, there was an institutional structure. That structure, a sort of backbone or spine, was provided by household offices: sometimes these were exercised hereditarily and/or honorifically by nobles in the service of the ruler; sometimes the nobility (especially its younger members) served in a domestic capacity themselves as members of the prince's upper household. The increasingly large personnel of carving squires, cup-bearers, esquires of the stable and pantry, as well as the greater officers such as steward (or seneschal), constable, marshal, first chamberlain and grand master of the household, served to enlist the service of nobles and their kinsmen (especially in the Burgundian lands, the German empire and, increasingly, among the Italian princes). Even within the lower household – the sphere of the servants of the prince – offices were distributed which included those held by artists, sculptors, musicians and artisans. Jan van Eyck was a *valet de chambre* (chamber valet) to Philip the Good of Burgundy, and other artists, sculptors, musicians and painters held similar positions, some described as that of court painter. As a vehicle of cultural patronage, the court thus played a fundamental role in this period.

That role was shared with the city and the town. Although the concept of a specifically 'bourgeois culture' is highly questionable, there is certainly plenty of evidence for sentiments of civic pride and independence. During the fifteenth century, moreover, the decline of Italian city-republics in favour of princely despotisms was not echoed in Northern Europe. The privileged 'imperial' cities of Germany, the Flemish and Dutch towns, the Hanseatic urban league, the greater of the *bonnes villes* of France, and the ports of Scandinavia all possessed a distinct identity of their own and a flourishing cultural, as well as commercial, life. It was a period of increasing wealth for many urban patriciates in the North. But, as we have seen, these were by no means solely 'bourgeois' social and political structures. Many of the members of urban patriciates and governing classes were either already noble or aspired to nobility. The phenomenon of the town-dwelling noble, linked to his peers by a network of both kinship and business, but often also in possession of rural lordships, was well known across Northern Europe, from the North Sea coast to the Eastern shores of the Baltic, and from South Germany to the Slavonic borderlands. And the surviving evidence from the more urbanized regions of Northern France, the Low Countries and the German-speaking lands suggests that, in political terms, contrasts between city independence and princely power can be overdrawn. So can the disparities between 'courtly' and 'civic' culture. There was a degree of reciprocity between court and city. Throughout Europe, the spheres of 'courtly' and 'civic' culture may, therefore, have to be redrawn by future historical enquiry. That there was a considerable degree of overlap is at least arguable. The proximity of the ruler's court to a city or town – at Paris, Westminster, Brussels, Bruges, Ghent, Lille, Mons, The Hague, Milan, Ferrara, Mantua, Naples, Prague, Vienna, Nuremberg, Krakow, Buda, Innsbruck – became an increasingly marked feature of both political and cultural life. The resources of the towns were critical for the elaborate styles of court life which developed during this period to be sustained. What we see in the fifteenth century is merely one, highly developed, version of those lifestyles. The towns increasingly held the credit facilities, the banking houses (both indigenous and Italian), the luxury tradespeople, the craftsmen, artists, courtesans, musicians and players that were essential to that mode of life. There were also common aspirations and activities which were to some extent shared by the princes, the nobility and the upper ranks of the citizens. One such activity was the tournament: the place of 'chivalric' culture in this context has also to be reassessed. The patricians and burghers of many cities, including the great German towns of Nuremberg, Regensburg, Cologne or Augsburg, engaged in urban jousts, and the role of town-dwelling nobilities in mediating between court and civic culture remains to be properly studied.

HYPOTHESES

This book proposes a number of hypotheses for the interpretation of Renaissance culture and the applicability, or non-applicability, of the term 'Renaissance' to Northern Europe. Some of these, or versions of them, were first proposed more than a century ago. Others are more recent. The premises upon which the cultural history of this remarkably creative and inventive period have been built have undergone significant revisions, and that process continues. Concepts of evolution, adaptation, shifts of emphasis and eclecticism, rather than radical departures, rifts, stylistic hegemonies, or terminal decay and decline, may more convincingly explain the cultural history of Northern Europe at this time. As this book argues, metaphors which depend on analogies between human civilizations and biological, botanical or seasonal processes – 'flowering', 'awakening', 'waning', 'decaying', 'autumnal' – may exert an alluring power over our imagination but do not always satisfactorily analyse or elucidate the cultural phenomena which we seek to explain. But, that said, they should not be dismissed out of hand. As stimuli to debate, discussion, revision and reconsideration – the lifeblood of ongoing historical enquiry – they have proved their worth.

1

WHAT WAS THE 'NORTHERN RENAISSANCE'?

We are reluctant to acknowledge how medieval the man of the Renaissance really was, the man whom we salute as a superman, the liberator of the individual from the dark prisons of the church. (Aby Warburg, *Flanders and Florence* [1901])[1]

THE CONCEPT OF A RENAISSANCE

To embark on any account of the so-called Renaissance in Northern Europe, we must first attempt to define what we mean by the term 'Renaissance'. The idea of a 'Renaissance' or 'rebirth' (from Fr. *renaitre*, Lat. *renascere*, It. *rinascita*) has been linked to notions of renewal, renovation and sometimes reformation, in many epochs of human history. We hear of a 'Carolingian Renaissance', a 'Twelfth-Century Renaissance', a 'Christian Renaissance', an 'Elizabethan Renaissance' or, most recently (2017), a Franco-German 'renaissance' of the European Union. The Renaissance which is the subject of this book is that which is normally thought to have taken place in Western Europe between the fourteenth and sixteenth centuries. But what was actually 'reborn' during these periods? What, if anything, has prompted the desire to represent an age as one which gave birth to a renewed and reinvigorated world? Is the Renaissance, it has been asked, nothing but a metaphor, which obfuscates rather than illuminates, forming a 'mere figurative intrusion' into historical thought and historiography? But a tendency to lament, often in nostalgic terms, the decline or decay into which a civilization, culture or some aspects of their specific forms were judged to have fallen, can be found in many past – and indeed present – societies. A renewal or revival is awaited. The Renaissance is no exception to this rule. To be 'reborn', something has presumably had to die, or at least to have degenerated and broken down into a condition in which it is either unrecognizable or unacceptable, or both. Rebirth can take place in a religious context – Christian, Buddhist or Hindu – and assume very different forms in each case. A 'born again' Christian, for example, in a Protestant Evangelical context, is one who has experienced a spiritual rebirth or regeneration. Their former, tepid faith has been renewed and reinvigorated by an injection of life-giving fervour, through the tonic of Bible reading, preaching and witnessing, thereby committing them to a new, personal and often emotional relationship with Christ. And Christ's stricture to Nicodemus that 'no one can see the kingdom of God unless they were born again' (Jn 3.3-5) could, for instance, be secularized to apply to a theory of evolution or progress whereby a state of artistic, political or any other degree of perfection – a secular 'kingdom of God' – can ultimately be attained.

But in order for a rebirth to take place, we must know at least something of what had gone before. The 'new' faith can only be understood in contrast to the 'old'. In historical thought about the rise, fall and changing nature of civilizations, cultures or art forms, analogies and metaphors of a pseudo-biological or anthropomorphic kind, attributing to them human or other characteristics, and giving rise to theories of organic development, are common. Civilizations and the arts, it is argued, 'like human bodies, are born, grow up, become old, and die'.[2] The visual arts, literature, music, and other of man's acquired habits and attributes, are all part and parcel of that process. Hence, it is claimed, they undergo transformation through a succession or cycle of births, deaths and rebirths. This metaphorical underpinning of cultural history has, perhaps surprisingly, had a long lifespan. In 1919 the Dutch cultural historian Johan Huizinga (1872–1945), in his masterpiece, *The Waning of the Middle Ages* (perhaps more accurately translated from the Dutch *Herfsttij der Middeleeuwen* as *The Autumn of the Middle Ages*) wrote:

> In history, as in nature, birth and death are equally balanced. The decay of overripe forms of civilisation is as suggestive a spectacle as the growth of new ones. And it occasionally happens that a period in which one had, hitherto, been mainly looking for the coming to birth of new things suddenly reveals itself as an epoch of fading and decay.[3]

Together with seasonal, botanical and even meteorological metaphors, a quasi-biological image has loomed large in cultural history from the sixteenth to the twentieth centuries. Allusions to an 'autumn', a 'dawn', a 'sunset' or a 'flowering' have also not been absent from the titles and texts of books on the declining later Middle Ages and the emergent Renaissance. The 'Renaissance' phenomenon is therefore one product of a tendency to holistically depict whole civilizations within a given period as possessing a biological, seasonal or 'dawn-to-dusk' character. Metaphors which depend on analogies between human civilizations and biological, botanical or seasonal processes may exert a highly stimulating power over our imagination. But they do not always analyse or elucidate the cultural phenomena which we seek to explain.

The perennial question which is usually asked about the European Renaissance is this: What was it that was actually reborn? And at what time, and by what process, was that achieved? A pattern was set in 1568 by the Florentine artist and writer Georgio Vasari (1511–74) in his *Lives of the Artists*. His book has been profoundly influential ever since. Vasari set out to trace the organic development of Italian art – with a few glances outside Italy – in three stages. The first, comprising the beginning of a rebirth of the arts after the demise of Roman civilization in the fifth century AD, followed by a long period of decay, he associated with stylistic innovations by the Italian artists Cimabue (1240–1302) and Giotto (1266–1337) in the later thirteenth and early fourteenth centuries. This was followed by the experiments and achievements of Masaccio (1401–28), Brunelleschi (1387–1446) and Donatello (1386–1466) in the fifteenth century (the Italian *Quattrocento*). Finally, the summit of absolute perfection in the arts was attained by the collective consummate genius of Leonardo da Vinci (1452–1519), Raphael (1483–1520) and Michelangelo Buonarroti (1475–1564). Central to Vasari's thought was the notion that a revival of the study and appreciation of classical (i.e. primarily Roman but also the less well-understood Greek) antiquity had led to the direct imitation of nature in the arts. This was the supreme aim of great art – to represent the visible world naturalistically, and to render both human and divine subjects in as realistic a manner as possible. A teleological process had been set in train in the course of the later thirteenth century which was, he thought, to reach full fruition only in Vasari's own time. The ancient world of Greece and Rome could never be physically recreated or reincarnated. But its thought, art and literature, and the principles behind them, could be revived and 'reborn' as a *rinascita* (Vasari uses the word). It could be argued that this was the narrower vision and conception of the 'Renaissance', as a revival of interest in, and appreciation of, classical antiquity. A broader and much more comprehensive one, seeing the 'Renaissance' period as introducing fundamental changes in the ways in which men and women viewed and explained the world, was to follow. But that was only after another 250 years or so had passed. And the geographically limited scope of the concept (confined very largely to Italy alone) inevitably raised questions about conditions and developments in other parts of Europe, especially in the North. Why had the Renaissance phenomenon only affected Southern Europe, and the Italian peninsula in particular? What was happening elsewhere on the continent? Historians have certainly identified a 'Northern Renaissance', but have disagreed over its nature and chronological span.[4] Some would place it, as an art-historical period, between about 1380 and 1580; some as beginning even earlier in the fourteenth century; others would limit it to the reception in the North of Italian humanist thought and Italian, or Italianate, artistic styles between about 1480 and 1540. And the Protestant Reformation, beginning in the 1520s and 1530s, provides, for some, a terminal dividing line. So significant questions still remain to be discussed and this book attempts to provide some answers to at least some of them.

It has been argued that the 'Age of the Renaissance' was an 'age of transition' from the Middle Ages to modern times. The history of the emergence and development of this notion dates from its first appearance, as we shall see, in the early nineteenth century. We need to trace the course, and vicissitudes, of the concept of the Renaissance, especially in its Northern manifestations, through the works of some of the many scholars and others who have embarked on its study from the early 1800s until the present day. I make no apology for discussing the historiography of the concept of a Renaissance at some length, above all in its Northern forms. It is fundamental to our understanding of how that concept has evolved, changed and adapted to different schools and traditions of historical thought. But its artificial nature has not gone without critical responses. A recent historian of the art of printing and its impact has questioned whether the Renaissance represented simply 'a hypothetical transition rather than an actual occurrence'.[5] The notion of a passage from 'medieval' to 'modern' is, after all, a construct of historians and their need to periodize European history. The claims made for the Italian Renaissance, in and of itself, as forming the transitional period between medieval and modern times, have been challenged. It has been argued that 'when one considers what was happening elsewhere on the Continent between 1350 and 1450, one may wonder if an encounter with peculiar local conditions [in Italy] has not been mistaken for the advent of a new age'.[6] One aim of this book is to discover what was in fact happening outside Italy between 1350 and 1450 (and beyond). Can some form of indigenous, if not self-contained, 'Renaissance' be seen in Northern Europe? How far, if at all, did this indicate the 'advent of a new age'? Or, before any 'Renaissance' characteristics can be discerned in Northern Europe, did it have to receive the influence of Italian humanistic thought and a revival of classical antiquity, stemming largely from Italy? But to speak of a transition to 'modern times' does not take account of the essentially time-bound nature of that concept. For example, what may have appeared 'modern' in 1860 might not have been thought so in 1960, let alone 2019. As with other conceptual constructs, change over time is of the essence here. The very concept of a 'Renaissance', whether in Southern or Northern Europe, or both, underwent profound changes between, say, 1530 and 1830, as well as in the course of the nineteenth and twentieth centuries.[7] Alongside the artificial abstractions embodied in terms such as the 'Renaissance ideal' or 'Renaissance man', a search for concrete evidence for the new, innovatory and what has been called 'the gradual'(or less gradual) 'erosion of existing presuppositions'[8] has to be undertaken.

THE MIDDLE AGES AND THE RENAISSANCE

Perhaps more than any other period in pre-industrial European history, the Renaissance has been portrayed as possessing a 'spirit' of its own. The notion of a Zeitgeist, or 'spirit of the age', has descended to us from the lofty heights of Friedrich Hegel's (1770–1831) philosophy. It presupposes that every age or epoch has a 'supra-individual collective spirit'.[9] This permeates, informs and unifies every area of life, especially the arts, social habits, morals and conventions, laws, and all of a society's other cultural attributes and acquisitions. This holistic interpretation of cultural history (Ger. *Geistesgeschichte*) has also not been without its critics. At a very early stage, Hegel's near-contemporary Goethe (1749–1832) made his Faust declare that 'what you call the spirit of the ages is really no more than the spirit of all those people in which the ages are reflected'.[10] The Zeitgeist is thus simply a historian's metaphysical construct or artificial abstraction, lacking concrete existence in reality. The implicit notion, moreover, that there was a unity between the various, sometimes disparate, manifestations of an entire civilization, could be a mere illusion. More recently, art historians and cultural historians have tended to reject such a holistic approach, preferring to concentrate on the particular and the individual. Since Erwin Panofsky, Edgar Wind and Ernst Gombrich, among many others, began to concentrate on iconography and the elucidation of the 'hidden meanings', symbolism and allegory inherent in Renaissance works of art, the shift away from a Hegelian-influenced approach has been almost total.

It has been argued that the apparent unity ascribed to the 'spirit of the age' is fictitious and takes no account of what is disparate and different within a given civilization, society or art form. Disparate, sometimes dissenting, forms coexist within a given culture. There is, it is claimed, 'no unbreakable unity between every branch of knowledge',[11] just as there is none within the arts or literature. During the Renaissance, Raphael's or Leonardo's art may represent the 'Renaissance ideal', but that ideal was completely rejected, in its Florentine heartland, by the rabble-rousing preaching of the Dominican friar Savonarola (1452–98) against the worldly vanities which, for him, it represented. To gain any credibility, the Renaissance had, therefore, to define itself against what may be seen as its antithesis, and that antithesis was, for its early historians, provided by the Middle Ages.[12] As a generic term for a set of assumptions and presuppositions, expressed in a wide range of forms, the Renaissance could only exist in relation to what had preceded, and indeed what followed, it. And to discover its predecessor, which provided the conditions for a 'rebirth', an agreed concept of the 'medieval' had to be born.

Just as the 'Enlightenment' presupposes the existence of a former, unenlightened period in the history of thought, so the Renaissance posits a previous, relatively benighted age in which 'renascent' qualities or characteristics were absent. But beneath the artificial abstractions and labels which we use to characterize commonly shared outlooks there lay considerable degrees of diversity and disparity. Shared 'Renaissance' ideals, or ideas held in common, were not always understood in the same way by different individuals or groups – controversies over Christian beliefs and doctrines, or over the nature and interpretation of classical thought and literature, are a case in point. What then gave the Renaissance, whether in Southern or Northern Europe, its essential characteristics and how was the contrast with the Middle Ages first made?

The Middle Ages as we know them today are largely a creation of the nineteenth century.[13] Much the same could be said for the Renaissance.

The advent of a battle of styles – classical/Renaissance versus Gothic/ medieval – in the early nineteenth century reflected two opposed and contrary images. On the one hand, there was the image of the Renaissance, depicted imaginatively as an age of 'purple and gold', the musical equivalent of which would be a positive and jubilant key of C major.[14] The Middle Ages, on the other hand, as the age of romanticism dawned, were set in a minor key, with a backdrop of moonlight, scudding clouds, Germanic forests, Gothic ruins, silhouetted cathedrals seen through the mist and the evocative sound of hunting horns, epitomized by Caspar David Friedrich's (1774–1840) paintings and Carl Maria von Weber's romantic opera *Der Freischutz* (1821). And, critical for our purposes, the 'medieval' came to be identified essentially with Northern Europe. But this did not preclude the injection of brighter, primary colours into the picture, as the Middle Ages were also viewed as the Age of Chivalry and all its pageantry. Against this, the Renaissance came to be defined not only as a movement in the arts, thought and literature but also as a distinct cultural period, free-standing and autonomous. Yet its essential character derived as much from what it was not, as from what it was. Its alleged escape, not only from two-dimensional icon-like images and an art regarded as wholly subservient to the Church but also from feudal and ecclesiastical oppression, gave it its fundamental character for many nineteenth-century scholars and writers.

The greatest and most influential of these were the French historian Jules Michelet (1798–1874) and the Swiss scholar Jacob Burckhardt (1818–97). The emancipation of the individual and the rise of an art of realism and naturalism made the Renaissance, for them, the birth of the 'modern' world. Yet, contrary to popular belief, Michelet did not coin, let alone invent, the term 'Renaissance', as an autonomous entity, denoting a specific historical period, in 1855. That distinction, if distinction it was, belongs to the French antiquary and archaeologist Jean-Baptiste Seroux-d'Agincourt (1730–1814) in his posthumously published, lavishly illustrated six-volume work entitled *The History of Art through Its Monuments, since Its Decadence in the Fourth Century until Its Renewal [Renouvellement] in the Sixteenth Century* (Paris, 1823). He described one of the three periods into which he divided the history of Christian art in the West as witnessing *the* 'Renaissance' (*Renaissance*). The term covered the period from the early fourteenth to the late fifteenth century and was used in contrast to, but as a preparation for, what he called the final 'Renewal' (*Renouvellement*) of the arts in the early sixteenth century. His scheme obviously owed much, but by no means everything, to Vasari's schematization and periodization of the history of art. In it, he included some examples from Northern Europe, but confined the origins and essence of his Renaissance to Italy. By compiling a vast compendium of engraved images, Seroux-d'Agincourt was attempting to do for Christian art what the German art historian and archaeologist J. J. Winckelmann (1717–68) had done for the art of classical antiquity. But there was also a source for the term 'Renaissance' which lay outside the confines of the scholarly world of art history, archaeology and antiquarianism.

In Honore de Balzac's novel, *Le Bal de Sceaux* (1829), the conversation of Emilie, the rather insufferable daughter of the Comte de Fontaine, is described as follows:

> She could argue fluently about Italian or Flemish painting, about the Middle Ages or the Renaissance, making erroneous judgements about old or new books, and could bring out with a cruel elegance the defects of a work.[15]

The French reading public, and the world of literature and the theatre, were clearly accustomed to the use of the term 'Renaissance' as 'a specific term for a circumscribed cultural period' (Huizinga) by the late 1820s. Balzac's prose may also suggest an awareness of a contrast or even antithesis between the Middle Ages and the Renaissance and between Italian and Flemish painting by that date. Some prominent writers and dramatists of the time, such as Victor Hugo, expressed an aversion to the Renaissance. It 'became', he wrote, 'pseudo-antique. ... This was the decadence we call the Renaissance. ... It was this setting sun which we take to be a dawn.'[16] The Middle Ages–Renaissance antithesis was already alive and well.

THE RENAISSANCE AS A HISTORICAL PERIOD

The emergence of the concept of the Renaissance as an autonomous historical period linked with the idea of modernity received perhaps its greatest endorsement in the works of Michelet and Burckhardt. Michelet's radical political standpoint led him to admire what he saw as fifteenth-century Italian individualism, and his anticlericalism evoked fervent denunciations of the Church which, for him, had put much of Northern Europe, especially the German-speaking lands, under a heavy and repressive tutelage in the Middle Ages. But, for Michelet, in 1855, the Renaissance was as French as it was Italian. Feudal France was released, in the early sixteenth century, he believed, from clerical oppression, thereby stimulating new forms of art and greater freedom of expression. Sensuality once again flourished, freed from the tyranny of the priests. Western civilization moved further towards the nineteenth-century liberal ideals of individual freedom, artistic creativity, vibrant civic culture and secularism. These themes were to be taken up by Jacob Burckhardt who, in his *The Civilisation of the Renaissance in Italy* (1860), set out what was to become the most pervasive and persuasive account of the Renaissance for the next 100 years. Burckhardt's chapter headings in that book are themselves enough to demonstrate the shape of his thoughts: 'The Discovery of the World and of Man', or 'The State as a Work of Art'. For him, the discovery of the individual, the 'unbridled, free sense of personality, pagan zest for the world, and indifference to, and disdain for, religion'[17] were the outstanding characteristics of the Renaissance which were to usher in the modern world. His vision was to become profoundly influential, especially for Northern Europeans, over the next century. As we shall see, it was not without its critics and dissenters, but the 'Burckhardtian' view increasingly, from the later nineteenth century onwards, took hold in both the academic and public arenas. It still informs many presentations of the Renaissance in the modern media today.

Yet the views of Michelet and Burckhardt were not universally shared. Romanticism and the rediscovery of the Middle Ages had inevitably influenced attitudes towards the Renaissance. The contemporary surge of Gothic revivalism meant that there was a vocal and influential body of opinion, especially in the British Isles, which saw the Renaissance as morally reprehensible, an expression of the 'Revived Pagan Principle'. This was largely because of its association with the culture of pagan antiquity and the egotistical cult of the self. Augustus Welby Pugin (1812–52) and John Ruskin (1819–1900) both denounced it, and Ruskin, in the 1840s, was to some degree responsible for pitting the 'medieval' diametrically against the 'Renaissance'. The pre-Raphaelite movement, so named because of its near-worship of both Italian and Northern art before the early sixteenth century, had also given Gothic revivalist styles an advantage over neoclassicism and this was to be reflected in British architecture. The new Houses of Parliament (1840–60), for example, are uncompromisingly Northern Gothic. Ruskin was outspoken in his distaste for the Renaissance, calling it 'an incubus in the history of the West', while Pugin, although a devout Catholic, found one of the High Renaissance's greatest monuments, St Peter's Basilica at Rome, 'disgusting'.

The movement at this time towards an appreciation of Gothic and the medieval was to bring a renewed, pan-European interest in Northern art, both religious and secular, of the fourteenth, fifteenth and early sixteenth centuries. But was the art and culture of Northern Europe to be described in any sense as part of the Renaissance? Was there evidence for an indigenous, self-engendered Renaissance in the North? Or was the period simply the end of the Middle Ages – a period of termination, in which an old culture had reached its apogee and the end of its natural lifespan?

THE CONCEPT OF A 'NORTHERN RENAISSANCE' AND ITS CRITICS

The idea of a 'Northern Renaissance' initially emanated from two art historians, one French and one Belgian, at the end of the nineteenth century. Louis Courajod (1841–96) and Hippolyte Fierens-Gevaert (1870–1926) are today quite unknown outside specialist art-historical circles.[18] But they formulated theories about the origins and provenance of the Renaissance which, though heavily criticized and often dismissed, still bear examination as more than mere historiographical curiosities. Both adopted extreme positions which favoured the notion of national or regional 'schools' of painting and consciously set French and Franco-Flemish identities against Italian ones. Courajod, teaching and writing in Paris between 1887 and 1896, sought the 'true origins of the Renaissance' in Franco-Flemish art between 1360 and 1440. In his lectures at the School of Art in the Louvre, he argued that the Gothic style 'regenerated itself quite independently, by turning towards an absolute naturalism'.[19] From this movement, the Renaissance sprang, rather than from any rediscovery of antiquity or liberation of the individual stemming exclusively from Italy. From the Franco-Flemish illuminated manuscripts, panel paintings and sculpture of the later fourteenth century to the strikingly realistic works of Jan van Eyck and Rogier van der Weyden in the fifteenth a 'new feeling for nature and reality' was born (Figures 1, 2, 3, 4). Courajod had devised the expression 'International Gothic' to describe a cosmopolitan artistic style which had developed by 1400, in which elements from both Italy and Northern and Central Europe were combined. But, he claimed, Northern France and the Low Countries remained the true source of that 'modern' realism, which stood in contrast to the emergent rhetorical, classically dominated styles of the Italian Renaissance. A Renaissance had therefore dawned in the North, while Italy provided only 'a varnish from antiquity' to the visual arts.

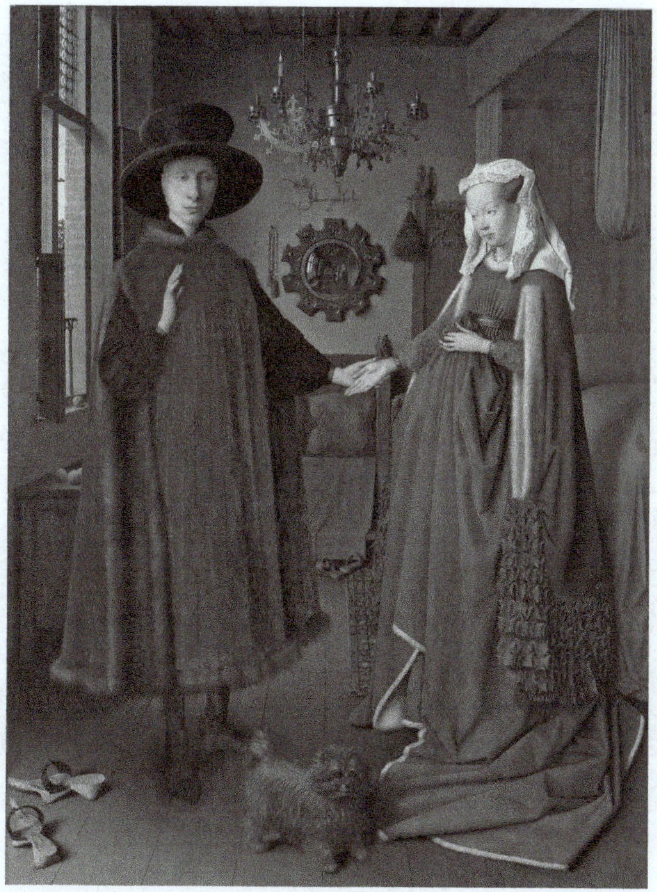

Figure 1 Jan van Eyck: *Giovanni Arnolfini and His Bride* (London, National Gallery).
(Photo by VCG Wilson/Corbis via Getty Images.)

This theme was taken further by the Belgian scholar, museum curator and educationist Fierens-Gevaert, working in Brussels and Liege, who seems to have been the first to coin the term 'Northern Renaissance'. In 1905 he published, at Brussels, his *La Renaissance Septentrionale et les premiers maitres des Flandres* (*The Northern Renaissance and the First Flemish Masters*). He followed Courajod's method and chronology, seeing the critical developments towards an art of realism occurring in the North, depicting the 'real properties of things', in which he discerned

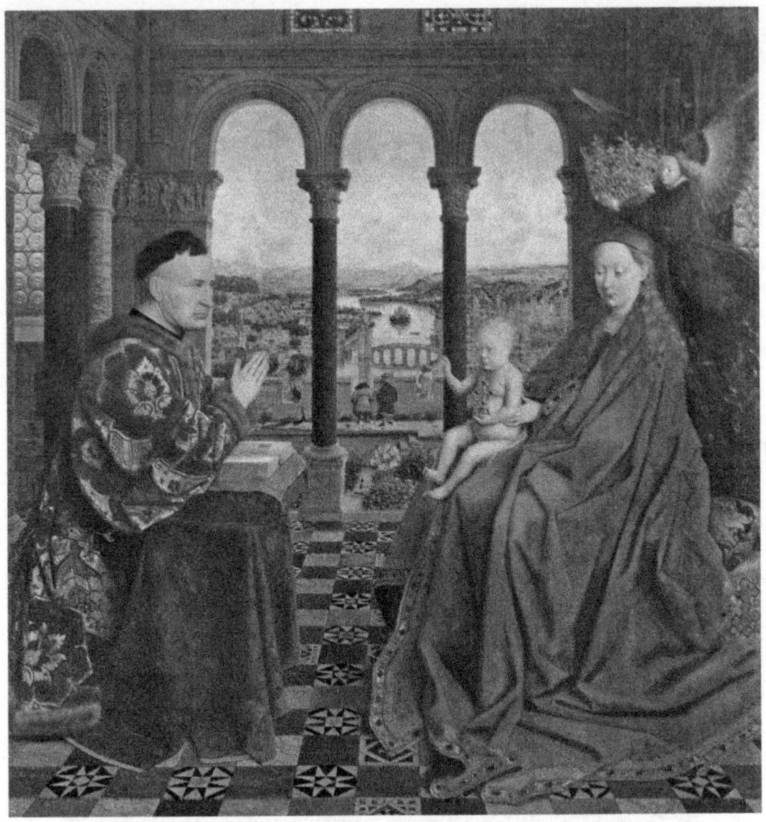

Figure 2 Jan van Eyck: *Madonna of Chancellor Rolin* (Paris, Louvre). (Photo by The Print Collector/Getty Images.)

the origins of 'modern naturalism'. There was, he claimed 'a fundamental evolution of the aesthetic sentiment … in the Northern lands',[20] where the portrait, the landscape and the still life were to be born. This, in the art-historical climate of his time, was sheer heterodoxy. Italian ownership of the Renaissance had become something of an article of faith. It was perhaps unsurprising that the term 'Northern Renaissance' then more or less disappeared from art-historical and cultural-historical discourse until a much later date. Only in the 1960s and later, as we shall see, did it begin to reappear. A textbook of documentary and other texts for the study of art history, published in 1966, was among the very first to use the term (in English) as a title. Wolfgang Stechow chose to call that volume *Northern*

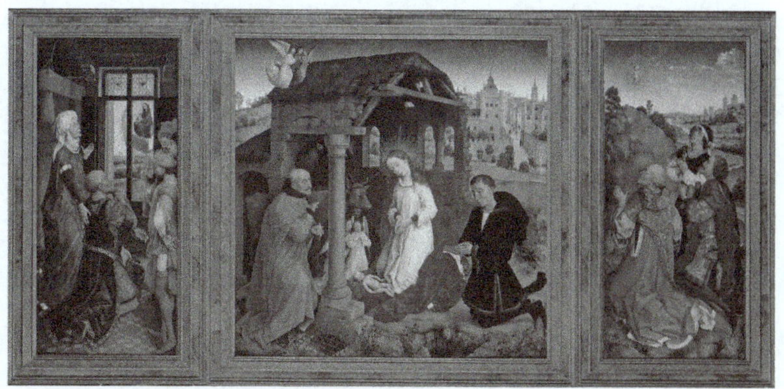

Figure 3 Rogier van der Weyden: Middelburg Altarpiece with Pieter Bladelin as donor.
(Photo by Fine Art Images/Heritage Images/Getty Images.)

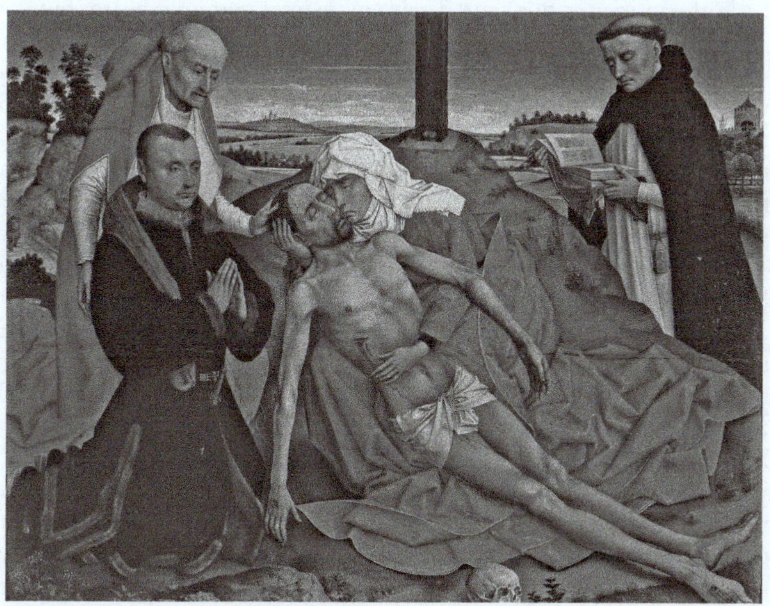

Figure 4 Rogier van der Weyden: *Pietà with donor* (London, National Gallery).
(Photo by DeAgostini/Getty Images.)

Renaissance Art, 1400-1600: Sources and Documents. In 1945, however, Otto Benesch had published his *The Art of the Renaissance in Northern Europe: Its Relations to the Contemporary Spiritual and Intellectual Movements.* While seeing Northern Europe possessing certain distinctive traits which marked it off from Italian developments, Benesch in effect addressed only the sixteenth century in his account. Van Eyck, Van der Weyden, Memling, Bouts, Geertgen tot Sint Jans, Bosch and the other fifteenth-century Flemish and Dutch masters were excluded from his analysis. Artists from Durer (1471–1528) to Bruegel (1525–69), and the reception of Italianate styles in the North after 1500, rather than any indigenous Northern Renaissance before that date, provided his body of evidence. For all the notice taken of them, Courajod and Fierens-Gevaert might well never have existed. The definition of a Renaissance was crucial in determining whether or not it was confined to Italy. Yet the exclusively Italy-centred, Burckhardtian view of the Renaissance had other critics at this time. Their voices were certainly heard, but they gained comparatively little ground in the debate.

One of those who became sceptical of Burckhardt's interpretation was Abraham Moritz Warburg, known as Aby (1866–1929), from the Hamburg banking family of that name. He had renounced his partnership in the finance house of Warburg and become an independent scholar, furnished (largely at the firm's expense) with a vast research library which formed the basis for the Warburg Institute. His background is not entirely unimportant as an influence on the directions taken by his work. Warburg thought that he could see some similarities between the banker dynasties of fifteenth-century Florence – the Medici, the Tornabuoni and the Sassetti – and the Hanseatic merchant-bankers of his own time. In one revealing comment on Domenico Ghirlandajo's frescos commissioned by the Tornabuoni family in the church of Santa Maria Novella (1485–90), he remarked, somewhat tartly: 'This is the kind of art a Renaissance banker's family likes, because they get a much better deal than do either religion or art.'[21] Warburg also became profoundly dissatisfied with the conventional view of the Renaissance which had dominated his student days and which he had in part absorbed. He intensely disliked the late nineteenth-century aesthetic cult of the Renaissance, which saw the Florentine *Quattrocento* as a kind of golden age, a triumph of individualism and secularism over the power of superstition and the Church. But his most original contribution, in the earlier part of his career, lay in his profoundly unconventional interest in the relationship between Northern realism and the Italian recourse to classical antiquity, not only for artistic subject matter but also for stylistic influences. He began to doubt the truth of the art-historical orthodoxy of his time which set Northern and Italian art completely apart. He was fascinated by the apparent taste of Italian art patrons for Northern devotional painting and portraiture, with its closely observed depiction of reality. His explorations, in the early 1900s, of the interactions between patrons and artists were highly original pioneering studies, grounded not only in the paintings and sculptures themselves but in documentary and textual sources. But there was still, he argued, an apparent conflict between what he saw as cool, stolid Northern realism and rhetorical, classically inspired Italian idealism. Much of the rest of his life was to be devoted to attempts at explaining, and reconciling, these and other tendencies. He was never to succeed entirely in this task. And the inherent tension within an essentially Christian civilization between religious and devotional art, on the one hand, and an art drawing upon pagan mysteries, mythology and pre-Christian ancient history, on the other, was never resolved by Warburg.

He came close to rejecting the Burckhardtian view of the Renaissance entirely. Reviewing the art patronage, and religious observances, of leading Florentine (and other) families, he ruefully observed:

> We are reluctant to acknowledge how medieval the man of the Renaissance really was, the man whom we salute as a superman, the liberator of the individual from the dark prisons of the Church.[22]

The way seemed now to be open to a reconsideration of a 'Northern Renaissance' which had already been hinted at, if only negatively, in the work of some of Warburg's academic teachers. Carl Justi (1832–1912) had suggested that 'the word "Renaissance" had been ... misused when artists such as Jan van Eyck were described as "forerunners" of that movement for no other reason than they were realists'.[23] Warburg, as a student, disagreed with Justi and left the University of Bonn for Berlin, to study with other professors. Courajod's work was clearly known to Justi, but was rejected by him out of hand. Another of Warburg's professors, Henry Thode (1857–1920) had, in 1885, developed a theory about the origins of the Renaissance which located it in the religious thought of the thirteenth century. The Franciscan 'admiration of God's creation' – the natural world – had, he argued, been a founding principle of the Renaissance, independent of any allusion whatsoever to classical antiquity. Why should the idea not be extended and applied to the realistic art of Van Eyck and the other Netherlandish masters of the fifteenth century? The case for St Francis as the (unlikely) midwife of the Renaissance was generally dismissed by art-historical opinion at the time. But here was the germ of a notion which, if developed and expanded, could mean that there could indeed have been a Northern Renaissance.

Warburg's thought was also shaped by his engagement with the new disciplines of both psychology and anthropology in the latter part of the nineteenth century. The influence of Karl Lamprecht (1856–1915) on him was marked. Lamprecht introduced collective psychology into the analysis of historical change, but still operated within a Hegelian, *Geist*-driven system. Art, for him, was the prime source for the psychological characteristics of a historical period. Influenced by early anthropologists, such as the Oxford professor Sir Edward Burnett Tylor (1832–1917), he widened the scope and definition of 'cultural' life to include ritual, folk customs, symbolism, rites of passage and gesture. Tylor, who was in effect a founder of social and cultural anthropology, gave, in his major work *Primitive Culture* (1871), a classic definition of

> Culture or Civilization, taken in its wide ethnographic sense [as] ... that complex whole which includes knowledge, belief, art, morals, laws, custom and any other capabilities and habits acquired by man as a member of society.[24]

Together with Lamprecht's influence, this was to become part and parcel of Warburg's own intellectual apparatus, inspiring his multidisciplinary approach to cultural history and the idiosyncratic organization of his library. In his study of art, Lamprecht, like Burckhardt, had identified the Renaissance with individualism, regarding the Middle Ages, which he believed had no knowledge of portraiture, or interest in the depiction of the natural world, as lacking in those objective and rational qualities which the Renaissance introduced. Without portraits, individualism could not develop, and the conventions of Gothic art precluded any progress along those lines. Warburg absorbed these lessons, but never fully subscribed to them. The implications of his position for Renaissance studies, and the further tensions which it engendered, will be examined in a later chapter.[25] But between 1902 and 1908 Warburg could, potentially, have transformed the study of art history. The prevailing, predominantly stylistic approach to the subject, in which questions of attribution, assessment of quality and an evolutionary interpretative narrative had dominated, was questioned by, at that time, his admittedly slender volume of published work. Yet that style-centred approach was not to be substantially challenged, let alone superseded, for many years.

HUIZINGA AND THE 'AUTUMN' OF THE MIDDLE AGES

The most important, most perceptive and perhaps most controversial figure in the study of Northern European culture in the later Middle Ages and Renaissance was the Dutch scholar Johan Huizinga (1872–1945).[26] Huizinga was, by early training, neither a medieval nor a Renaissance scholar, nor an art historian. His first academic work had been in Sanskrit studies, and his doctoral thesis was on the role of the court jester in Indian drama. This had led to an interest in the precocious disciplines of anthropology, ethnology and, like both Lamprecht and Warburg, psychology. His Dutch background also led him into the fashionable aesthetic movements of the *fin de siècle* Netherlands, and he was profoundly influenced by the current, no less fashionable, anthropological study of colonial peoples, such as the Indonesian population of the Dutch East Indies. His enthusiasm for the French and Belgian Symbolists, for writers such as Verlaine, Maeterlinck, Joris-Karl Huysmans, the Goncourt brothers and Mallarme, made Huizinga an exceptionally interesting and unusual figure among Dutch medievalists, whose ranks he was to join only when he was in his thirties. There was a poetic quality to his mind, and his historical imagination was acutely responsive to visual and aural stimuli, perhaps more so than any other writer of serious historical works. According to his own account, his conversion from Sanskrit and Indian studies to the European Middle Ages was in part the result of a walk, and of the impact of an exhibition. His conviction that the later Middle Ages represented a period of decline and decay came to him, he claimed, during a walk taken in the countryside around Groningen. In 1902, he had visited the first great international exhibition of early Netherlandish painting (*Exposition des Primitifs Flamands et d'art ancien*) which was held in Bruges. This brought together, for the first time, 413 Netherlandish, rather than strictly 'Flemish', paintings, as well as sculptures, tapestries and other objects from the applied arts. Its significance, and its influence on both academic and public reactions to the art of the Netherlandish 'primitives', so often eclipsed at the time by the primacy of Italian art, was striking and long-lasting.

The way towards a renewed appreciation of early Netherlandish painting had already been prepared, as one outcome of the German romantic movement, in the early 1820s. In 1822, the gallery curator and cataloguer G. F. Waagen (1784–1868) had published, at Breslau, a short monograph entitled *Uber Hubert und Johann van Eyck* (*Concerning Hubert and Jan van Eyck*). This contained a detailed catalogue of the surviving works of the Van Eycks, as they were known at the time, as well as a number of subsequently rejected attributions. It marked something of a milestone in the serious study of Northern Renaissance painters, comparatively neglected as they were in favour of Italian artists. Waagen witnessed the early stages of art history's emergence as an academic discipline, being appointed to a chair of art history at Berlin in 1844. The earliest professorship of the subject had been established at Gottingen in 1813, followed by Bonn in 1818. A reappraisal of Netherlandish painting, sculpture, and the applied and decorative arts in the North between the later fourteenth and early sixteenth centuries had been under way for some time. But it was the advent of large public exhibitions that began to have a real impact on a more general awareness and appreciation of Netherlandish painting outside the select circles of specialists and scholars.

During the 'age of the Van Eycks', the greater part of the Netherlands had come under the sway of the dukes of Burgundy, and then, by dint of a marriage alliance, of the Austrian and Spanish Habsburgs. The 1902 Bruges exhibition seemed, to many observers, including Huizinga, to point up a sharp contrast between the extravagant, 'decadent' splendour of the Burgundian court and the apparently deep devotional piety expressed by many of the paintings. Explanations were required, but before further conclusions were reached, there was also a need to establish a complete inventory, with detailed descriptions, of all surviving works from this period. A sustained effort, begun by Waagen, at cataloguing, attributing, dating and interpreting this art began, and was ultimately to lead to the appearance of perhaps the greatest contribution to its study – Max J. Friedlander's fourteen-volume *Early Netherlandish Painting* published between 1924 and 1937. Like Warburg, a product of a banking family (from Berlin), Friedlander (1867–1958) had become a museum curator, art expert and connoisseur, advising both public institutions and private individuals on purchases and acquisitions of Northern paintings. His shorter study of the subject, *From Van Eyck to Bruegel* (first edition 1916), was to become, with Bernard Berenson's *Italian Painters of the Renaissance* (1930), a standard textbook for students of art history. In the aftermath of the Bruges exhibition, moreover, the very idea of a 'Northern Renaissance' also received further important, but often critical, attention.

It was not the very first exhibition of 'Old Masters'. One of the earliest and largest had taken place in Manchester in 1857, when paintings from the Flemish, Dutch, Spanish and German schools were assembled from collections throughout Great Britain. It was followed by exhibitions devoted to individual Northern painters such as Rembrandt (Amsterdam, 1898), or Cranach (Dresden, 1899). The inspiration for the Bruges exhibition of 1902 came in part from an English émigré, who was to play a fundamental role in the re-evaluation of Netherlandish painting of the fifteenth century. W. H. J. Weale (1832–1917), an Anglican who had converted to Roman Catholicism, settled in Bruges in 1855, founded the Archaeological Society there and organized, with two Belgian associates, an exhibition, the Paintings of the Old Flemish School, in 1867. This brought together 150 early Netherlandish paintings, but did not, it seems, attract a great deal of public interest. Weale, however, continued to work intensively on the cataloguing and description of paintings in Bruges and other collections, largely because of his convictions as a devout Catholic convert and his belief, shared with others, that the Belgian public should be made more aware of the treasures housed in their midst. He did not consider those treasures to be part of any Northern Renaissance. If anything, they provided a welcome antidote to what he regarded as the pernicious secularism of his own age, and offered to the pious a haven of spirituality in a Godless world. His especial interest lay in the devotional paintings of Hans Memling (*c.* 1430–94), many of which were housed (and still are) in St John's Hospital (Figure 5). It had become a place popular among both tourists and Catholic pilgrims to Bruges in the second half of the nineteenth century, attracting 11,567 visitors in 1899 alone. Weale also founded a periodical devoted to the study of Flemish religious art entitled *Le Beffroi* (*The Belfry*), which made a more general public conversant with the masterpieces of early Netherlandish painting and sculpture. He was, moreover, to play a major part, with the Belgian aristocrat, museum curator, government commissioner and diplomat Henri Kervyn de Lettenhove, in organizing and cataloguing the 1902 exhibition.

Supported by the Belgian monarchy and state, but surprisingly not welcomed by the authorities of the city of Bruges itself, the Bruges exhibition received loans of masterpieces from across the world, and set the standard for a subsequent series of displays which were the precursors of the 'block-buster' shows of our own day. In 1904 the French, not to be outdone by little Belgium, mounted a large exhibition of early French painting dating from a similar period. National rivalries, aided and abetted by art-historical scholarship, now brought the so-called French, Dutch, German and Flemish 'primitives' to general public attention.[27] Between 15 July and 15 September 1902, the Bruges exhibition attracted

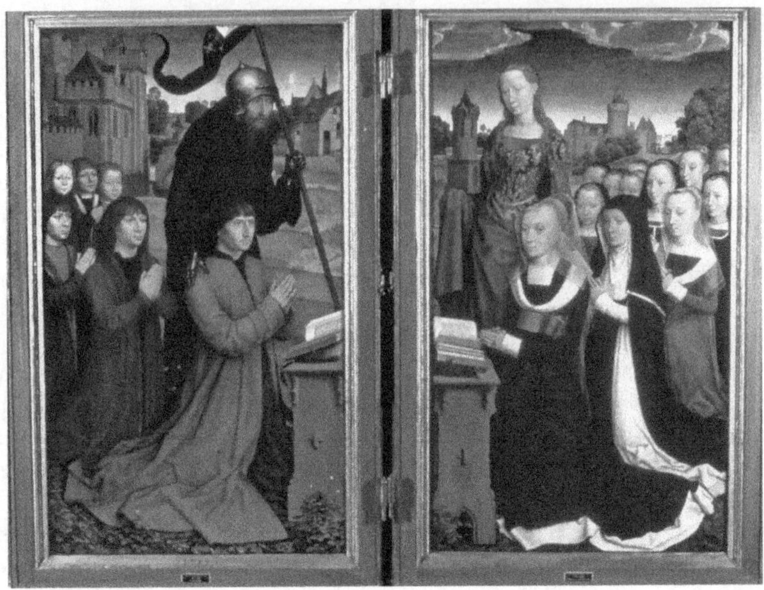

Figure 5 Hans Memling: Willem Moreel Altarpiece (Bruges, St John's Hospital).
(Photo by Universal History Archive/Getty Images.)

over 35,000 paying visitors, as well as citizens and working-class inhabitants of the city who gained free admission on certain days. It is essential to place the event in the context of its time. A revival of national and civic sentiment in much of Europe before 1914 had led to a heightened awareness of the past, especially of the medieval past, both actual and imagined. The invention, as well as the observance, of tradition experienced a halcyon period. This was expressed by the staging not only of exhibitions but also of pageants and re-enactments of significant events and episodes in a country's or a city's history. Bruges had its procession of the Holy Blood from 1850 onwards, and processions and parades celebrating events such as the victory of the Flemings over the French at Kortrijk (Courtrai) in 1302. Brussels had its *Ommegang*, a pageant and procession with later medieval origins in the celebration of a miracle of the Virgin Mary, and then commemorating the ceremonial entry of the Emperor Charles V into the city in 1549. In the German cities of Nuremberg, Augsburg, Cologne and elsewhere, processions and pageants were similarly organized. In 1879, the seven-year-old Johan Huizinga was deeply impressed by a pageant celebrating the entry of Edzard, count of East Friesland, into Huizinga's hometown of Groningen in 1506. His essentially visualizing approach to history was, he later said, stimulated and nourished by such early experiences.

Despite Huizinga's positive reaction to the Bruges exhibition of 1902, he, like Weale but for different reasons, was not prepared to see a 'Northern Renaissance' in the culture represented by the art of Van Eyck, Van der Weyden or Memling. Although, in a very perceptive article on the 'Problem of the Renaissance' in 1920, he criticized Burckhardt for not being 'well enough aware of the great variety and luxuriant life of medieval culture outside Italy' and for giving 'too restricted spatial limits to the emerging Renaissance', he was unconvinced that a 'Renaissance' civilization existed in the North.[28] The later Middle Ages were, for him, a period of termination, in which an old culture was dying and a new one was waiting to be born. In 1919, he was to set out that thesis in his masterpiece *The Waning* [or *Autumn*] *of the Middle Ages*. The book was to become one of the bestselling historical works of all time, going through twenty-two editions and reprints in Dutch alone up to 1997. It was translated into seven European languages in Huizinga's lifetime, and many more since then, including Russian, Lithuanian and Japanese. Huizinga took up a stance which seemed diametrically opposed to art historians such as Courajod or Fierens-Gevaert. The art of the period, he argued, was a product of an overripe and decaying culture, not of one infused with new ideas and attitudes. That was only to come, not with the advent of Italian Renaissance thought and Italian-inspired art in the North, but with the Protestant Reformation. There may have been an element of ingrained anti-Italianism in Huizinga, possibly one product of his Dutch background, coming as he did from a family with a long line of austere Mennonite preachers from North Holland and Friesland among his ancestors. What is not often realized is that he was as equally dismissive of the Italian Renaissance as he was of the 'decadent' culture of the North. His image of a 'dying away of things that had outlasted themselves' referred not only to France and the Burgundian Low Countries but also to Italy. In lectures given at Groningen in 1906–7 on the Renaissance in Italy, he described it as 'a short triumph of excessive individualism'.[29] In both areas of Europe, North and South, the political and social elites craved what he called 'a more beautiful life', seeking a way of escape from the harsh and cruel realities of daily life by entering a world of illusion and dreams. In later life, he modified this view somewhat, being convinced that great creativity could coexist with, and be aroused and sustained by, the desire to escape from or transcend present reality. He also revised his views on the intellectual impact of Renaissance humanism in the North as a result of his work, as we shall see in a later chapter, on Erasmus.[30]

But the Renaissance, he still concluded in his *Homo Ludens* (1936), was 'a gorgeous and solemn masquerade in the accoutrements of an idealised past'.[31] There was a *fin de siècle* quality about Italian Renaissance civilization, just as there was about that represented, for all its splendour, by the products of the 'Burgundian Age'. 'It had', he wrote, 'the greatness of despair, it was a course into the abyss.'[32] He quoted Paul Verlaine's poem IX in his volume *Sagesse* (1880): 'The great century [*siècle*] at its decline, when the setting sun, so beautiful, gilded life.'[33] The image was taken up by Huizinga, as a metaphor for his whole book, in an extraordinary passage, in the introduction to the first, original Dutch edition of the *Autumn of the Middle Ages* (1919) when he spoke of his mind, focused as it was

> on the depth of the evening sky, a sky steeped in blood-red, desolate with threatening leaden clouds, full of the false glow of copper.[34]

The allusion is clearly a direct reference to another of Verlaine's poems in *Sagesse*, 'The False Fine Days': 'And here they are, my poor soul, vibrant in the copper glow of sunset.'[35] He was echoing a common theme of the writers and poets of the so-called Decadence of the later nineteenth century. He may well also have had in mind what Theophile Gautier (1811–72) called the 'setting sun of decadence', contrasting it with the 'raw, white and direct light of a midday sun, beating down on all things equally, and the horizontal light of evening, firing the strange clouds with reflections'.[36] Much of Huizinga's critique of later medieval thought and art also rested on analogies with the 'decadence' perceived by nineteenth-century writers and critics in the Late Latin poets of the later Roman Empire (AD third to sixth centuries). They, like their fourteenth and fifteenth-century successors, indulged in literary and artistic artifice rather than 'moral vision', where 'ornament replaced substance, and false complexity replaced clarity of thought and language'.[37] The sun was setting on a tired world.

So, for Huizinga, tendencies within either Northern or Italian civilization in the fourteenth and fifteenth centuries towards the birth of a new conception of life, thought and even art rested upon a misapprehension. A 'false glow of copper' could also have represented the false dawn of the idea of modernity in either Italy or the Northern lands. Burckhardt's thesis, influential though it was, had in effect been seriously wounded, if not put to death, by Huizinga. He did not see the Renaissance, in any of its manifestations, as in any sense 'modern'. It did not, he argued in his 1920 essay, establish such 'modern' characteristics as the individual's right to self-determination. It did not cede to the individual the right and ability to determine his or her lifestyle, beliefs, convictions or personal taste. The authoritarian nature of its culture, or cultures, was paramount. It constantly referred back to the past, revering ancient authorities, learning lessons from the world of classical antiquity and attempting to imitate, emulate and even to surpass antiquity's artistic and literary styles. And, in both Northern and Southern Europe, the prominence and power of kings, princes and their courts, eclipsing republican modes of government, also made Renaissance culture, in many senses, a culture of autocracy and authority.

THE POST-HUIZINGA DILEMMA

In the wake of Huizinga's influential work, historians of culture and the arts in Northern Europe were left firmly impaled on the horns of a dilemma: Should they accept his vision of an 'autumn of the Middle Ages' in the North, or should they incline more sharply towards a view that allowed them to speak of a 'Northern Renaissance'? Was there sufficient evidence to sustain the notion of a dichotomy between two versions of the same phenomenon, one in Northern Europe, and the other in Italy? So much depended on definitions of 'rebirth' and the extent to which, in a post-Hegelian world, holistic interpretations of complete civilizations, cultures and societies were still tenable and acceptable. Some historians decided to abandon any reference whatsoever to 'Renaissance' elements in the North and resorted to more neutral terms such as 'early modern Northern European culture' or 'Northern art in the early modern period'. Yet the debate was not closed. From the mid-1980s onwards, books about Northern art began to appear in increasing numbers with 'Renaissance' in their titles. Among them were James Snyder, *Northern Renaissance Art: Painting, Sculpture and the Graphic Arts from 1350 to 1575* (1985); Craig Harbison, *The Art of the Northern Renaissance* (1995); Marina Belozerskaya, *Rethinking the Renaissance: Burgundian Art across Europe* (2002); Jeffrey Chipps Smith, *The Northern Renaissance* (2004) and Susie Nash, *Northern Renaissance Art* (2008). In 2009 *The Journal of the Northern Renaissance* was founded. Studies of individual Northern cities have also placed them in a Renaissance context: Maximiliaan P. J. Martens's *Bruges and the Renaissance: Memling to Pourbus* (1998) and Jeffrey Chipps Smith's *Nuremberg: A Renaissance City* (2014) are among the most noteworthy. Studies of important Northern artists have also equated them with a 'Renaissance', often stemming from major exhibitions of their works, such as Maryan Ainsworth and Maximiliaan P. J. Martens' *Petrus Christus: Renaissance Master of Bruges* (1994) and the catalogue of the exhibition held at Rome in 2014–15, entitled *Memling: Flemish Renaissance*, while *Man, Myth and Sensual Pleasures. Jan Gossart's Renaissance. The Complete Works*, edited by Maryan Ainsworth (2010) is the alluring title of another such erudite and scholarly study. It is, however, sometimes difficult to decide whether the title of a book, or an exhibition, has been determined more by publishers' and curators' commercial considerations than by the nature of the book's or exhibition's content and argument. Anything with 'Renaissance' rather than 'Later Middle Ages', 'Late Gothic' or 'Fifteenth Century' in its title is, it seems, more likely to play well – and pay well – with a general audience and readership. Be that as it may, the term 'Northern Renaissance' now has a general currency which was virtually unknown thirty or so years ago. It now appears to be a definite 'period-indicative' term in art-historical discourse, but in some instances it seems merely to refer to nothing more than a time period which is roughly coterminous with that of the Italian Renaissance.

Recent years have also seen some convergence between studies of social, economic and art history in Northern France, Italy and the Netherlands. Northern Italy and the Netherlands were the most densely urbanized areas of Western Europe during this period. An interdependence between the urban societies of Italy and, especially, the Southern Netherlands has been stressed, and the role of intermediaries between the two, such as the Florentine Medici bank and its northern branches, has been highlighted. This has led to a reappraisal of the influence not only of Northern art but also of Netherlandish music and musicians, on Italian developments. Elisabeth Crouzet-Pavan's and Elodie Lecuppre-Desjardin's edited volume *Les Villes de Flandre et d'Italie (xiiie – xvie siècle). Les enseignements d'une comparaison* (2008), the many articles of Wessel Krul and Reinhard Strohm's *Music in late medieval Bruges* (1985) and *The Rise of European Music, 1300-1500* (1993) are among the more significant contributions. Similarly, studies of relations and cross-currents between the princely courts of the period, above all those of Burgundy, Naples, and the northern and central Italian despotisms, have emphasized the links between them. A major contribution to the debate on the question of artistic and cultural interactions was Paula Nuttall's *From Flanders to Florence: The Impact of Netherlandish Painting, 1400-1500* (2004) which, perhaps not before time, more or less took up the subject from where Aby Warburg had left it in the early 1900s. The former hermetically sealed compartments of Italian art, on the one hand, and Northern art, on the other, have effectively been broken open in recent years. Similar advances have been made in urban history. Although there may be a risk of creating further false dichotomies, recent interest in the relationships – political, social, economic and cultural – between princely courts, cities and towns in the Netherlands, Northern France, Germany, Eastern and Central Europe has proved fruitful. Closer study of the 'court-city dichotomy', as Hanno Wijsman and others have suggested, may prove productive of further debate about the interactions, as well as distinctions, between 'court' cultures and 'civic' cultures during the period of the Northern Renaissance. The evidence may suggest that there was less of a dichotomy between them than had previously been assumed, especially by historians of the Burgundian Netherlands.

In the history of ideas, despite long-standing assumptions to the contrary, the innovatory role of new devotional movements, trends in biblical and patristic scholarship and changes in Northern attitudes towards classical antiquity have been pointed out. This has given some grounds for arguing that the later fourteenth and fifteenth centuries had formed a seedbed, and a fertile soil, for innovation and experiment. Claims have been made in favour of a pre-Reformation 'Christian Renaissance' in Northern Europe and a 'Religious Renaissance of the German humanists' and their Netherlandish contemporaries. The quiet 'interiority' of the Netherlandish *devotio moderna*, represented by Thomas Kempis's *The Imitation of Christ* (1424–7), has been reconsidered, and placed in a more positive relationship with the development of the ideas of Erasmus and other Northern humanists and theologians. Inward spirituality was clearly a prominent feature of Northern European piety, marking it off from its more extrovert and theatrical Italian or Iberian counterparts, during the century or so before the Reformation. As we shall see, the Northern European invention of printing with movable type during the 1450s also had a profound effect, throughout Europe, on the dissemination and availability of texts and ideas. Italy had no monopoly of the radical and novel, especially in the field of applied science and technology.

It would, however, be difficult to see the penetration of these cultural trends much further down into Northern European societies. Clearly, rising levels of lay literacy (though never approaching anywhere near modern norms), combined with the impact of printing, made the written word available and accessible to a much larger body of the reading public than perhaps ever before. It also, through woodblock prints, engravings and etchings on paper, released a larger body of visual images into more general circulation over a wider social range than before. But these were, numerically, still largely illiterate and formally uneducated societies, the greater part of whose populations, especially those engaged in agricultural and manual labour, remained an illiterate peasantry and underclass. Urban proletariats, disenfranchised and often exploited, were in a similar condition. The gap between rich and poor, between the haves and the have-nots, does not appear to have narrowed significantly over this period. Poverty, rural and urban, was still a universal characteristic of the age, although drastic demographic decline during the period of the fourteenth-century plagues may, paradoxically, have improved conditions for some of the survivors. Post-plague conditions were productive of a range of reactions across Northern Europe. Although many of those conditions predated the onset of the mid-fourteenth-century epidemics of 1347–9, the ever-present proximity of sudden death and disease could only have led to a heightened state of awareness of the need to provide for the fate of the soul in an afterlife. 'Renaissance' men and women were, in general, no less conventionally pious than their predecessors and in many cases they were more so. Cults associated with Christ's Passion, and with the agony of the cross, were rife, especially in Northern Europe. The arts took up the theme, and although it should never be exaggerated, the extreme expressiveness of Northern painting and sculpture was, as we shall see, in part nourished and sustained by the lived experience of suffering, both actual and vicarious.[38]

Death, disease and epidemics spared no one, high or low, rich or poor, clerical or lay. The indiscriminate nature, and large scale, of plague deaths could hardly promote the cause of reason, while there were simply no rational explanations for the ubiquitous ravages, plague or no plague, of infectious diseases and the deaths that they caused. It was perhaps hardly surprising that Northern Renaissance thinkers addressed the issues of wisdom and folly in the forms that they did.[39] The irrational, the non-rational and the supra-rational all had parts to play in both the psyche and working repertoire of writers, artists and their patrons. As we shall see in our final chapter, there was an underside to this culture, a darker vision which sometimes led to bitter satire and polemic, sometimes to real mental and spiritual trauma. Much lay outside reason, including faith, and a notion, held by many Catholics and Reformers alike, that God's wisdom was untouched, and untouchable, by either human reason or human folly, was current. It was accessible to men and women only through divine revelation, trust and belief. Playfully mocking those who claimed to be wise, Erasmus contributed his Latin *In Praise of Folly* (1509, with revisions between 1511 and 1514) to the corpus of Renaissance satirical literature. Sebastian Brant, in his German vernacular *Ship of Fools* (*Narrenschiff*) (1494), lambasted folly of every conceivable kind for didactic purposes and effect. And the enigmatic art of Hieronymus Bosch (1450–1516), with its images of folly, sin and what seem like pre-Surrealist dreams and nightmares, still remains to be convincingly explained. Themes and motifs from popular folklore, superstition, sadism and ribaldry here met the tastes and preoccupations of upper- and middle-class patrons.

These were the classes of society – the social, political and economic elites – to whom 'Renaissance' values in the North very largely belonged. Any attempt to 'democratize' the Northern Renaissance is doomed to fail. The only approach towards that notion would lie in the impact of printing which made a greater volume of 'educational' material available and accessible to a wider, albeit necessarily literate, audience than before.[40] But humanism in the North did not go very far beyond the relatively restricted circles of humanist intellectuals both inside and, perhaps more importantly, outside the universities; beyond the classrooms of a relatively small number of schools for the urban middle classes; or beyond the rarefied, if not always very sober, air of courtly societies, with their increasingly common predilection for classically inspired rhetoric and erudite allusions intended for a more broadly educated body of princes, nobles and civil servants. Humanists, such as Erasmus or Brant, were no friends of the common people. Yet this did not mean that there was no evidence for a vigorous and thriving popular, secular culture. As we shall see, themes, motifs and beliefs, as in the case of Bosch, coming from the lower ranks of society, could have a marked effect on its upper levels. The later divorce between 'high' and 'popular' culture was not yet absolute – if it ever was. And although humanism did not imply humanitarianism in any discernible form, the work of Christian charity went on, firmly based on its medieval roots in the doctrine of good works. Almshouses, hospitals, orphanages, schools and colleges proliferated. A society, as Northern ones were, afflicted by recurrent epidemics and outbreaks of plague, at the mercy of weather conditions which could destroy a harvest or inundate an area, with disastrous results, continued to function as it had always done, Renaissance or no Renaissance. Huizinga's pessimistic picture of the period is only partially borne out by evidence from economic and social history – evidence which he himself did not in fact use. But the resilience and adaptability of Northern European society in the face of its many vicissitudes remains striking. And there were signs, particularly in the latter part of the period, of a shift northwards in the European centre of economic gravity. While some Northern cities, such as Bruges, underwent a slow decline, others, such as Antwerp, Amsterdam, Brussels, Strasbourg, Basel, Augsburg and Nuremberg, experienced rising prosperity, at least for their patriciates, both noble and merchant, and their enfranchised burghers. There was no necessary or inevitable correlation or connection between economic growth and cultural efflorescence, but any increase in the possession and circulation of readily available, disposable liquid capital was likely to be beneficial to the arts. This was as true for Northern Europe as it was for Italy.

There have, moreover, been recent efforts to depict a separate, free-standing Northern Renaissance which was to some degree independent of Italy. These studies attempt to make a clear distinction between some aspects of an indigenous Northern Renaissance and one which was directly inspired and influenced by Italian developments in thought and the visual arts. Similar patterns have been detected in the German-speaking, Slavonic and Nordic lands, as well as in the Netherlands. Arguments have tended to be concentrated on the later fifteenth and early sixteenth centuries, in both intellectual and art history, rather than the pursuit of ideas similar to those of Courajod or Fierens-Gevaert. An outstanding recent example is Marisa A. Bass, *Jan Gossart and the Invention of Netherlandish Antiquity* (2016), who argues that Netherlandish scholars and humanist thinkers of the later fifteenth and early sixteenth centuries strove to create a local or regional Renaissance, which was shared and participated in by artists, writers and their patrons. Bass trenchantly rejects 'the long-held understanding of this period in Netherlandish art and intellectual history as defined by revelatory encounters with Italy and the rediscovered antiquities of Rome. Classical rhetoric, antique forms, and antiquarian pursuits did not seep into northern Europe passively and inevitably, like silt water after a deluge.'[41] They were the result of conscious effort. An independent Northern European contribution to the 'rebirth' of antiquity is therefore proposed. This view will be discussed in a later chapter.[42]

To use the term 'Northern Renaissance', we argue in this book, is permissible and justified. Faute de mieux, it can be used to describe not only a period in cultural history and the history of art but also, with important regional and local variations, a more general, multifaceted movement. Its chronological limits, like all such periodizations, cannot be precisely fixed, but we propose to date it from *c.* 1380 to *c.* 1540. Some, but by no means all, recent art-historical opinion has inclined in favour of this kind of periodization.[43] This period brought innovations and new modes of thinking and perception into religious and secular thought, while new forms of representation and expression emerged in the visual arts and literature. A renewed emphasis on the individual and an intense interest in the natural world, as much as a rediscovery of classical antiquity, informed much of the art and literature of the time. But far from rejecting all aspects of the medieval past, including the indigenous Gothic and popular culture of the North, it built upon some of them and, in the process, adapted or transformed them. It is, therefore, one purpose of this book to reopen the debate about the nature of a Northern Renaissance and establish whether one can discern relationships, continuities or discontinuities, between the world of Jan van Eyck, Rogier van der Weyden and Thomas Kempis and that of Albrecht Durer, Hans Holbein and Desiderius Erasmus.

2

REALISM AND THE VISUAL ARTS

In Italy, Germany, Flanders, especially the latter, these artists had revealed the unsullied self-sufficiency of pious souls; their subjects, caught in life-like postures amid entirely authentic settings, with not a detail out of place, were rendered with mesmerizing sureness; from these heads, many of them common enough in themselves, and these physiognomies, often ugly but powerfully evocative as a group, emanated celestial joy or acute anguish, spiritual calm or turmoil. (J.-K. Huysmans, *La-Bas* (1891))[1]

THE 'EYCKIAN REVOLUTION'

The period of the Northern Renaissance witnessed something not far short of a revolution in the visual arts. Some will claim that it is easy to exaggerate its nature and significance. Since the rejection of the views put forward in the past by proponents of quasi-Hegelian holistic theories of artistic progress and profound changes in the Zeitgeist, purportedly expressed through the visual arts, art historians have tended to err on the side of caution. Nevertheless, the rise of representational realism in painting, sculpture and the applied arts signified a rediscovery of pictorial space and verisimilitude more or less unparalleled since the demise of the Western Roman Empire in the fifth century AD. Whatever causes, motives and attitudes lay behind this development, the fact remains that the art of the fifteenth century simply did not look like the art of the eleventh or twelfth centuries. The revolutionary aspects of the changes can be overdrawn, because there was a strong evolutionary, and sometimes counter-revolutionary, current flowing beneath them. But it would be difficult to deny that the realism and naturalism which reached its early peak in the art of Jan van Eyck (1390–1441) were such that they could hardly fail to influence the manner in which a viewer might react when contemplating such works of supreme artistic virtuosity. But the so-called Eyckian revolution was not simply a product of developments in artistic techniques. The notion, promoted by Vasari, that Jan van Eyck had invented the technique of painting in oils has long since been disproved and discarded. Van Eyck's innovations may have been both symptoms and causes of much wider and deeper changes in both aesthetic and religious sentiment. It has been said of Van Eyck's so-called *Arnolfini Marriage* panel (1434) that its truthfulness to observed reality, however illusionistically achieved, creates 'a fresh relationship ... between what art expresses and what a human being perceives and feels'[2] (Figure 1). If true, this conclusion has very wide implications indeed.

We therefore need to trace the advent and development of strikingly 'realistic' representations of people, animals, objects, landscapes, townscapes and even seascapes in Northern art. How and why had convincing representations of pictorial space, peopled with realistically rendered figures, more or less completely materialized in all major art forms by the end of the first quarter of the fifteenth century? The congruence between what is expressed by art and what is seen, perceived and felt was particularly marked as artists set their human subjects into defined spaces created by means of an empirical use of perspective. It has been said of those human subjects that

> they stand in groups as though they could move in a moment into a different relationship with one another. Instead of seeming to be merely superimposed on a background, the manner of rendering a room, a street or a stretch of countryside puts them at ease within its space.[3]

This congruence, and much of its underpinning, owed nothing whatsoever to humanist – or any other – theorizing. How these innovations were greeted by those who first witnessed them is difficult to gauge. Unlike the state of the Italian evidence, we are hampered in our understanding of how Northern European contemporaries saw, evaluated and appreciated works of art produced in the North. There is, until Karel van Mander's *Het Schilderboek* (1604), no Northern equivalent of Vasari's *Lives of the Artists* (1568) and we are reliant for information about reactions to the arts, on the writings of Italian visitors and Italians who had seen works by Northern masters in Italy. Again, unlike the Italian evidence, there are few surviving contracts for artistic commissions which relate to surviving works of art. The contract between Dieric Bouts and the confraternity of the Holy Sacrament in the church of St Peter at Louvain (March 1464) is a notable and rare exception. There was also no Northern fifteenth- or early sixteenth-century Leon Battista Alberti (1404–72), Bartolomeo Fazio (*c.* 1410–57) or any other writer of treatises on art and architecture which not only discussed techniques but also offered evaluative judgements and opinions on the works of individual artists and architects. The one major exception to this rule were the theoretical and critical writings of Albrecht Durer. In Fazio's case, the list of outstanding artists included Northern Renaissance painters such as Van Eyck and Van der Weyden, praised for their verisimilitude and (especially Van der Weyden) their expression of feeling and emotion. Fazio's treatise *De viris illustribus* (1456) was a panegyric on famous men, including the artists of his time, and provides us with some guide as to how viewers might react to contemporary works of art. Fazio, a humanist, historian, civil servant, diplomat and educator, had seen some of the Netherlandish painters' works in Naples. It would not be unreasonable to suppose that what this Italian humanist and critic thought would not be entirely out of line with the attitudes and assumptions of his Northern contemporaries.

That said, it is clear that what is known as 'illusionistic realism', that is the accurate, precise and detailed representation of people, animals, objects and space, had entered (or re-entered) Western art at this period. To its earliest observers, its effects must have seemed not far short of magical. In the *Arnolfini Marriage* panel, the extraordinary virtuosity with which the mirror at the back of the picture space is rendered, entirely through the medium of varnished oil paint applied in layers to a wooden board, is part of what amounts to an artistic conjuring trick. This conjuring up of what appears to be reality depended upon the artist's command of illusionistic three-dimensionality, of artificial, empirical, but not necessarily strictly mathematical, perspective, and the techniques of representing light, shade and colour convincingly. This 'realistic' art has also been described as naturalism, illusionism, or mimesis – the imitative representation of the real world in art or literature. But since the early to mid-nineteenth century, 'realism' and 'naturalism' have tended to be conflated, or become synonymous, in discussion of the art of the Northern Renaissance and its precursors. And it is a significant fact that its emergence in no way depended upon the inspiration or influence of, or from, classical antiquity.

To combine figures, objects and landscape features within a convincing spatial context meant opening up vistas of the natural world with what appears – deceptively – on the surface to be near-photographic realism. The stylized landscapes of the past, with their impressionistic rocky outcrops, randomly placed trees and forests, often set against a background of gold leaf, were increasingly eclipsed by images which corresponded strikingly to what one actually saw. Van Eyck's *Madonna of the Chancellor Rolin* (*c.* 1435) sets the donor, portrayed as he was in life, against a vista viewed from a high point on a terrace above a river, which meanders – in a totally convincing perspective – into a distant mountainous terrain (Figures 2, 6). The techniques of representing receding distances, reflections in water and the play of light on surfaces are exercised with something nearing perfection in this panel. The scene,

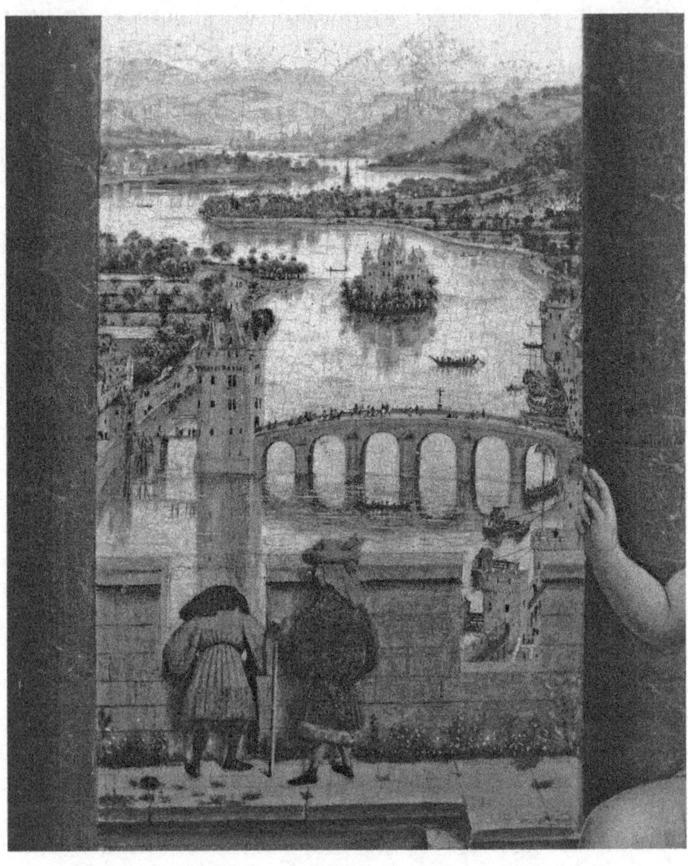

Figure 6 Jan van Eyck: *Madonna of Chancellor Rolin* (close-up).
(Photo by DEA/G. DAGLI ORTI/De Agostini/Getty Images.)

probably intended to be set in a chamber in the palace of Syon above the city of Jerusalem, represents it as in fact taking place in an entirely fifteenth-century setting. That setting could be the Burgundian town of Autun, Rolin's birthplace, and the panel was intended for his own chapel in his burial church there. The little figures looking out over the parapet in the middle distance, leading towards a busily trafficked bridge over the river, and then into the far distance, wear exactly the costumes current in the 1430s. There is a coalescence here between the sacred and the secular, between the spiritual and the temporal, and between the eternal and the transient. It is these dualities that have tended to dominate the debate as to whether the art of Van Eyck was truly 'realistic' in the modern sense.

The origins of these developments can be traced back to an earlier period. They also had contemporary and later manifestations which saw the emergence of independent portraits and independent landscapes, divorced from any religious or devotional meaning or context. It will be one purpose of this chapter to investigate them. The coexistence, in the works of Van Eyck (1390–1441), Van der Weyden (1400–64) and Memling (1430–94) of both donor portraits and independent portraits, requires some explanation. We are still in the world of 'functional' art, and both species of portrait had their specific purposes. The emergence of the independent landscape came somewhat later, in the works of Albrecht Altdorfer (1480–1538) and Albrecht Durer (1471–1528). But the seeds of the essentially topographical character of Altdorfer's and, especially, Durer's landscape studies were sown in the works of the later fourteenth- and fifteenth-century Netherlandish masters. As with the development of portrait types, lines of affinity can be traced between Van Eyck and Van der Weyden, on the one hand, and Durer and Holbein on the other. We can see continuities here, rather than any abrupt break from a firmly rooted, though innovative, Northern tradition. And curiosity about the natural world, its close observation and careful depiction, was a product as much of the fourteenth, as of the sixteenth, century.

REALISM IN THEORY AND PRACTICE

Any discussion of 'realism' must first attempt to elucidate the many and varying definitions of the term, which are essentially time- and context-bound. In the fourteenth century, a philosophical and theological concept known as realism had developed, set beside and against a rival concept of nominalism. The debate between the two 'schools' was, it is argued, to dominate scholastic disputation between university scholars, their pupils and followers, for the next century or more.[4] Whether realism in this sense bore any relation whatsoever to artistic realism, and whether the intellectual innovations of the fourteenth century had any influence on the visual arts remains to be seen. It was the belief of Erwin Panofsky, in his *Gothic Architecture and Scholasticism* (1951), that there was some correlation between contemporary intellectual movements and developments in art and architecture in the twelfth and thirteenth centuries.[5] Can anything similar be detected at a later period?

In later medieval metaphysics, scholastic thought, after the Aristotelian controversies of the later thirteenth century, began to revolve around the categorization of entities, things with a distinct and independent existence. One result of those controversies was to create distinctions which were often formulated in binary terms: the ideal was confronted by the real; faith was offset against experience and the substance of things was contrasted with their 'accidental' qualities. Debate over the nature of entities took on a distinctly novel form as a retreat, and reaction, from the formulations and propositions of St Thomas Aquinas (1225–74), or what came to be known as Thomism, began. Exponents of realism argued that all entities could be gathered into two categories: particulars and universals. Nominalists, on the other hand, acknowledged a single category: particulars. Realists thought that particulars were related to each other by sharing some universal qualities and characteristics. So the particular could exemplify the universal. A particular horse, for example, shared such features as four legs and a tail with other horses. Nominalists, on the other hand, denied all universals and all universal abstractions. They concentrated on the particular, the individual and the unique. They believed universals to be simply a product of human invention which grouped objects or ideas into artificial categories (such as 'gender' or 'virtue') with no independent existence of their own. These two opposed positions were not merely examples of scholastic hair-splitting, as some Renaissance humanists believed, but had wider implications for assumptions about the nature of knowledge and scientific observation, about religious truth and the nature of God, and possibly about the manner in which the natural world might be depicted.

The fourteenth century was a critical period in what has been called the 'Dissolution of the Medieval Outlook'.[6] Scholastic thought was at something of a crossroads or watershed. The great systematizers, such as Aquinas, were now succeeded by thinkers with a greater concern for the division of inquiry among the various fields of knowledge – metaphysics, logic, optics, mathematics and so on – rather than their being brought together in the form of *Summae*, or other encyclopaedic compilations. It would be misleading to see all so-called realist and nominalist thinkers in either of the two camps as expounding exactly similar ideas because there were significant differences among them. But warring factions certainly emerged, with realism represented by the followers and supporters of Aquinas, Duns Scotus (*c.* 1266–1308) and Albertus Magnus (1200–80). Nominalism was professed by a younger generation of thinkers, including Thomas Bradwardine (1290–1349), Jean Buridan (1300–58) and, above all, William of Ockham (1288–1348). The following two generations of nominalists included Pierre d'Ailly (1351–1420), Jean Gerson (1363–1429), Nicolas of Cusa (1404–64) and Gabriel Biel (1420–95). They were all from Northern Europe, products of the universities of Paris, Oxford, Heidelberg and Cologne. Nominalist thinkers such as these rethought the bases of both philosophical and theological truth. They attempted to explain the natural world in natural terms, pioneering a more recognizably scientific means of studying natural phenomena, employing mathematics, physics and logic rather than metaphysics, as the inquiry required. This approach, or approaches, produced highly original work, especially in the natural sciences. For example, Nicolas Oreseme (1320–82), Parisian scholar, astrologer and early student of monetary issues, is considered to be one of the most significant early investigators of velocity, acceleration, projectile force and other forms of motion. This fourteenth-century movement rested upon a logic-based and evidence-led understanding. What was actual and particular, having a concrete existence in the visible world, was strictly separated from the conceptual, living in the mind. Ockham represented what was termed the *via moderna* ('new' or 'modern way') while Aquinas and his later disciples followed the *via antiqua* ('old way'). By a paradoxical reversal of nomenclature, it could be argued that 'nominalism' had in effect more in common with the emergence of realistic representation in the visual arts than philosophical 'realism'. But, in religious thought, which was in turn reflected and expressed by visual art, the particular could carry universal characteristics within it. A representation of a particular saint could also be interpreted as a representation vision of a universal truth, namely the role of the saints as mediators between man and God. This would be in accord, in some respects, with a realist position. Such labelling can therefore be highly misleading and susceptible to misinterpretation. Be that as it may, the fourteenth-century shift in thought certainly qualifies for inclusion in any account of a Northern 'Renaissance' or, perhaps more appropriately, 'renovation' which introduced a 'modern way' (*via moderna*) in the world of the intellect.

It was in nominalism's concern for detail, for the individual and the particular, that some affinity with developments in the visual arts might conceivably be found. It would be difficult, if not impossible, and probably undesirable, to try to trace a concrete causal link. But these developments took place within a broadly common climate of thought. The issue of the individual and individualism may be a case in point. Individuality at this time was seen not so much in terms of the free-standing self-definition of a human being, but in the relationship of the individual soul with its creator. Self-awareness, in a religious context, and in that of devotional art, both Northern and Italian, was subordinated to a relationship with God through Christ, the Virgin Mary and the saints. Donors of altarpieces were represented, as individuals, in the presence of their objects of adoration and veneration, and were often shown as presented to Christ and the Virgin, with a benevolent hand on their shoulder, by their name saint or patron saint. The altarpiece provided a visible means of invoking the intercession of the saints, pleading for God's mercy on behalf of the donors. They could be depicted in settings that they might recognize, sometimes including familiar landmarks, well-known buildings and other features of these idealized background landscapes that they might find familiar. It has been said of fourteenth-century thought that 'the unitary mould of the past, enclosing men from direct contact with what lay outside them was being broken, bringing them into the presence of a new diversity and a new freedom in their conception of God'.[7] That diversity and freedom may have led to a curiosity about the natural world which expressed itself in close observation, exemplified in visual art by Hubert and Jan van Eyck's *Ghent Altarpiece* (1432) with its meticulous depiction of many species of plants and trees, many of which can be botanically identified (Figure 7). Unless one follows the more extreme approaches of some iconographers, Erwin Panofsky among them, whereby every single object in a painting contains a hidden or symbolic meaning, the careful rendering of such details seems one product of the opening up of the natural world to observation in its own right. It is perhaps not always necessary to introduce, in this instance, the notion of a search for a meaning which went beyond the objects represented or was subsumed within them. This would accord with, for example, Ockham's view of the primacy of the particular.

The greater or lesser degree to which an apparently realistic rendering of the natural world in visual art may, wittingly or unwittingly, have

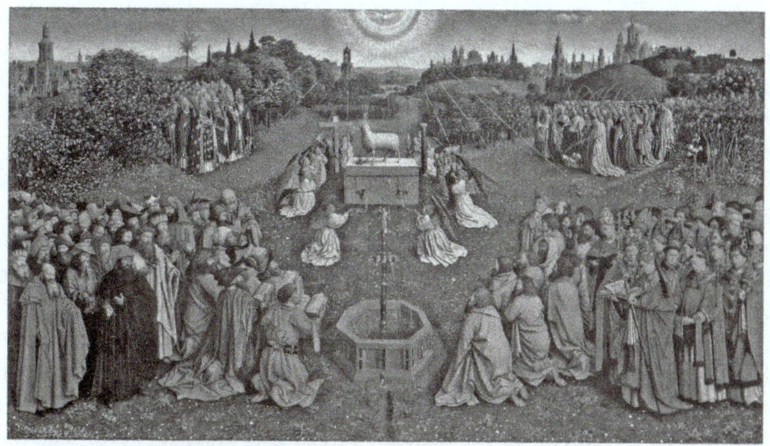

Figure 7 Jan and Hubert van Eyck: Altarpiece of the Mystic Lamb, Ghent
(Ghent, St Bavon).
(Photo by Electa/Mondadori Portfolio/Getty Images.)

reflected broader intellectual and aesthetic tendencies is at least arguable. If ways of seeing are undergoing changes, then ways in which what is seen is depicted may also shift in similar or related directions. The emphasis on 'imitation' (*imitatio*) at this time, especially in religious life and thought, whereby patterns of thought and behaviour consonant with those of Christ were advocated and adopted, also appears to have had some influence on the visual arts. As we shall see in a later chapter,[8] an increasing emphasis on moral and pastoral theology during this period led to a re-exploration of the humanity of Christ and its implications. The Christian doctrine of the Incarnation, whereby God assumed human form and walked upon the earth with the rest of common humanity, could hardly fail to suggest, and indeed stimulate, visualizations of many aspects of the Christian story. These found their way into the visual arts, arts which were now thought to be suitable vehicles for depicting those stories in concrete form, in a more 'realistic' manner than ever before in the Middle Ages. If the quality of the Christian life, and the spirituality of both clergy and laity, could be in any way enhanced by visualization of biblical doctrine and narrative, then the Church could only be favourably disposed towards it. Similarly, the lives and actions of the saints could be brought with greater immediacy into the consciousness and imagination of lay people by visual means. And the laity themselves, at least among the literate and educated classes, clearly wished to be more closely associated with, and participate more actively in, a more inclusive style of worship and religious observance. What could be more inclusive than representations of themselves, exactly as they were, or wished to be seen, in life, in the company of Christ and the saints, on the altarpieces which they themselves had commissioned?

It has been claimed, from Burckhardt's work (published in 1860) onwards, that the more realistic and convincing representation in art of human beings, animals and the natural world carried elements of secularism or secularization within it. Did it indicate the coming of a new, secular Renaissance, throwing off the bonds of the Church? A fundamental objection to this line of argument lies in the purposes behind the adoption of illusionistic realism in the visual arts of this period. It has been said that the Van Eyck's and their contemporaries' 'striking achievements in the depiction of the natural world were always subservient to transcendental ideas'.[9] If religious and devotional art, as it had in fact always done, 'visualises a theological program, and aims at giving immediate presence to all holy things, how can it be realist at all'? An example of this would be the way in which the Van Eycks depicted and located the source of the light which illuminates the central panel of the *Ghent Altarpiece* (1432) (Figure 7). This emanates from a point directly above the Eucharistic Lamb of God in the very centre of the altarpiece. A sixteenth-century engraving shows the altarpiece as it then was including, at that point, a tabernacle which housed the sacrament of bread and wine and which was set in a now lost horizontal layer, or intermediary register, of the work. It was from there that the Light of the World came, from the sacrificial Lamb, spilling its blood into a chalice, as victim of the Eucharistic feast. The 'realism' of the altarpiece was thus tempered by the intervention of a transcendental, theological concept, perfectly expressed by the Van Eycks in visual terms.

This art may thus never have held up a scrupulously exact mirror to reflect every aspect of the world in which it had been created. But, by placing holy and sacred scenes in a contemporary fifteenth-century setting, it both recorded and, to an extent, sacralized the mundane, and less mundane, details of the secular world. The everyday Netherlandish interiors, for example, in which images of the Annunciation to Mary were set, were instantly recognizable to the viewer (Figure 8). But they gave an immediacy to the presence of the divine and the sacred in the visible, material world. As we shall see, this reflected and indeed mirrored some of the trends and movements in the devotional piety of the age.[10] The transcendental nature of the subject matter posed problems for the arts.

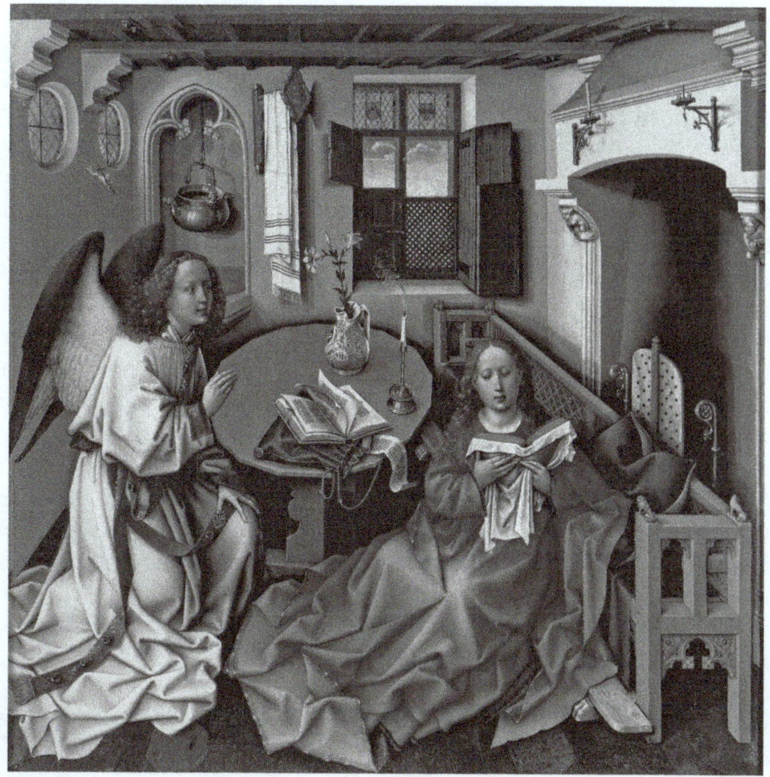

Figure 8 Robert Campin/Master of Flemalle: Annunciation (Mérode Altarpiece),
(NY, Met. Museum of Art).
(Photo by De Agostini/Getty Images.)

How was the invisible world of the Godhead, Paradise and its antithesis,
Hell, to be made visible, if at all? Did they need to be represented in
this way? Earlier medieval art had tended to emphasize the distance
between God and man. Images were either icons themselves or icon-
like – two-dimensional, sometimes remote, certainly distanced from the
visible world of common humanity. Icons represented the other-worldly
presence of Christ and the Holy Spirit in this world, giving much art of
the earlier period a detached, stylized, remote and elevated character.
Religious art of the eleventh and twelfth centuries did not hold up a
mirror in which worldly reality was in any way reflected. The thirteenth
century, however, undoubtedly saw the emergence of a number of

works and written texts described as 'Mirrors' (*Specula*) – of Nature, or Salvation – but the reflections which they presented and contained were cast in the form of highly symbolic, non-realistic images, full of inner and often hidden meaning.

However, movements within the theology of the doctrine of the Incarnation, that is, of Christ's assumption of humanity in the form of God made man, had begun to have some impact on the visual arts from the twelfth century onwards. Cults of the Virgin Mary, mother of Christ, also began to introduce another, more human, sometimes domestic dimension, into both devotional religion and devotional art, certainly from the early thirteenth century. But modern realism was still a very long way off, and was to remain so for a long time. It could be claimed that there was very little in common between these early manifestations of apparent realism and the nineteenth- and early twentieth-century movements towards artistic realism and naturalism. Modern Realists from Gustave Courbet (1819–77) onwards were determined to depict the 'ordinary, everyday, uninteresting' aspects of life, because their desire for 'realism, in both life and art, may [have been] the result of a sense that fantasy, imagination, speculation have all run away with human attention'.[11] This concentration on the fantastical, imaginative and speculative in the arts had, it was claimed, relegated the realistic depiction of observed reality to a minor place. Courbet and his followers stressed, on the contrary, the importance of letting things and their appearances stand for themselves. He proposed that artists should aim for objectivity. A painting's character and appearance was not to be determined or dictated by its subject matter, narrative content or moral message. A work of art should speak for itself. Unsurprisingly, more recent reactions have rejected this cult of realism. The artist Georges Braque (1882–1963) summarily dismissed the arguments for realism in painting and adopted an anti-realistic stance: 'Writing is not describing, painting is not depicting. Verisimilitude is merely an illusion.'[12] He and other critics opposed the idea of 'imitating what one wishes to create'.[13] For them, imitative realism therefore killed artistic creativity.

On grounds such as these, Renaissance realism, whether Northern or Italian, could not be 'modern'. If the depiction of scenes, human figures, narratives and objects, both exotic and everyday, was infused with symbolic and allegorical meaning, then fifteenth- and sixteenth-century realism does not, and cannot, stand or speak for itself. Inner meaning, it is argued, has to be teased out of the images depicted, and Renaissance art has therefore been fertile soil for the great iconographers of the past to cultivate. For most fifteenth-century patrons and viewers, it seems, the subject matter and content of a work was of equal, if not greater, importance than the manner in which those subjects were represented and the means by which the painting or sculpture was produced and created. Transcendental ideas may well have reigned supreme in religious art, but secular subject matter might be thought to have required different treatment. Yet, in the depiction of mythological, historical, astrological, didactic and even erotic subjects, some similar considerations prevailed. Symbolism, allegory and allusion were also present in representations of a purportedly secular character, such as depictions of episodes from classical mythology, ancient and more recent history, or the Arthurian legend. It was not only pagan mysteries from antiquity that were represented in Renaissance art of a secular nature. A strong and vigorous Northern tradition, rooted in indigenous Gothic but subject to changes affecting all the visual arts, flourished in its depiction of secular, profane and erotic subjects. As we shall see,[14] the new techniques of woodcut- and metal-plate engraving, etching and printing, enabled a much wider dissemination of such images. The Northern Renaissance had its own versions of themes depicting secular life and thought. Italy possessed no monopoly in this respect.

THE ORIGINS AND DEVELOPMENT OF REALISTIC REPRESENTATION

It is a characteristic of developments in the visual arts, as in many other spheres, that different art forms and different geographical areas do not always move together in unison. The pace of change, development and sheer coexistence can vary widely from one form to another and from one area to another. It seems that, during the medieval period in Western Europe, the first art form to adopt more expressively realistic styles of representation was sculpture. Free-standing sculpture is of course an entirely three-dimensional medium, and it can render images in a more immediately lifelike manner than a two-dimensional painting or drawing. The earliest surviving evidence for this tendency originated not in Italy but in Northern Europe. In the West choir of the cathedral at Naumburg, a remarkable series of twelve figures, dating from the 1240s, survives[15] (Figure 9). Although, as Andrew Martindale pointed out, these figures were 'all remote in time, the sculptor gave them a vivid and individual contemporary presence'.[16] They represented the eleventh-century ancestors of the counts of Meissen, who were the original benefactors

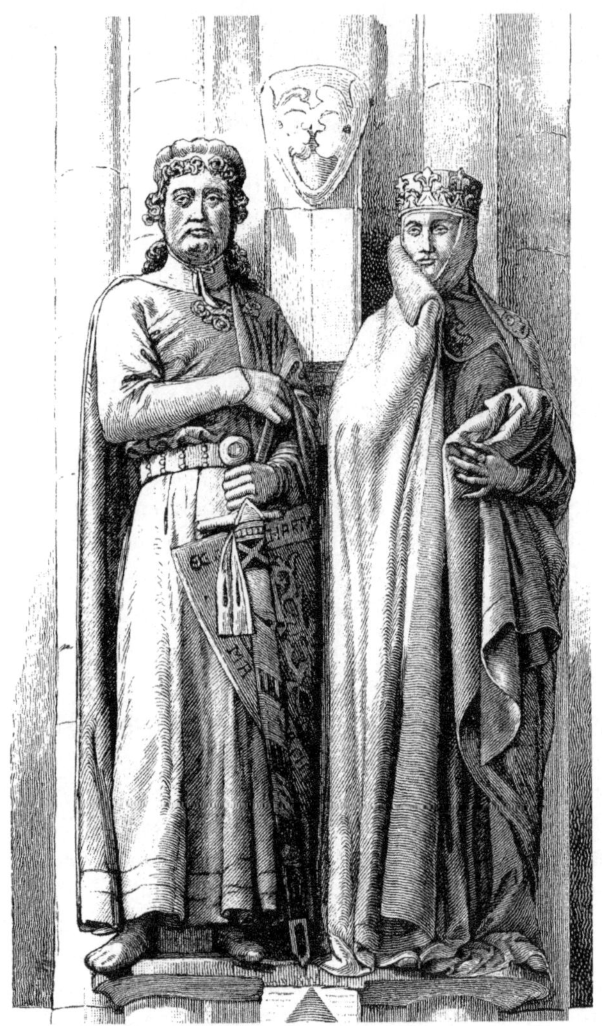

Figure 9 Costume of princes (1885 woodcut).
(Photo by Bildagentur-online/Universal Images Group/Getty Images.)

and protectors of the bishopric of Naumburg, which had been created under their patronage in 1028 as a result of its transfer from the see of Zeitz. What is more, the lifelike features, expressive gestures and body language of these ancestral figures appear to be narrating a story, of family discord as well as of harmony. Although no one had the remotest idea of what they might have actually looked like in their lifetimes, they were given contemporary thirteenth-century costumes and facial features which are vividly expressive. They must have been based on real, living models from the 1240s.

These sculpted, and then painted, galleries of ancestors began to appear and proliferate more widely in the early to mid-fourteenth century, at Paris, Prague and, in heraldic stained glass, as commemorative windows in great churches such as Tewkesbury abbey in England. From the mid-thirteenth century, moreover, for the very first time in the Middle Ages, the individual images of some famous, and not-so-famous, people were rendered in a lifelike, convincing fashion. In Italy, statues and tomb effigies, such as those of Charles of Anjou (1227–85), king of Naples and Pope Clement IV (1190–1268) were rendered with the features that they possessed in life. Apart from the Naumburg series, and the near-contemporary equestrian figures of former German emperors at Magdeburg (*c.* 1232–40) and Bamberg (*c.* 1235–40), the pace of change initially accelerated in Italy rather than in the North. In the sculpted representation of figures from the Bible, and of saints and martyrs, realistic and varied human types, expressing a wide range of different emotions, began to appear from the workshops of Arnolfo di Cambio (*c.* 1240–*c.* 1310) and Nicola (*c.* 1220–*c.* 1284) and Giovanni (*c.* 1250–*c.* 1315) Pisano. By the later fourteenth century, the genius of Claus Sluter (1340–1406), sculptor of the great 'Moses fountain' figures at the Burgundian Charterhouse of Champmol, had made its presence felt in the North (Figure 10). The vivid characterizations of the figures of the prophets around the Carthusian monastery's well and fountain were unparalleled in Northern Europe at the time. In the realm of painting, Giotto (1266–1337), Simone Martini (1282–1344) and Ambrogio Lorenzetti (1290–1348) all produced lifelike, profile images of their patrons as donors of frescos and altarpieces. The first recorded fully independent portrait appears to have been the lost image of Petrarch's beloved Laura, which Simone Martini painted in about 1336. But Northern Europe was soon not only to emulate these Italian examples but to surpass them.

It is clear that the rise of the portrait at this time in Western art was closely connected to the creation of visual memories and the commemoration of the individual.[17] The visual recording and commemoration of ancestors and predecessors in a line of succession evidently functioned as a means of stressing continuity, and giving (often spurious) antiquity to new or upstart dynasties. Bishops might record the apostolic succession to their sees in this way, as the bishop of Prague did in 1301. Not only royal but

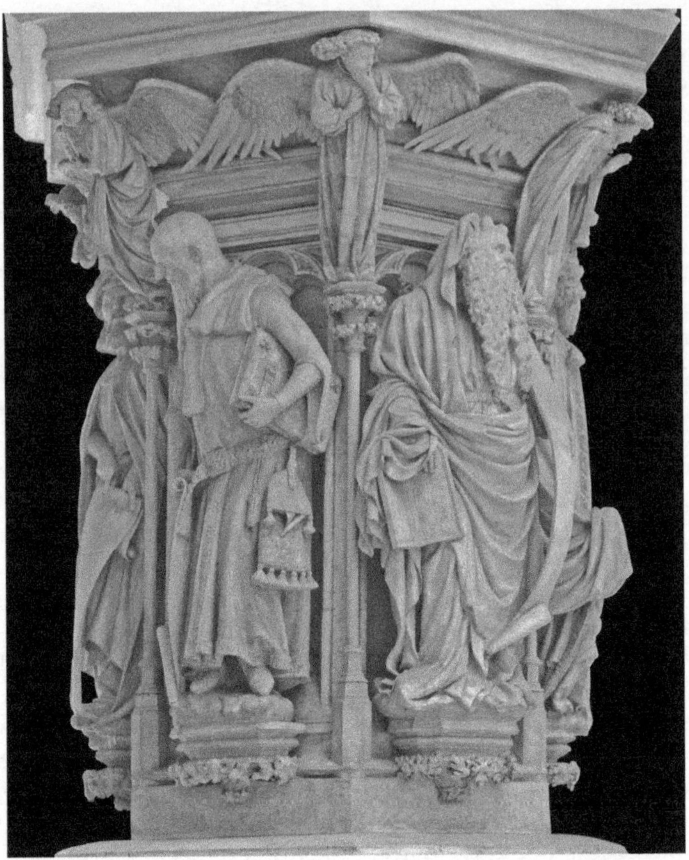

Figure 10 Claus Sluter: *Well of Moses* (Champmol, Chartreuse).
(Photo by Christophel Fine Art/Universal Images Group/Getty Images.)

princely dynasties similarly emphasized their past in this fashion, as did the counts of Flanders, dukes of Brabant and dukes of Burgundy. In the course of the later thirteenth and fourteenth centuries, it thus became increasingly common to create lifelike characterizations of the faces of the dead whether any record of their features survived or not. They were a means by which mortality and the physical reality of death could be transcended and overcome. In the public sphere, tombs, galleries of portraits and monumental sculptures provided the vehicles whereby rulers and nobles, both recent and distant, were commemorated. This was to continue for centuries to come. In a more private sphere, the self-contained portrait, emerging in the mid-fourteenth century, offered a personal memento, a souvenir or means of remembrance or, rather more publicly, a diplomatic gift. These images tended to be portable, without any very clear function apart from that of a keepsake. Charles V of France had four such small paintings in his possession in 1380. The practice of taking premarital likenesses of possible husbands and, more particularly, brides also led to such examples as Jan van Eyck's lost portrait of *Isabella of Portugal* (1428) before her betrothal to Philip the Good, Duke of Burgundy. Marriage alliances could be aided, abetted or even broken by the accuracy or inaccuracy of such images. Henry VIII of England's marital history was not uninfluenced by them. But all these images were in effect autonomous and self-contained, without reference to any evident religious or other meaning. The independent portrait had been born from a combination of factors in which identification, commemoration and remembrance of both the living and the dead played very important parts.

In the devotional sphere, the figure of the donor and his or her family on the altarpieces and wall paintings commissioned for their private chapels, in both Italy and Northern Europe, was critical to the evolution of the portrait. Depictions of the donor's wife and children were ultimately to lead to, and influence, the emergence of the group portrait of non-royal, non-noble and commoner families – represented by such works as Hans Holbein the Younger's collective portrait of Sir Thomas More and his family (*c.* 1527). But even in this case, what may appear to be an entirely secular subject can be interpreted as an essentially devotional image, as the More family appear to be preparing, in their household, to celebrate the Hours of the Virgin. They seem to be holding their Books of Hours, ready to follow the liturgical text. In the later thirteenth century, Books of Hours – service books containing the order of services and prayers for all the canonical hours of the liturgical day – also began to include the figure of the book's owner, normally to accompany the *Obsecro te* ('I beseech Thee') prayer addressed to the Virgin Mary[18] (Figure 11). This could form a kind of frontispiece to the personalized service book, which might also contain prayers to certain saints, universal, regional and local, to which the owner had a particular devotion. These volumes, many of them readily portable, were produced for the laity by the laity. They were not the products of monastic *scriptoria* (writing offices) but of lay workshops. They largely escaped ecclesiastical and episcopal supervision and are therefore vital sources for the currents of lay piety at this time. Representation of individual donors in panel and wall painting had

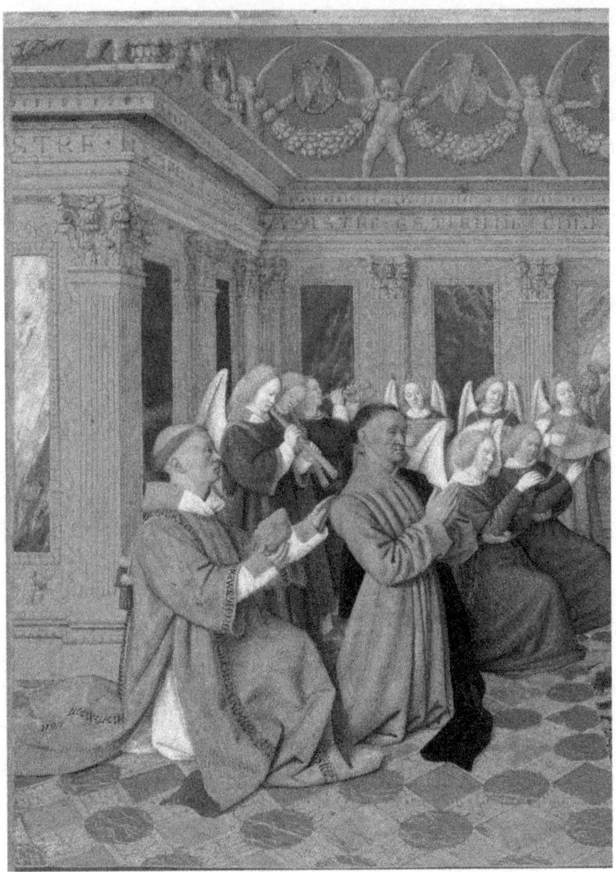

Figure 11 *Hours of Étienne Chevalier* (1455), *Obsecro te* folio
(Chantilly, Musee Conde).
(Photo by Fine Art Images/Heritage Images/Getty Images.)

begun in the later thirteenth and early fourteenth century, when small figures began to appear on the *predella* panels and elsewhere in Italian, German and Bohemian altarpieces. These often relegated the diminutive donor and his or her family to a relatively inconspicuous position, at the very base of the panels which made up the complete altarpiece. They were on a much smaller scale than the figures of God the Father, Christ and the saints which formed the main focus of the work. In some areas of Italy and Germany, such as the Marches, the Romagna and Westphalia, this convention persisted for a long time, well into the fifteenth century, as in the works of Carlo Crivelli (1430–95) or Antoniazzo Romano (*c.* 1430–1510). By 1305, however, when Giotto completed his frescos for Enrico Scrovegni in the Arena Chapel at Padua, the donor had already begun to appear on more or less similar scale to the sacred figures, on this occasion in a depiction of the Last Judgement. Simone Martini similarly depicted donors such as Cardinal Gentile Partino da Montefiore dell'Aso at Assisi, venerating St Martin, in 1315 and Robert II, king of Naples, in an altarpiece of 1317 which shows him, on a slightly reduced scale, in obeisant prayer before St Louis of Toulouse. All these lifelike images conformed to the contemporary notion of the 'counterfeit' portrait, as an imitation of the donor *contrefais al vif* ('imitated from life') but without the derogatory modern connotations of the word.[19] They were also all depicted strictly in profile, perhaps the least potentially expressive and searching of portrait types, but one in which a simple likeness can be more easily achieved.

By the later fourteenth century, three portrait types had emerged: the profile portrait, the frontal portrait, often reserved for kings and princes such as the Emperor Charles IV of Luxemburg or Richard II of England and, as the most novel and recent form, the three-quarter or half-profile portrait. This depicted the subject with his or her face turned, normally towards the spectator, looking out of the picture space. The earliest surviving example comes from Central Europe, when Rudolf IV, Duke of Austria, was represented in three-quarters profile, probably by a Bohemian artist, between 1360 and 1365. It was roughly contemporary with a portrait of John the Good, king of France, dated to the 1360s, but this is in simple profile. Both these works appear to be 'independent' or autonomous portraits, unrelated to any known devotional or commemorative project or other evident function. But the emergence and continuance of the three-quarter representation of the face may bear some relation to the demands of donors to be depicted within sacred spaces in as close a relationship to the Godhead, the Trinity, Christ, Mary and the saints as was doctrinally and theologically acceptable. These panels, portraying donors and their families in this way, were essentially and intrinsically functional works of art, and they appear to have originated in Northern Europe. They formed altar furniture, often merely one part of much more comprehensive pious endowments of private chapels in which masses for their souls, as well as for those of all the faithful departed, were to be said or sung in perpetuity.[20] The full liturgical apparatus of later medieval ritualized piety – vestments, altar frontals, chalices, ciboria, patens, pyxes, incense boats, censers, holy water pots and buckets, bells, asperging brushes, sprinklers, tabernacles and other housings for the sacrament – was part and parcel of an elaborate and expensive provision for the fate of the soul after death and entry into, and subsequent release from, Purgatory. The painted altarpiece was simply one element in that package or investment whereby, it was believed, the passage of the soul towards Paradise might be eased. Although donors may not, at this period, have been shown as active participants in the biblical and other episodes depicted on their altarpieces, they were no longer physically detached from those sacred scenes, nor shown on a smaller scale than the objects of their adoration and veneration.

It is striking that in the representations of donors by Jan van Eyck, Rogier van der Weyden, Hans Memling, Petrus Christus (1410–75), Dieric Bouts (1415–75) and other subsequent fifteenth- and early sixteenth-century masters, the angle of the donor's vision is always directed away from the images of God the Father, Christ, Mary and the Trinity. Nicolas Rolin, canon George van der Paele, Pieter Bladelin, Willem Moreel and countless other donors and patrons gaze in prayerful meditation out of the picture space towards some point to the left or right of the spectator (Figures 2, 3, 5). Any visual representation of an individual in the presence of God was subject to doctrinal constraints and theological objections. There is evidence that donors consulted ecclesiastical authorities, from university theologians to personal confessors, as did the confraternity at Louvain in 1464, to ensure that adherence to orthodox doctrine was maintained in their commissions. The doctrine of the invisibility of God to human vision, hidden behind the blinding, all-consuming light of divine radiance or refulgence, came into play here. Donors were represented exactly as they were in real life, with the closest of attention paid by the artist to their individual features. Images were so lifelike that later observers commented that these people seemed to be on the verge of actually speaking. Holbein's (independent) portrait of the Hanseatic merchant Derich Born (1533) carries a Latin inscription incised into the stone parapet (a Van Eyckian device) at the base of the picture space reading, 'Add but the voice and you have his whole self, that you may doubt whether the painter or the father made him.'[21] Such was the degree of lifelike immediacy that the painter could achieve in the representation of the features of an individual. Whether the space they inhabited was that of the real, visible world, or the invisible world of the Spirit, they could not physically see God. Thomas Kempis, in his *The Imitation of Christ* (1424–7, 1441), makes his 'Disciple' (i.e.

the priest, about to celebrate the Eucharist) address his 'Master' (Christ) with the words: 'I could not bear to gaze on You in the total glory of Your divinity, nor could the whole world cope with the brightness and glory of Your majesty.'[22] The notion was encapsulated in a hymn of 1867 written by, surprisingly, not a Roman Catholic nor an Anglo-Catholic Tractarian, but a Free Church of Scotland minister, based upon biblical texts:

> Immortal, invisible, God only wise, / In light inaccessible hid from our eyes. ... All laud we would render; O help us to see / 'Tis only the splendour of light hideth thee.

God is 'pure father of light' whose 'angels adore Thee, all veiling their sight', just as Christ is the Light of the World. Biblical authority was provided by 1 Tim. 6.15-16: 'God immortal ... lives in unapproachable light, whom no one has seen or can see.' The light emanating from the deity was therefore all-consuming, and God could only be 'seen' through Christ, whose humanity brought God's light, albeit figuratively, into the visible world. Observance of physical distance from the Godhead was therefore still imperative, close though the donor of an altarpiece might wish to be to his or her objects of adoration or veneration.

But in some devotional works of the later fifteenth and early sixteenth centuries, the donor and his or her family could hardly be closer to the sacred figures. In Holbein's *Meyer* or *Darmstadt Madonna* (1526), Jakob Meyer, sheltering under the Virgin's cloak, still looks not towards the objects of his adoration – Mary and the Christ child – but upwards, out of the picture space, towards another, heavenly realm (Figure 12). The figure of his deceased infant son, however, stands on the hem of the Virgin's robe. The panel is in some ways a summation of the evolution of the donor portrait since its inception. Both profile and three-quarter profile types are employed by Holbein in his depiction of the Meyer family members. Although the impact of Italianate forms and styles is evident in the work, with its Leonardo-esque rendering of both the Christ child and Meyer's deceased son, it owes far more to the Netherlandish masters of the fifteenth century than to anything recently emanating from Italy. It has been said of Holbein that a 'feeling for the surface and texture of nature remained characteristic of the art of Northern Europe for many years, and in this respect Holbein was truly the heir of van Eyck'.[23] But there were other ways in which the heritage from the fifteenth-century Netherlanders was transmitted to their successors. The independent portrait stood in a direct line of succession from the likenesses of

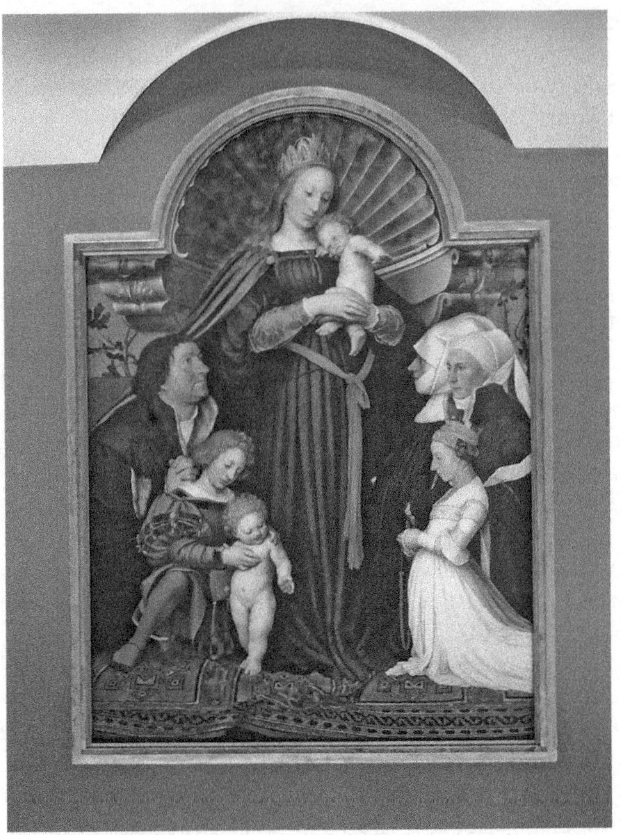

Figure 12 Hans Holbein: Meyer/Darmstadt altarpiece: Getty ed. 1131130136; object name b8020916jpg. (DEA/ALBERT CEOLAN/Getty Images.)

donors on the triptychs, diptychs and single panels which they had commissioned. Holbein and his contemporaries, including Durer and Cranach, adopted the portrait formulas first employed by Van Eyck and Van der Weyden. The three-quarter profile, lit from one side, set against a monochrome background of, normally, green or blue, became one of the most characteristic forms of the Renaissance portrait (Figures 13, 14). And it was also adopted by Italian artists. Ideal beauty and idealized portrayals of the dignity of man, those much-admired qualities of Italian Renaissance art, were found wanting in many respects. Not least in the desire to represent individuals as they were in life, with a cool, objective concentration upon realities. This was Northern Renaissance realism

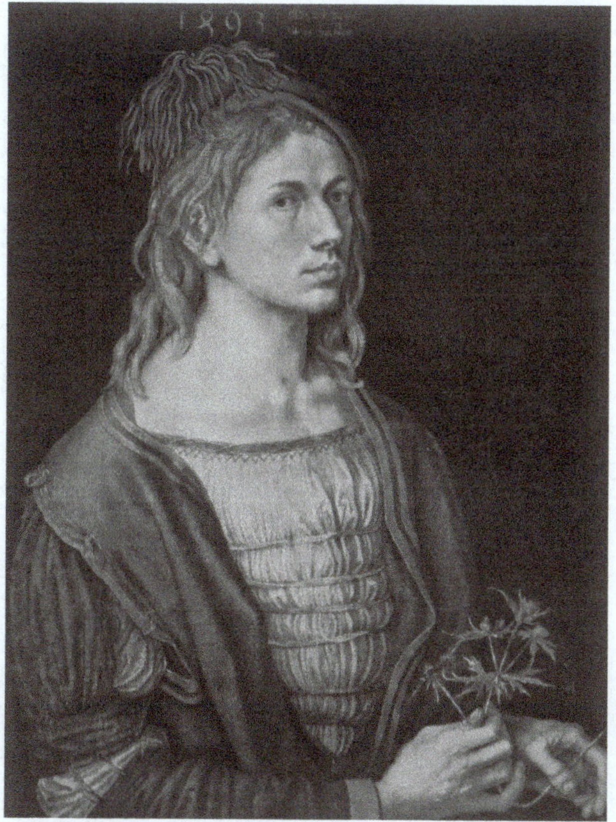

Figure 13 Albrecht Durer: *Self-portrait aged twenty-two* (1493) (Paris, Louvre).
(Photo by Archiv Gerstenberg/ullstein bild/Getty Images.)

at its most convincing and, for some, including Italians, most alluring. And there can be no doubt that great cultural and other historians, such as Huizinga or Warburg, were profoundly affected by the simple fact that there was now an accurate surviving record of the features of those whom they studied. These people could never be 'known', but the lifelike depictions of these recognizable human beings gave a greater degree of immediacy to our contact with the past. Huizinga's Hegelian-inspired concept of *Ahnung* – presentiment or intuitive feeling – must have come into its own when portraits as convincing and thought-provoking as these acted as profound stimuli to the informed and prepared historical imagination.

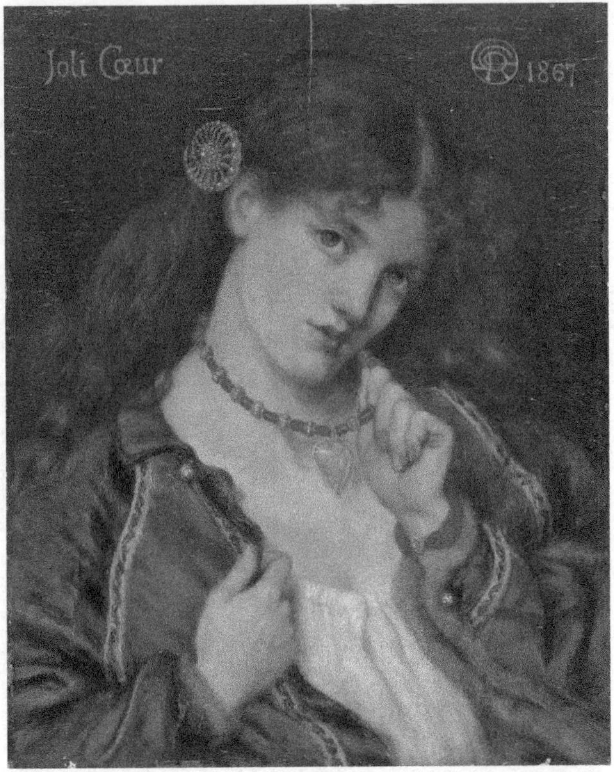

Figure 14 Dante Gabriel Rossetti: *Joli Cœur* (1867) (Manchester): (wikicommons).

The later medieval concern for the afterlife, and the knowledge, derived from Christ's teaching, that entry into the kingdom of Heaven by the worldly affluent and advantaged was no easy task, gave an urgent impetus to their pious endowments, foundations and commissions. Remission from the pains of Purgatory, and consequent reception into Paradise, was of particular concern in Northern Europe.[24] Endowment of Masses on a near-industrial scale – in various forms, including that of the perpetual chantry in England – created a demand for armies of Mass-celebrating clergy and essentially private, not public, space in which they could operate.[25] The tombs and chantry foundations of the rich, powerful and well-to-do clustered around the chancels, choirs and aisle side-chapels of cathedral, collegiate, conventual and parish churches throughout Western Europe. Hence the appropriation of sacred space by the laity, rivalling and sometimes outdoing the clergy, became a prominent feature in the devotional art that they commissioned as part of their Mass-celebrating endowments. In their altarpieces and devotional panels, donors began to be placed in ever-closer proximity to Christ, Mary and the saints. In some instances, such as a *Pieta* or *Lamentation* from Rogier van der Weyden's workshop (*c.* 1460–5; London, National Gallery) (Figure 4), the furred hem of the as yet unidentified lay donor's gown is actually touched by one finger of Christ's hand, in rigour mortis, after the bringing down of His body from the cross. We can only speculate on the possible psychological effects on donors and patrons of seeing themselves, just as they were in life, represented in this highly realistic, albeit illusionistic, fashion within the sacred, invisible space once reserved only for the divine and the sanctified. Huizinga, fascinated but also to some extent repelled by the phenomenon, accused them of worldly, over-weening arrogance and presumption, for considering themselves worthy of keeping such close company with God, the Holy Family and the saints. Over-familiarity with the sacred, he argued, led to disrespect, profanity and debasement. But, alternatively, such images might suggest a deep-seated devotional piety, no doubt moved by fear and apprehension about the fate of the soul in an afterlife, but nonetheless betokening a very high degree of self-awareness in relation to the divine. That self-awareness, initially springing from the spiritual life, could be, and was, translated into secular terms. The three-quarter profile donor portrait provided one source for the independent, secular, autonomous portrait, which has, for many, been seen as an example of Renaissance individualism. And the rise of the portrait, as well as the naturalistic tomb effigy, had opened up a new world of visual commemoration or remembrance (*Gedachtnis*) in which the individual, as the Emperor Maximilian I wrote, was no longer 'just forgotten with his funeral bell'.[26]

REALISM, LANDSCAPE AND THE NATURAL WORLD

The first surviving realistic representations of independent, autonomous landscapes in Western European art were drawn and painted between *c.* 1490 and *c.* 1520. A striking early example is a forest landscape painted by Gerard David of Bruges (1460–1523) in the 1510s on the two outer wing panels of a *Nativity* altarpiece (Amsterdam, Rijksmuseum). The meticulously observed trees, the reflections caught in a stream and a pond, at which two oxen drink, and a small, turreted, fortified *manoir* all carry a high degree of verisimilitude. On one panel, an ass lies resting beside the stream. This may possibly not be an entirely 'independent' landscape, because it would make sense to represent here the location of the place of Rest on the Flight into Egypt, a subject closely related to the depiction of the Nativity on the inner panels. It may therefore be telling a story. Be that as it may, the quiet calm of the scene, and the characteristically virtuoso treatment of the trees and their foliage, cannot fail to appeal to the viewer. It also bore all the hallmarks, or trademarks, of Gerard David's style and might, by comparison with other similar works from his hand, advertise his merits to potential patrons. But it was by no means the first time that apparently closely observed renderings of the natural world had appeared in both Northern European and Italian painting. Their function had, however, always been to provide backgrounds or accompaniments to devotional, narrative or decorative works, rather than standing as independent and detached studies of nature. The German artists Albrecht Altdorfer and Albrecht Durer, from Regensburg and Nuremberg respectively, were among the earliest and most prominent creators of truly independent landscapes. Altdorfer's finished landscapes, and his sketched, etched and engraved landscape studies, depicting mute and untitled scenes, of which a few include tiny human figures or animals, tell no stories(Figure 15). They have no known iconographical underpinning, religious or secular. But they are not simply images of nature as it actually was, or would be, seen by the naked eye. Artistry and fantasy was an essential part of Altdorfer's creative process. In Durer's work, however, there may be more attention to the accurate representation of the natural world as it appeared to the eye, albeit to a painterly eye (Figure 16). Durer was much influenced by the thoughts of, among others, his humanist friend Willibald Pirckheimer, who advised his readers in 1517 to 'observe and study nature' and 'inquire into the hidden and powerful workings of the earth'.[27] Durer himself, in two of his treatises on the visual arts, wrote that 'the more exactly one equals nature, the better the picture looks'.[28] It was to nature that one went to discover beauty, proportions and the fundamental principles of true art. This, in Durer's case, may not have led to the creation of finished independent landscapes for public consumption, but only to investigative studies, sketches and the accurate recording of views and prospects observed on his travels. But he nonetheless, with other German Renaissance artists, clearly considered the natural world worthy of representation in its own right.

Convincing depictions of landscapes in Northern Europe had originated in Franco-Flemish manuscript illumination of the later

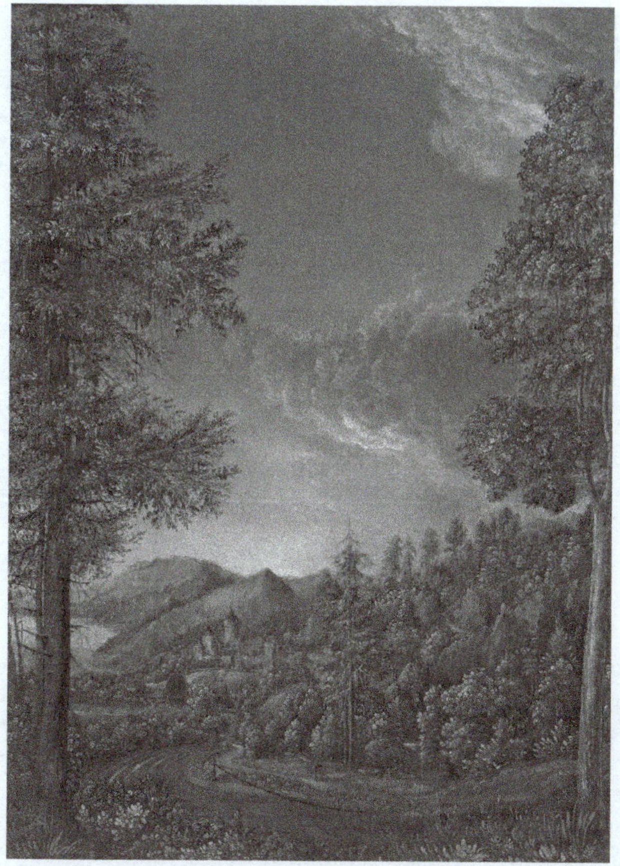

Figure 15 Albrecht Altdorfer: *Landscape with Castle* (*c.* 1515)
(Munich).
(Photo by Fine Art Images/Heritage Images/Getty Images.)

fourteenth century. The calendar pages of Books of Hours, depicting the labours of the months and seasons, offered an opportunity to illuminators to introduce landscapes, some stylized, some more naturalistic, into their work. These scenes were peopled by peasants working in the fields, tending their flocks and herds, or warming themselves by the February fireside while the outside world is shown covered in ice and snow, as in the *Tres Riches Heures* of Jean, Duke of Berry (*c.* 1416) (Figure 17). The upper classes were also represented, riding in their green May-day finery through the spring landscape, in celebration of the month of May. These

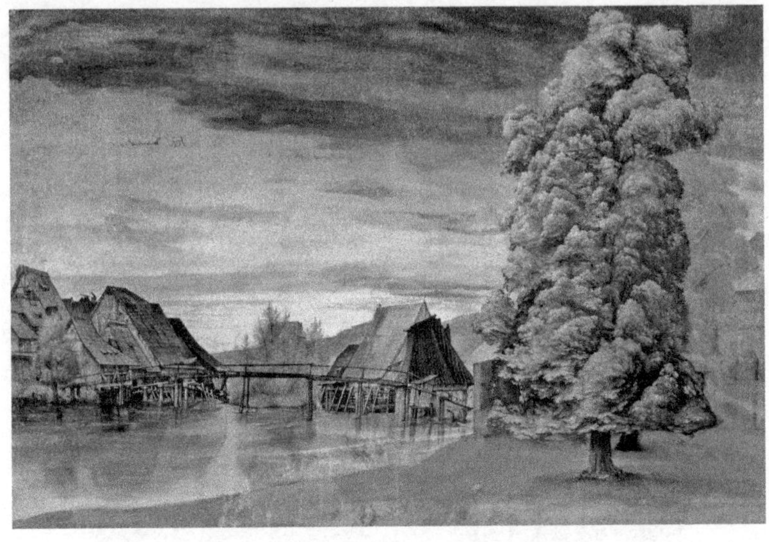

Figure 16 Albrecht Durer: *The Watermill.*
(Photo by Photo12/Universal Images Group/Getty Images.)

were in no way fully independent landscapes. Nor were the scenes of hunting and hawking, in forest or more open countryside, contained in such treatises as the *Livre de Chasse* of Gaston Phoebus, count of Foix and *vicomte* of Bearn, which survive in many manuscripts of that hunting treatise dating from the period *c.* 1380–1410. During the same period, the Limburg brothers, Jean of Berry's illuminators, had strong affinities with panel painters such as Melchior Broederlam, working for Philip the Bold, Duke of Burgundy, in the 1380s and 1390s. The Van Eyck brothers stood in a direct line of succession to them, coming from a similar area of the Low Countries as the Limburgs. The landscape depictions in the *Ghent Altarpiece*, for example, owed much to these earlier visions of the natural world in the devotional paintings and illuminations of the time. Although the attribution is now disputed, there can be little doubt that the full-page miniatures, and the *predella*-like scenes at the base of the surviving pages and photographic copies of the so-called Turin/Milan Book of Hours, were closely related to the art of Hubert and Jan van Eyck.

These images have, confusingly, received dating attributions from art historians ranging from the 1420s to the 1440s or even 1450s. But the extraordinary rendering of the seashore in the illumination of William,

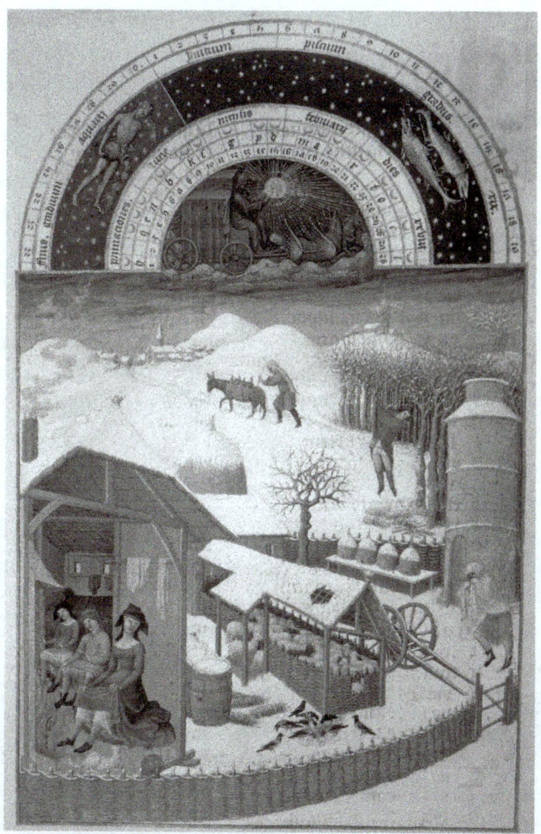

Figure 17 *Tres Riches Heures* of Jean, Duke of Berry (February page) (Chantilly, Musee Conde).
(Photo by Leemage/Corbis/Getty Images.)

count of Hainault and Holland, landing, probably at Veere on the Walcheren peninsula in Zeeland, riding a white horse which might have come straight out of the Knights of Christ panel of the *Ghent Altarpiece*, must surely point in the direction of extremely strong Eyckian influence. There can be no question that the artist or artists, if not the Van Eycks themselves, who were responsible for such images as the seashore scene, or the baptism of Christ, with its riverside castle, superbly reflected in the water, or the birth of John the Baptist, with its *Arnolfini Marriage*-like representation of a domestic interior, stood in a highly productive and symbiotic relationship with them. Their work would also stand comparison with the landscape, and townscape, in Jan van Eyck's *Madonna of the Chancellor Rolin*. This work, as well as the central panel of Rogier van der Weyden's *Bladelin* or *Middelburg Altarpiece* (1445–50) (Figure 3) with its view of the new Flemish town of Middelburg (now Maldegem), founded in 1450 by the donor Pieter Bladelin himself, or Gerard David's inclusion of recognizable buildings from Bruges in his devotional paintings, indicates the birth and early infancy of the townscape. In all these instances, however, the background representation of a Netherlandish urban scene was a device whereby Jerusalem, Bethlehem or other sacred sites were transposed into a recognizable contemporary setting. These images, among others, also provided models and exemplars for later topographical woodcuts and engravings of towns and cities in Renaissance atlases and chronicles. The copiously illustrated *Nuremberg Chronicle* (printed in 1493) is full of them.

The Northern Renaissance landscape, however, may have carried other connotations. It has been argued that the independent landscape, perhaps more so than any other subject, offered unrivalled opportunities for the development and demonstration of an artist's individual, even idiosyncratic style. Thus 'the independent landscape was born directly of this radical intrusion of the German artist's personal authority into his works'.[29] Signed by the artist, often dated, and identifiable by characteristic techniques, effects and eccentricities, these outdoor images allowed the expression of the artist's self-definition and self-advertisement to the full. Without the constraints of clearly defined rules, whether aesthetic, technical or iconographical, it could be claimed that the Northern Renaissance painter, etcher and engraver was here at his most free and uninhibited. Durer was clearly at their head, and was declared to be outstanding in his own time, but self-awareness, if not self-aggrandizement, was also present in the landscape studies of Lucas Cranach the Elder (1472–1553), Altdorfer, Hans Burgkmair (1473–1531) and Hans Baldung Grien (1480–1545). Landscapes simulating the Garden of Eden provided the backdrop to Cranach's and Baldung Grien's provocatively erotic nude renderings of Adam and Eve, with the apple and the serpent to represent their sin (Figure 18). In such cases, where the landscape *was* linked to a known theme or narrative, freedom from rules, especially for secular subjects, allowed the representation of profane, erotic and unorthodox material. For example, the forests depicted in Netherlandish and German Renaissance art are inhabited by often lustful, feral wild men and women and their children, savages, comic rustic and bucolic characters, satyrs, strange beasts and mythical beings

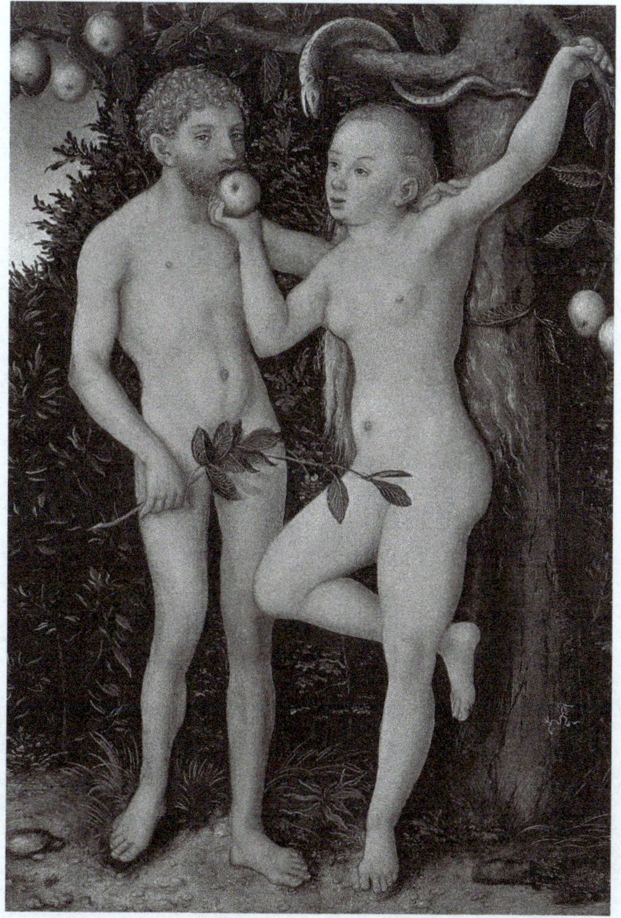

Figure 18 Lucas Cranach: *Adam & Eve* (1538) (Prague). (Photo by DeAgostini/Getty Images.)

from the indigenous pagan and pre-Christian, as much as the classical, past.[30] Landscape thus provided a ready medium for the exploitation and display of artistic individualism. The period also saw the rise of the artist's self-portrait, in which Durer again led the field, but he was not alone. So-called Renaissance self-awareness and self-presentation were by no means confined to Italy, and their spurs and roots did not lie exclusively in reference back to classical antiquity. The Northern landscape, as well as the self-portrait, had become a vehicle whereby artistic personality and reputation might be expressed and conveyed to a wider audience.

The much-extolled Renaissance cult of fame was also not confined to Italy. Jan van Eyck had pioneered the authentication of his works with a signature, and dated them precisely by means of inscriptions, carved into the *trompe l'oeuil* stonework parapet in the foreground of a portrait, or

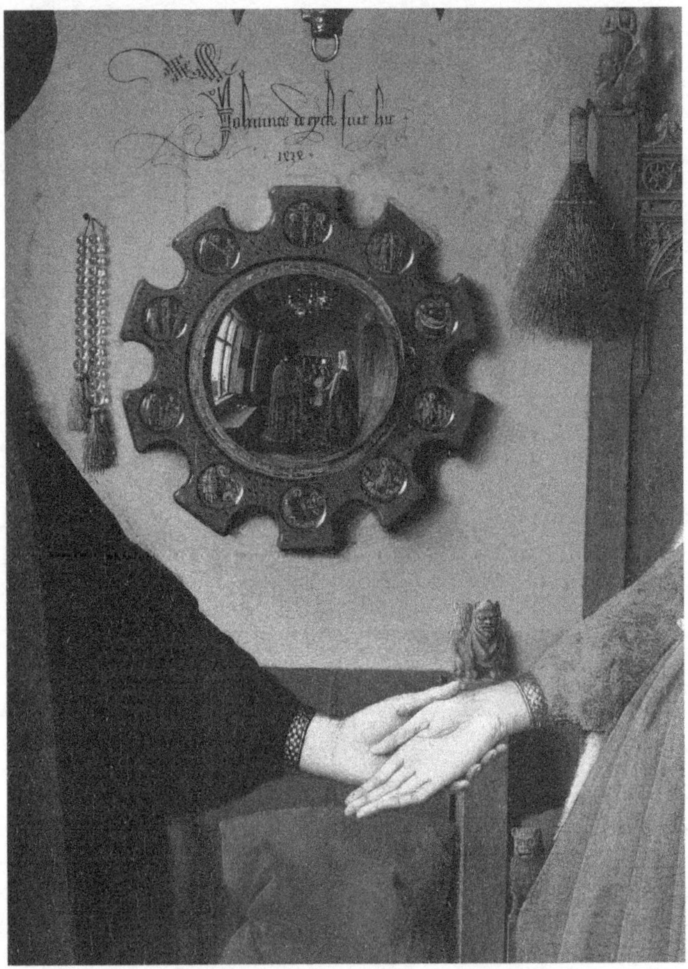

Figure 19 Jan van Eyck: *Arnolfini Portrait* (detail): Mirror and inscription. (Photo by DeAgostini/Getty Images.)

painted on the picture frame. Memling and other later artists followed this practice. In 1433, Van Eyck had produced what is thought to be his self-portrait, with his personal motto or device painted on to its frame (Figure 47). Most remarkably of all, the elaborately crafted inscription *Johannes de Eyck fuit hic 1434* ('Jan van Eyck was here 1434') in the background of the *Arnolfini Marriage* panel leaves no doubt as to the identity of the artist and his presence at the scene – whatever its meaning and significance really was – which he witnessed[31] (Figure 19).

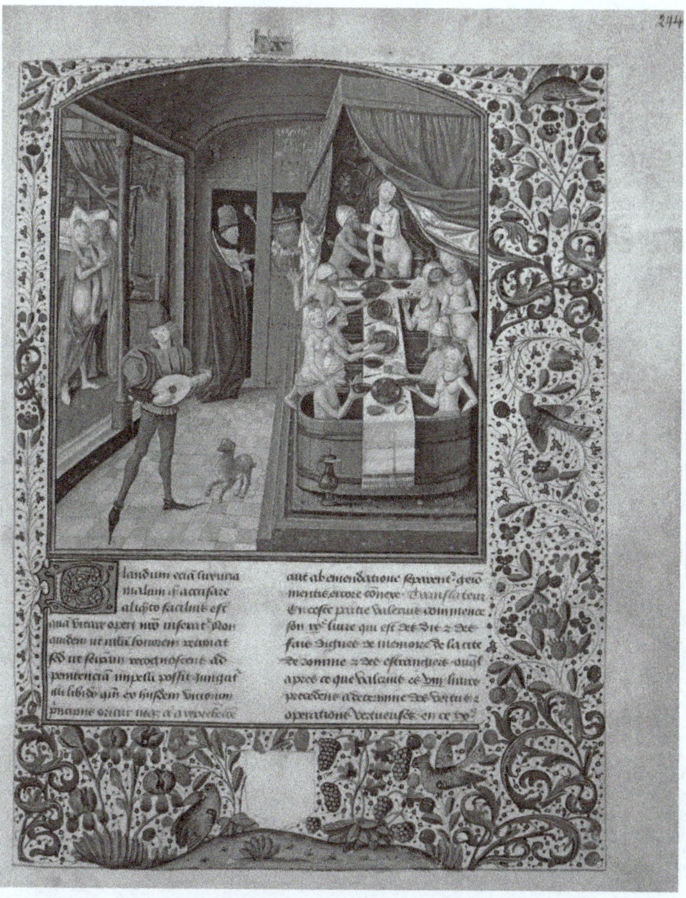

Figure 20 [Miniaturist, German] Valerius Maximus manuscript (Berlin): *Sexual License in a Public Bath* (*c.* 1470). (bpk/Staatsbibliothek zu Berlin/Ruth Schacht (00001095)).

The practice was taken further, and vastly more widely disseminated, by the advent of multiple copies of woodcuts, etchings and engravings. Martin Schongauer from Colmar (1448–91) monogrammed all his engravings, thereby building a reputation for himself in Northern Europe (Figure 21). Durer was not slow to follow suit and, early in his career, he began authenticating his prints and woodcuts with the famous 'AD' monogram from about 1495 onwards. His book illustrations, following in the steps of his mentor Michael Wolgemut (1434–1519), also began to be monogrammed. A public reputation was thus established, and Durer's close contacts with humanists and intellectuals meant that he received adulation from them. Erasmus and the Latin scholar Conrad Celtis (1459–1508) praised him for his consummate skills. South Germany became a cradle in which artistic fame and reputation was nurtured. By 1520, many German artists had created public careers for themselves, both on the open market and as the organizers of large workshops, in the service of the Emperor Maximilian I (1459–1519) and other princes and electors of the German empire. As we shall see, the advent of printing,

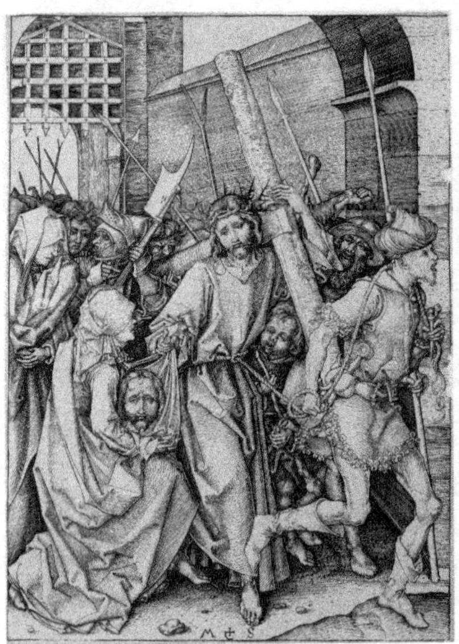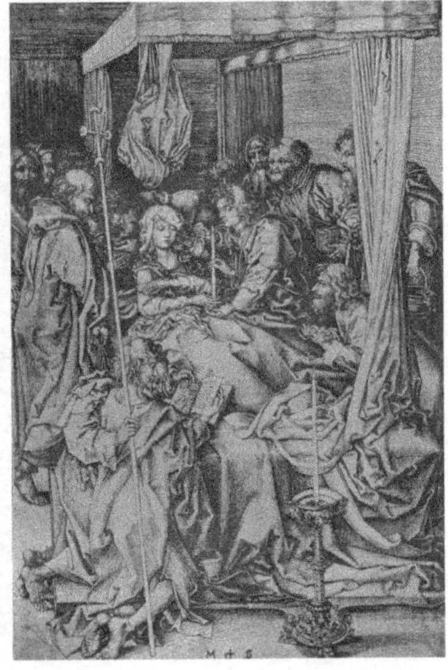

Figure 21 Martin Schongauer: *Christ Carrying the Cross* (engraving) (Ashmolean). (Photo by Ashmolean Museum/Heritage Images/Getty Images), and *Death of the Virgin Engraving* (*c.* 1475). (Photo by Print Collector/Getty Images.)

and the rise of the woodcut and engraving as an acceptable vehicle of 'high' art, helped to transform the career patterns and trajectories of many Northern European artists.[32] Their choice of subject matter was, of course, determined by the demands of both the market and individual patrons. Novel and less well-explored and exploited material came from various quarters. One impact of the coming of humanism to the North lay in its effects on the visual arts. Realism, illusionistic and deceptive though it might be, had been firmly established in all branches of the visual arts as a result of the 'Eyckian revolution' and its immediate, and longer-term, precursors in Northern Europe. The means to portray humanistic and mythological subject matter in an entirely convincing manner now lay at the disposal of painters, sculptors and engravers. How that subject matter blended, was incorporated into, or merely coexisted with the indigenous Gothic of the North will be considered in Chapter 3.

3

HUMANISM IN THE NORTH

RENAISSANCE HUMANISM

In any discussion of Renaissance humanism, there are at least two important distinctions to be made. The first lies in the differences between modern humanism and its Renaissance namesake. As we saw in the case of 'realism',[1] modern usage differs considerably from that of its Renaissance predecessor. A common definition of present-day humanist thinking would see it as an essentially rationalist outlook, centred primarily on human, not supra-rational or supernatural, concerns. Although there were certainly rationalist and secular aspects to Renaissance humanism, and a marked emphasis on the importance of the individual, it emerged within an essentially Christian culture and mindset. Many humanists were themselves members of the clergy – Leon Battista Alberti (1404–72), the Renaissance's 'universal man', was a canon of Florence cathedral, as was the Neoplatonist thinker Marsilio Ficino (1433–99). Erasmus, doyen of humanist scholars, was an (admittedly reluctant) Augustinian monk, but a cleric nonetheless (Figure 22). The textual critic Lorenzo Valla (1407–57) was also in Holy Orders. There were very few – if any – people who could truly be called 'humanists' in the modern sense, while the connotations of atheism or agnosticism which the term can carry today were all but unknown.

Second, Renaissance humanism represented one phase in a longer-term cultural movement which, at its most basic level, was characterized by an initially Italian rediscovery and further study of classical antiquity which subsequently embraced the rest of Western Europe. It was also a reaction against the cerebral abstractions of medieval scholasticism which many humanists dismissed as the narrowest kind of pedantry. But these are in

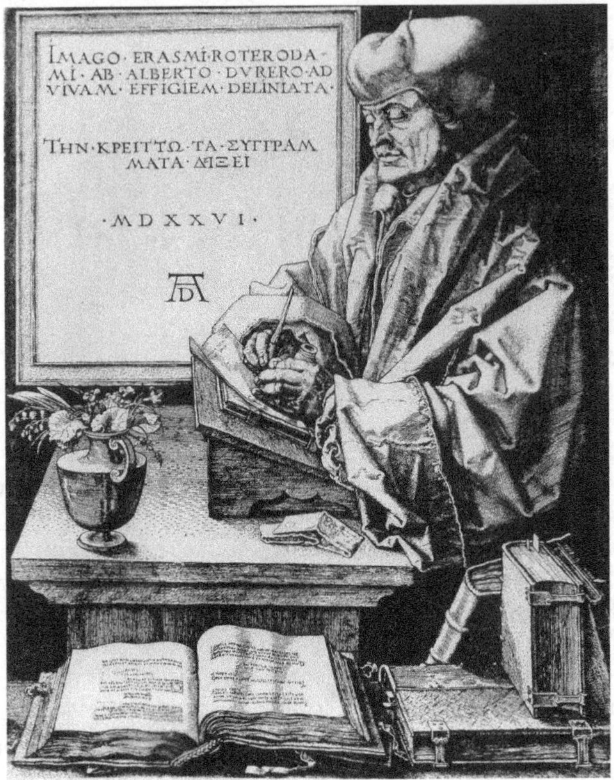

Figure 22 Albrecht Durer: *Portrait of Erasmus* (engraving).
(Photo by ullstein bild/ullstein bild/Getty Images.)

themselves narrow definitions, and some historians have sought to widen and deepen their scope and application. Humanism is, for instance, also seen as an essentially educational movement, seeking through urban grammar schools to promote the civil life of a literate laity, ideally encouraging virtue, prudence and a sense of civic responsibility among its pupils. At a higher social level, humanists frequented princely courts and made it their business, as advisers and tutors, to instruct rulers, their children and their nobilities, in the arts of responsible and conscientious government. They attempted to inculcate the persuasive arts of rhetoric into their pupils, developing those arts from their medieval roots in the scholastic curriculum. Diplomats and civil servants also received such training, enabling them to become, quite literally, orators skilled in the verbal formulation of policy, presentation of reports and dispatches, as well as the production of written instruments in Ciceronian Latin. It was part of a secularized celebration of the active over the contemplative life and, as such, had a long pedigree in Christian thought stretching back to Pope Gregory the Great in the sixth century AD.

Another important distinction lies in the manner in which Italian Renaissance humanism resembled, or differed from, its equivalent – if it had one – in Northern Europe. The movement is often seen as intrinsically and fundamentally Italian, spreading across Western Europe on varying timescales. It is argued that it was only after 1500, or at least only during the last two decades or so of the fifteenth century, that humanistic ideas and interests effectively began to take hold in the North. There is also a subsidiary distinction to be made, namely that between Italian usage of the principles and techniques of critical humanist textual scholarship and its applications in Northern Europe. Although the study of classical texts was fundamental to both Italian and Northern humanism, it was the application of humanist scholarship to the Bible and to the patristic works of the Church fathers and other Christian thinkers that tended to mark off Northern humanism from its Italian counterpart.[2] One notable exception to this tendency was the textual work on the New Testament by Lorenzo Valla. A form of 'Christian humanism' has therefore been identified in France, England, the Low Countries and the German-speaking lands, which was to contribute to both Catholic and early Protestant movements towards religious revival and Church reform in the North. In Italy, meanwhile, efforts to reconcile the pagan thought of antiquity with Christian belief produced the more mystical and cryptic forms of Neoplatonism associated with the humanists Marsilio Ficino and his pupil, the lay nobleman Giovanni Pico della Mirandola (1463–94).

In the North, concentration was more clearly focused on the roots and origins of Christianity itself, motivated (but only in part) by a desire to return to the supposed simplicity and purity of the earliest Christian congregations. These could only be discovered by rigorous examination of early Christian texts according to the principles and techniques of humanist criticism. Above all, the Old and especially the New Testaments, available in the inaccurate and sometimes demonstrably erroneous Latin translation of the Vulgate version, had to be restored by the application of rational critical norms to their original authenticity. Italian humanists, on the other hand, spent much time searching the works of Plato and other ancient thinkers for evidence that, had they lived in the Christian era, they would have been Christians. Ficino and Pico made valiant efforts to prove that pagan and pre-Christian thought did not contradict Christian teaching. It was presented as a fundamental source of 'ancient God-inspired wisdom'.[3] Northern scholars, on the other hand, devoted much of their energies to treating biblical and patristic texts in a manner comparable to that in which non-Christian classical texts were treated. One by-product of this was to provide reformers with material from which to discredit the Church of Rome, its Latin Vulgate Bible and its divergence from what was regarded as the simplicity of the early Church. There was, of course, no equivalent Protestant Reformation in Italy, and a wider-ranging reform of the Catholic Church came only with the counter-reformation of the mid- and late sixteenth century. Italian humanism before that date did not go out of its way to embrace the cause of Church reform.

In secular life and thought, a tendency to graft elements of early Italian humanism on to indigenous forms in political and didactic thought, prose literature and poetry can already be detected in the North from the mid-fourteenth century onwards. But there was also a contrary movement from North to South, as French and Provencal poetry was clearly well known among literate Italians. Dante was clearly conversant with it. Avignon, seat of the papacy from 1305 to 1378, and home to Petrarch, 'founder and father of humanism', as a papal secretary, had provided a meeting point for Italian and Northern European writers and thinkers. The international Church councils of the period from 1409 to 1417, at Pisa and Constance, had also served as points of contact. The Alps were no barrier to the transmission of ideas. But the rise of vernacular literatures, both religious and secular, in the North tended to offset the onward march of humanistic Latin as the prime medium of Renaissance thought. A robust, pre-existing, vernacular literary tradition, together with the continued presence of Gothic – or Gothic-influenced – styles in the visual arts, also ensured the distinctiveness of Northern Renaissance culture.

The origins of Renaissance humanism lie beyond the scope and remit of this book. But recent studies have tended to trace those origins back well beyond the normal time frame in which they have often been set. Padua, Vicenza and Verona in the later thirteenth century have been singled out as centres of 'proto-humanism'. Notaries, lawyers and civil servants were among those who formed the first circles of humanist intellectuals. Continuities rather than abrupt or sudden transitions have therefore been emphasized. What has been identified as the humanists' fundamental concern with the legacy of antiquity – above all its literature – has, furthermore, been traced back to the work of the ninth-century scholars of the 'Carolingian Renaissance', rediscovering, restoring, editing and interpreting those texts in Northern Europe as well as in Italy.[4] Monasteries at Auxerre, Tours, Fulda, Reichenau and St Gall produced, in their scriptoria, copies of classical texts which remained in their libraries, and in those of cathedral chapters, waiting to be 'rediscovered' by fourteenth- and fifteenth-century humanists. The very existence of the raw material for the later Renaissance's retrieval of the classics was a direct product of earlier medieval interest in many kinds of Latin text. The search for those texts had been renewed and reinvigorated in the twelfth century by the purposeful recovery of the 'wisdom of the ancients', deemed to be contained in the ethical, moral and didactic legacy of antiquity. But the Church's emphasis on canon law and Aristotelian logic meant that in the course of the later twelfth and thirteenth centuries, the 'pagan' literature of ancient Greece and Rome underwent something of an eclipse. A polarity between scholasticism and humanism was to emerge, albeit often overstated by fifteenth-century humanists in their somewhat self-serving and self-aggrandizing claims to novelty and innovation. As we shall see, this was to become a major issue in the age of Erasmus. But scholasticism was by no means only of one colour and contrasts can be overdrawn.[5]

A fundamental issue in discussion of Northern Renaissance humanism revolves around the question: Are we dealing with essentially similar movements emerging from similar conditions, in Italy and in the North? The rediscovery, reappraisal and reinterpretation of classical texts was certainly common to both. But intellectual and cultural life in the two regions was significantly different. The role of universities, for instance, in Northern Europe, the majority of them new or recent foundations, was critical in this respect. As in more recent times, new university foundation could provide an opportunity to innovate and absorb innovations into mainstream curricula, as these institutions were likely to be less hidebound by long-established traditions and vested interests. In Northern and Central Europe, in the 150 years between 1348 and 1498, no less than 26 new universities were created, 19 of them during the fifteenth century. Among them were Prague (1348), Krakow (Jagiellonian University, 1364), Vienna (1365), Heidelberg (1386), Cologne (1388), St Andrew's (1413), Louvain (1425), Glasgow (1451), Basel (1459), Mainz (1476), Tubingen (1476), Uppsala (1477) and Copenhagen (1479). Many of them were to provide the conditions in which the so-called new learning of humanism could be introduced and sustained. Within them, and in some of their longer-established predecessors, what has been called an 'academic revolution of the first magnitude' took place.[6] This was the decentralization of university teaching, whereby 'secular' (as opposed to monastic) colleges were established beside the central faculty institutions which had formerly provided all lectures, academic exercises and disputations. But their academic personnel, with the exception of some who taught and studied law and medicine, were all members of the clergy, and had much in common with the colleges of non-monastic canons which had sprung up in such numbers, often as chantry foundations, in the later Middle Ages. In Oxford, ten such secular colleges were created, as acts of piety and charity, between the later thirteenth and the end of the fifteenth centuries. The prototype for the Oxbridge college was established by Merton College (founded in 1264). The pattern was also to be found at Paris, pioneered by the foundation of the College of the Sorbonne in 1257–8, and in Scotland and Germany. It was far less common in Southern Europe. The endowed, self-governing college was to survive, especially in Britain, for many centuries. A centrifugal rather than a centripetal form of university structure thus characterized many Northern European academic institutions. Furthermore, humanistic studies were introduced at a relatively early date into some of these collegiate bodies: Lincoln and Magdalen Colleges, Oxford, in the fifteenth, and Corpus Christi and Christ Church (Cardinal College) in the early sixteenth, century. At Cambridge, Christ's, St John's and Trinity colleges provided institutional support for the new humanist learning. Their libraries carried substantial collections, increasingly in printed editions, of humanist texts. This aspect of the Northern Renaissance therefore had a strong institutional underpinning.

Italian universities, largely non-collegiate, were renowned for their law faculties, rather than for theology or the liberal arts. In Italy, a generally higher level of lay literacy had encouraged the growth of a larger reading public among the urban middle classes. The relatively high proportion of notaries, merchants and bankers in Italian cities and towns helped to produce a more broadly literate and numerate citizenry. The well-to-do university student, often from a mercantile or legal background, was far more of a feature of Italian universities than of those of the North. In Northern Europe, an entrenched scholasticism, wedded to Aristotelian logic and the study of theology and canon law, had tended to be dominant, as distinct from the primacy in Italy, since an early date, of rhetoric and Roman law, its study and practice. Theology was led, Europe-wide, by the University of Paris and no Italian institution came anywhere near challenging that hegemony. There was a degree of resistance, in some quarters at least, among some northern university masters – especially at Paris and to a lesser extent at Louvain – to the introduction of a humanist curriculum. Humanistic thought in the North thus tended, on the one hand, to privilege the study, edition and restoration of religious and devotional texts, both biblical and otherwise. On the other hand, it was also concerned to apply the lessons of humanist scholarship to the study of classical philology, ancient numismatics, canon and civil law, and to the histories of Northern humanists' countries of origin. The French humanists Robert Gaguin (1433–1501) and Guillaume Bude (1467–1540), the English scholars Thomas Linacre (*c.* 1460–1524) and William Grocyn (*c.* 1446–1519), and Netherlandish scholars such as Rudolph Agricola (1443–85) or Gerard Geldenhouwer (1483–1542) were representatives of this kind of Northern Renaissance intellectual.

Before the 1420s there was no university in one of the most prosperous and urbanized areas of Northern Europe, that is, the Low Countries or greater Netherlands. Flemish and Dutch students, masters and professors studied and taught at Cologne or Paris. But in 1425, Duke Jean IV of Brabant founded, in collaboration with the town councillors, a *studium generale* at Louvain (Leuven). As with other university foundations of the time, its function was in part to educate those clergy and laity who would go on to serve in ducal, noble and civic administrations. But its theology faculty also produced some distinguished alumni, including the humanist Jan Standonck (1454–1504) who became rector of the College de Montaigu in Paris. Another early professor, the Fleming Carolus Viruli alias Carolus Maneken (*c.* 1410–93), has been called 'the first native teacher at Louvain who might properly be called a humanist'.[7] He was regent of the early College of the Lily in the Arts Faculty there from 1438 onwards. In 1476 he published his *Formulae Epistolarum*, a manual of Latin letter-writing, citing examples largely drawn from Cicero. It was ultimately superseded by Erasmus's later treatise on the subject. The new university soon established connections with Italian scholars, especially in the field of law. Raimondo Marliani (*c.* 1420–76), a graduate of Padua, was professor of canon law at Louvain from 1461 to 1463, and was an early writer on the history and topography of the Low Countries and Germany, drawing largely on the works of Caesar and Tacitus. He proposed modern identifications and localizations of toponyms in Caesar's *Commentaries*, and his *Veterum Galliae locorum ... descriptio* (*Description of the Ancient Places of Gaul*, printed in

1482) became a standard work on the place names of Roman Gaul (*Celtica*). He also endowed a scholarship for Louvain students to study in Italy. Louvain harboured Erasmus for a time, but he was intolerant of its relatively conservative position theologically and left for what he regarded as more fertile fields. In 1519 the university was among the first to condemn Luther's ninety-five theses.

With the accession of Philip the Good of Burgundy to the duchy of Brabant in 1430, the University of Louvain was to become an important feeder of civil servants and lawyers into the Burgundian administration. But the Faculty of Arts also included a significant number of members of the Burgundian nobility among its matriculated students, and the university received its first lay chancellor in 1509, under Habsburg rule. Louvain's earliest matriculation register (1426–53) is an instructive source for the education not only of the clergy and urban middle classes but also of the nobility, some of them of the highest rank. The number of young men styled *nobilis* ('noble') in the register suggests that any residual belief in a poorly educated, semi-literate nobility in this area of Northern Europe must be totally discarded. The Northern Renaissance witnessed the emergence of the literate, articulate nobleman, skilled in the arts of persuasion, diplomacy and rhetoric as well as of war. The leading Flemish and Dutch noble families of Lannoy, Croy, Lalaing, Brederode, van Borselen and Glimes were all represented among early Louvain students. Some, such as Edmond de Dynter, of noble birth, became authors of significant works of literature. Dynter, who was also a ducal secretary, compiled a Latin history of the duchy of Brabant. That the universities of the fifteenth century were providing an education for the lay nobility, as well as for preachers and teachers, is evident from the moving letter which, on 3 May 1465, the Flemish nobleman Jean de Lannoy addressed to his infant son, Louis. Lannoy realized that he might never live to see his son reach an age 'when he can understand me', so he advised him 'to enter the Latin schools of Louvain, Cologne or Paris, with a priest of Netherlandish language (*de langue thioise*) so that you may become fluent in that tongue'.[8] In the multilingual Burgundian Low Countries, that was sensible advice. Equipped with a sound education, his son – unlike his father, who claimed that he lacked such skills – would then be able to speak his own opinion in royal or ducal councils, and not have to defer to the 'learned, eloquent legists and *ystoryens*'.[9] The humanist emphasis on rhetoric and public speaking clearly had a strong practical dimension.

As we have already seen, it has often been claimed that Italian humanism only reached the Low Countries and the German-speaking lands in the very late fifteenth and early sixteenth century. But to attribute some kind of superiority to the Italian Neoplatonism of that period over what had gone before tends to play into the hands of Italian humanists' self-promotion, if not self-aggrandizement. The new universities of the Burgundian dominions appear to have reached a compromise in their curricula between the scholastic and humanist positions. In any case, continuity with some aspects of the past rather than abrupt change often makes more sense in the study of the history of ideas. What we know about the new University of Louvain could, to a lesser degree, also be said of another newly created academic institution in the Burgundian lands. In 1422–3 Philip the Good of Burgundy had founded a new *studium generale* at Dole, near Besancon in his dominion of Franche-Comte. It had three faculties: canon and civil law, theology, and medicine. It became known as the 'university of the two Burgundies', that is of the duchy and the county of Burgundy. Like Louvain, it attracted members of the lay nobility among its students, who were granted exceptionally extensive privileges by the duke himself. The best teachers were sought for the new establishment, from Italy, the Low Countries and Germany. In 1452, the duke created a chair of civil law for 'foreign' professors, and its first occupant was the distinguished Italian legist Anselme de Marenches (d. 1499). The post became a permanent one in 1454, and Marenches entered ducal service in 1460 as an adjudicator of petitions and ducal councillor. The new – nor indeed the old – universities of Northern Europe in the fifteenth century could therefore never be written off as irrelevant 'ivory towers'. They were recruiting grounds for service not only to the Church but also to the state.

The humanist credentials of Dole as a centre of the *studia humanitatis* were slower to develop than those of Louvain. But its capacity to attract some of the most notable humanists of the age was demonstrated by the arrival there in 1509 of the German astrologer, occultist and alchemist Cornelius Agrippa of Nettesheim (1486–1535) who was an outstanding example of the Renaissance polymath. A graduate of Cologne, in arts and medicine, he was proficient in eight languages, including Greek and Hebrew, and had been influenced by Marsilio Ficino, Johann Reuchlin (1455–1522) and Nicholas of Cusa (1404–64). When at Dole he composed what amounted to an early feminist treatise for Margaret of Austria, regent of the Habsburg Netherlands, entitled *On the Nobility and Pre-Excellence of the Female Sex* (1509, printed in 1529) thereby securing her (and no doubt other noble women's) favour. While Dole, however, remained primarily a law school, Louvain gradually took on the character of a more wide ranging, intellectually 'progressive' institution. Its Faculty of Arts became very distinguished indeed. Although it was not originally a part of Louvain's collegiate structure, the *Collegium Trilingue* (College of the Three Languages), established in 1517–18, represented an attempt to translate Erasmus's and other humanists' educational programmes into reality. The college taught Latin, Greek and Hebrew. It aimed to spread humanistic thought and revive classical studies in a new form. Greek was taught there by the Limburger Rutger Ressen from 1518 to 1545, the first in a long line of professors of that language. The study of Latin and Greek poetry also found a place at Louvain at a relatively early phase of its existence. Rudolph Agricola was one of its graduates (MA, 1465) and became perhaps a northern echo, at the very least, of the 'universal man' Leon Battista Alberti, in his broadly based interests. Not without a certain arrogance, Agricola claimed to be the self-styled 'first teacher of Latin and Greek poetry [who] first led the Germans into the camp of the Muses'.[10] He had been at Pavia, then Ferrara, and had clearly learnt the art of self-promotion from his Italian contemporaries.

Such Renaissance humanist scholars might well, with some justification, feel superior to their predecessors. But a renewed interest in the Latin, and subsequently Greek, classics was not solely a product of their own times. There had been an active movement in the North, from the mid-fourteenth century onwards, towards the translation of classical texts, and also of Italian works based on classical models and exemplars, into vernacular languages. The courts of Charles V (1364–80) and Charles VI of France (1380–1422) have been identified as centres of 'proto-humanism' in Northern Europe. The work of able translators such as Laurent de Premierfait (*c.* 1365–1418), of remarkable intellects such as Nicolas Oresme (1320–82), and others, brought ancient texts, often of a didactic kind, to the attention of a reading public which received its classics in French, rather than Latin or Greek. Oresme was responsible for the first accomplished translations of Aristotle's *Politics*, *Ethics* and *Economics* into French. Premierfait also produced a translation of the *Economics* (in 1418), as well as translations of works by Cicero, Seneca and contemporary Italian humanists, above all Boccaccio. This movement was to be sustained at the fifteenth-century court of Burgundy. Charles the Bold, Duke of Burgundy, read Livy and Xenophon in translation, continuing his father's accumulation of classics in French translation in the ducal library. Charles was in the habit of quoting from Livy and other Roman authors in his speeches and letters.

Although some of them, as university graduates, were clearly literate in Latin, bibliophile Burgundian nobles from the families of Lannoy, Croy, Lalaing, Luxembourg, Cleves, Nassau and Gruuthuse owned copies of these, and more recent, translations. In France, the sixteenth-century humanist translators of Virgil and Homer under Francis I of France (1494–1547) owed much to this tradition. A wider lay readership and audience was now in possession of direct access, in their own vernacular language, to both classical texts and more recent Italian humanistic literature.

It is worth noting that all the scholarly efforts made by the early humanists to recover and reappraise classical texts had been directed towards Latin works. Until the mid-to-late fourteenth century, Greek studies had languished in the West. The legacy of the Hellenic world – Aristotle, Plato and the literary and scientific masters of ancient Greece – had been transmitted through Latin and Arabic translations. Apart from some evidence of activity in Greek studies at the court of the Angevin kings of Naples, it was not until 1360 that the first teaching of Greek in Italy was undertaken, at Florence. But the most significant change occurred in 1397, when the Byzantine scholar and émigré Manuel Chrysoloras (*c.* 1355–1415) came to Florence at the invitation of the Florentine chancellor Coluccio Salutati and began a series of lectures on Greek. This has been described as a 'key date in the history of humanism and even of European culture'.[11] Chrysoloras had some distinguished Italian humanists among his pupils, and the teaching of Greek received an impetus with the publication of his *Erotemata*, the first Greek grammar book to be produced in the West. It existed in manuscript copies from *c.* 1415–17 onwards, but became more widely disseminated in both Southern and Northern Europe after the printing of an abridged version, at Venice, by Adam von Ambergau in 1471, of its full version in 1496, and the definitive edition in 1512. It was much studied by Erasmus, Thomas Linacre in England and Johann Reuchlin in Germany. It became the standard textbook for instruction in Greek for the whole of the sixteenth century. It spawned some Northern European variants and successors, some of which were designed with the specific needs and capabilities of students in mind. Among them was the German humanist Philip Melanchthon's (1497–1560) publication at Tubingen in 1518 of his *Institutiones Grammaticae Graecae*, modelled on Chrysoloras's work, but containing many more Graeco-Latin comparisons to aid Latinate students. In the Netherlands, Nicolaas Cleynaerts (1493/4–1542) from Brabant published his *Institutiones in Linguam Graecam* at Louvain in

1530. Northern European scholars and students were thus well provided for in Greek studies at this time.

The earlier Renaissance humanists had become interested in Greek texts merely as 'tools for the better understanding of Latin literature and history'.[12] By the later fifteenth century, however, Greek was beginning to be studied in its own right, not simply as an ancillary aid to the elucidation of Latin texts. The great works of ancient Greek literature, poetry and drama by Homer, Sophocles and Thucydides now became a part of the curriculum of the so-called *studia humanitatis* (study of human nature) in humanist schools and some university faculties. Beginning in Italy, it spread very quickly, if not near-simultaneously, to Northern Europe. This was to be one origin of a long tradition of classical studies in Northern European universities. At Oxford, it became known, by 1800, as *Literae Humaniores* comprising Latin and Greek languages, Rhetoric, Moral Philosophy derived from classical – not Christian – authors, Logic and Latin composition. By its title, literally translated as 'the more humane letters', it was distinguished from *Literae Diviniores*, 'the more divine letters', that is, Theology and Patristics. It provided a humanistic education in classical languages, philosophy, literature and history experienced by many generations of young men and, to a lesser extent, women, until the toppling of classics from its intellectual and academic pinnacle in the twentieth century. But its inauguration represented perhaps one of the greater, latter-day triumphs of Renaissance humanism.

HUMANISM, SCHOLASTICISM AND POLEMIC

It is striking that perhaps the most acute and erudite Renaissance humanist of his age – Desiderius Erasmus of Rotterdam – was not an Italian. He was apparently not very impressed by what he saw, heard and learnt in Italy. Nothing in his letters or observations suggests that he was in any way affected by the artistic or architectural achievements of the Italian Renaissance. Dutch by origin, but cosmopolitan, Erasmus (1466–1536) apparently found more to interest him, and to discover, in Basel, Antwerp, Louvain, Cambridge or Oxford than in any Italian centre of humanist thought and scholarship. Visiting, residing and lecturing in England in 1499–1500 and 1509–14, he eulogized English learning and knowledge of the classics. He lavished praise on Colet, More, Grocyn and Linacre. He claimed to have found there 'so much humanity and erudition ... that he need hardly any more long to go to

Italy'.[13] With the exception of Venice, which he admired for its embrace of the new art of printing classical texts (and some of his own works) by Aldus Manutius's press and publishing house, Erasmus's main sphere of activity lay in Northern Europe. But for nine months in 1507 Erasmus worked in Venice as a scholar-editor and proofreader at the Aldine press, and in 1508 Aldus published Erasmus's *Adages*.

Erasmus was not entirely happy with his Venetian publisher and subsequently preferred to use the press owned by his humanist friend Johann Froben (*c.* 1460–1527) at Basel. His voluminous correspondence was in Latin and was pan-European, but his personal contacts with other humanists were very largely confined to England, France and the German- and Dutch-speaking world. As we shall discover, there were circles of humanist intellectuals, writers and poets in the North who compared favourably with the denizens of the Platonic academies and schools of Italy. Although their knowledge of classical texts, including poetry and drama, was often copious and comprehensive, a major contribution was also made by them not only to biblical but also to legal and historical scholarship. The critical examination and edition of ancient and more recent texts and documents were among their prime activities. A concern for authenticity and accuracy accompanied Northern humanism, perhaps enabling us to see the origins of a long Germanic tradition in the study of philology and textual criticism as stemming from this period. *Literae humaniores* and the *studia humanistica* ('humanistic studies') flourished both inside and outside the world of academia. They helped to ensure the continued deployment of Latin for affairs of state, diplomacy and pan-European scholarly and other correspondence, as well as the continued study of the Greek and Latin classics in grammar schools and universities. The practical uses of humanist textual criticism became particularly significant in Northern Europe and were to play their part in the inception of the Protestant Reformation. Advances in Greek studies were especially important for biblical criticism in Northern and Central Europe at this time. It was here that many Northern humanists began to part company from their Italian counterparts. From the 1520s onwards, the divergence of substantial areas, especially of Northwest and Central Europe, from allegiance to the Church of Rome was to some degree driven and justified by humanist scholarship and polemic.

The concern for authenticity, for the urtext, and thus for the best edition of classical literary, historical and philosophical texts did not stop with those texts. Humanist scholarship was also brought to bear on non-literary, historical documents. In the visual arts, it is often argued that the achievement of historical distance and archaeological accuracy in depictions of ancient Greek or Roman themes first appeared in Italy during the second half of the fifteenth century. The works of Andrea Mantegna have been singled out in this respect. But in the world of the written word, some sense of historical distance, and some awareness of what was appropriate to a particular period of the past, came earlier. The beginnings of a concept of anachronism, of what was *in*appropriate to a particular period, have been identified in the course of the fourteenth century. Humanist scholars embarked on the critical study of ancient – and not-so-ancient – sources, deciphering inscriptions, detecting forgeries and questioning the authenticity of deeds, charters, decrees, notarial instruments and other formal documents. The best-known example was the Italian humanist Lorenzo Valla's demonstration, in 1439–40, that the so-called Donation of Constantine was in fact a forgery. But there were precedents for Valla's scepticism and its conclusions. In 1360, the Emperor Charles IV of Luxembourg was shown an alleged letter of the Emperor Henry IV (1056–1106), confirmed by the Emperor Frederick I Barbarossa in 1156. This claimed that the duchy of Austria was a principality independent of the Holy Roman Empire, and that its duke should be ranked among the imperial electors. The claim was in part based on two 'privileges' alleged to have been granted by the emperors Julius Caesar and Nero, the *Privilegium Maius* ('Greater Privilege') and the *Privilegium Minus* ('Lesser Privilege'). These referred to the Roman province of Noricum, deemed to have been the region of which the fourteenth-century duchy of Austria was a large part. Charles IV, on the advice of his chancery staff, sent the documents to Petrarch, as an acknowledged authority on texts emanating from the Roman Empire.

After subjecting the documents to textual criticism, using his knowledge of antique styles of address, appropriate vocabulary and epistolary prose, Petrarch declared them to be a forgery. It has been said that this represented 'a landmark in the humanist criticism of documents', revealing a 'new attitude to the antique basis of political authority'.[14] Be that as it may, Petrarch's dismissal of the five forged charters, edicts and deeds, some alleged to have been issued by ancient Roman emperors, served as a model and precedent for subsequent humanist detection of spurious documents. It preceded Valla's work by eighty years. It was discovered that the documents had been forged in 1358–9 for Rudolf IV of Habsburg, Duke of Austria, in his ducal chancery. Petrarch praised Charles IV's chancellor for his alertness and vigilance in doubting the authenticity of the privileges – perhaps a testimony to the extent to which knowledge of classical Latin styles had already become current in rulers' chanceries by the mid-fourteenth century. And an attempt, admittedly an unsuccessful one, had clearly also been made by the Austrian chancery's forgers to imitate those styles as well. Valla's demolition of the Donation of Constantine was thus not without precedent, at least in principle. Nor was it the first time that the Donation, an imperial decree, whereby the Emperor Constantine the Great (AD 272–337) purportedly transferred authority over Rome and the Western Roman Empire to the pope, had been challenged. Valla's demonstration had been preceded by the German humanist Nicholas of Cusa's declaration in 1433 that the Donation was apocryphal and, at the very least, of doubtful authenticity. In his treatise *De Concordantia Catholica*, Cusa stated that he had collected and consulted 'all the histories I could find, acts of emperors and Roman pontiffs' and other sources, but 'could find no confirmation of what is said about that donation'.[15] His rejection of the Donation rested upon an appeal to historical texts, and his exposure was based on a wide-ranging collation of sources. The Donation was then exposed as a deception based upon a lie. Cusa did not attempt Valla's line-by-line examination of the document but simply argued that it was not referred to in any known fourth-century or later source. The affair of the Donation was to be taken up by advocates of the Protestant Reformation, and in 1518 the German humanist Ulrich von Hutten published an edition of Valla's *De falso credita et ementita Constantini donatione declamatio* ('Discourse Concerning the Falsity and Forgery of the Donation of Constantine') which took account of, and included, Cusa's work. The Donation was regarded by some reformers as the root of many evils. Luther, who, like Erasmus, greatly admired Valla, then translated his text into German in 1537, thus ensuring its wider dissemination in print, and using it as a weapon to attack an allegedly corrupt Church and its claims. An English translation was already circulating among radical evangelicals in Thomas Cromwell's reforming circle by 1534. William Marshall (d. 1540), an evangelical lawyer, royal official and confidential agent of Cromwell, published translations of Valla's, Cusa's and von Hutten's work, and of the early humanist Marsilius of Padua's *Defensor pacis* (1324), in 1533–5. Humanist criticism, vernacular language and the printing press had joined forces to discredit papal authority and ecclesiastical privilege. Catholic censorship ensured that in 1559 Valla's refutation of the Donation was placed on the Tridentine Index of Prohibited Books.

By engaging with such questions of the authenticity and the reliability of sources, humanists were distancing themselves from the major concerns of scholastic study. The humanist antipathy towards scholasticism had many roots. They were partly intellectual, partly methodological and partly simply stemmed from a desire to be innovative, defying convention and tradition. The fourteenth century had certainly seen radical changes in the nature of scholasticism. But it was in the fifteenth century that its foundations were first effectively undermined. It has been said that Nicholas of Cusa (1404–64) played a major role in this process, and that 'not until ... Cusa did a Christian thinker north of the Alps ... completely break with the entire basis of scholasticism, which by then was contracting into the separate warring schools of Nominalism and the revived forms of Thomism, Scotism, and Albertism'.[16] Cusa's stance, with its Neoplatonizing tendencies, was to be taken up and pursued further by Erasmus and his contemporaries. But it could be (and has been) argued that, far from opening the way towards 'modern' thought, Renaissance humanism in effect represented something of an aberration and departure from a line of development initiated in the fourteenth century which was only restored in the nineteenth and twentieth centuries. The logic-based, more scientific, mathematically grounded thought of the fourteenth century, and its more broadly nominalist underpinning, had an intellectual rigour sometimes lacking in later medieval and Renaissance Neoplatonism and its derivatives. Huizinga, describing Erasmus's engagement with humanist discourse, pointed up the contrast well: 'Humanism since Petrarch had substituted for the rigidly syllogistic structure of argument, the loose style of the antique, free, suggestive phrase.'[17] Mystical experience, a heightened spirituality, a near-pantheism among some, an addiction to rhetoric and, as we shall see, an awareness of the irrational were among the characteristics of much humanist thought.[18] There was a tendency to advance the claims of the heart, the imagination, the emotions and aesthetic sentiment over the head in both religious and secular thought. Humanist mockery of scholastic arguments which were regarded as sterile and unproductive was sometimes unwilling to acknowledge the merits of those arguments as intellectual exercises. But the immediate future, throughout Europe, lay with humanism.

ERASMUS AND NORTHERN RENAISSANCE HUMANISM

Erasmus's influence on the shape, character and development of humanism in the North was profound. In part, this was due to his self-conscious creation and promotion of his own reputation. The significance of that reputation to the European intellectual world was thus to some extent a product of his own self-fashioning. His eulogy of Lorenzo Valla, for instance, was in effect a statement of his own credo and belief in humanist scholarship. Much of what he said of Valla could have been said about himself. Valla, wrote Erasmus, was

> a man who with so much energy, zeal and labour, refuted the stupidities of the barbarians, saved half-buried letters from extinction, restored Italy to her ancient splendour of eloquence, and forced even the learned to express themselves henceforth with more circumspection.[19]

The correction of the errors and misunderstandings of his predecessors, the rescue of ancient texts, the revival of eloquence and the need for scholarly caution, not necessarily accompanied by humility, were among Erasmus's own aims and objectives. And his expenditure of energy and unremitting labour was exemplified by the prodigious volume of his scholarly output. Not only did he praise Valla's refutation of the Donation of Constantine, but also his guide to refined Latin composition and style, the *Elegantiae linguae latinae* (1441-9, printed 1471), and his *Adnotationes Novi Testamenti* (1442), that is, annotations criticizing and correcting the Latin Vulgate New Testament. Erasmus's own re-translation of the New Testament owed a good deal to Valla's earlier work. Nicholas of Cusa had also obtained a copy of the *Adnotationes*. Erasmus had found a manuscript, dating from *c.* 1460, of Valla's unpublished annotations in the monastic library of the abbey of Parc, near Louvain, in 1504. Erasmus printed them in 1505, and his own annotations to his New Testament edition of 1516 certainly made good use of them.[20] But, unlike Valla, Erasmus was rather more cautious in his edition and publication of a text and critical notes which could be used, like Valla's demolition of the Donation, as a weapon of attack on the Church's abuses and the authority of the papacy. The sting and vitriol of Valla's prose was thereby to some extent diluted. Erasmus's relative moderation was, however, soon to be swept aside by the polemical use of these texts by Luther and the early Protestant reformers. Humanist textual criticism did not stay confined to academic and intellectual circles in Northern Europe. Its results could, in the appropriate hands, become powerful weapons with which to attack and undermine Valla's and Erasmus's own Church of Rome. Both, it should be remembered, were themselves members of the clergy, as indeed was Luther. As with earlier movements of religious dissent, such as Lollardy in England or Hussitism in Bohemia, the enemy within could be as potent, if not more potent, as the enemy without.

Erasmus's formative experiences destined him for the Church. The illegitimate son of a priest, he was schooled by the Brethren of the Common Life who prepared him for a monastic career. He claimed that the Brethren were prone to 'destroy all natural gifts' but he emerged as a first-rate Latinist from their hands. The natural progression was into the Augustinian order, which he entered and in which he took his vows of poverty, chastity and obedience in 1488. As we shall see,[21] the Brethren, originally a lay brotherhood, had become increasingly clericalized and in effect partially merged into the monastic order of Augustinian canons. Yet this did not exclude the cult of intellectual, spiritual and no doubt other forms of brotherly friendship among them, and Erasmus, in the convent at Steyn near Gouda, benefited from the opportunities for reading, learned conversation, Latin composition and letter-writing that the order offered. Erasmus became a witty and ironic Latinist, well versed in classical poetry and prose. He wrote, at this stage of his life, secular poems and discourses, and became increasingly intolerant of monastic discipline and the constraints it imposed upon him. In April 1492, he was ordained priest by David of Burgundy, the reforming bishop of Utrecht, one of the many bastard sons of Philip the Good of Burgundy. He escaped from the monastery at Steyn by being appointed secretary to Henry of Bergen, bishop of Cambrai, a member of the Burgundian noble family of Glimes and a patron of humanism. For three or so years, he worked as a Latin secretary, drawing up episcopal letters and memoranda, while continuing to pursue his classical studies.

In 1495, Erasmus entered the College de Montaigu in the University of Paris, which he disliked greatly. Its food was particularly appalling. Nor did the warring factions of Thomists and nominalists who dominated the Theology Faculty of the Sorbonne elicit anything but contempt from him. But at Paris he fell under the influence of the veteran French humanist Robert Gaguin, to whose history of the French (*Compendium de Francorum origine et gestis*, 1495) he contributed a eulogistic letter of homage. After four unhappy years in Paris, Erasmus went, as tutor to the sons of rich men, to England and it was here that he was persuaded (by Colet and others) to devote his talents to biblical criticism and thereby to achieve a better understanding of the original texts of the scriptures. This movement from poetics and rhetoric to biblical and patristic studies was a characteristic of Northern humanism that was to become increasingly common. By 1501, he was aiming to edit the works of St Jerome, learn Greek and begin to address the textual problems of the New Testament. His work led to the appearance, in 1516, of his *Novum Instrumentum*, a new edition of the New Testament with a Latin translation. Huizinga thought that Erasmus reunited the 'antique and Christian spirit', becoming a 'biblical humanist'.[22] In 1522 Erasmus spoke of 'Saint Socrates' and argued that Virgil, Cicero, Cato and Horace all conformed to a Christian spirit, as he claimed to discern the presence and workings of the divine in them. Although some Italian Neoplatonists shared such views, Erasmus went further, rejecting the Italian humanists' essentially aesthetic enjoyment of the formal beauty and elegance of classical thought and literature. He reacted, especially after 1527 or so, against the apparent paganism, pantheism and pedantry of some classicists, and had little time for rhetoricians, intoxicated with the orotund splendour of their own prose and, no doubt, the sound of their own voices.

But Erasmus did not follow the path which led some humanists from biblical criticism to Reformation theology. He contested Luther's denial of man's and woman's autonomous power of self-determination, especially in regard to their salvation. Simple faith was not quite enough for Erasmus and he remained wedded to the Catholic doctrine of works.[23] Although he assumed a position quite closely related in some respects to Protestant Evangelical theology, the sacrament of the Mass was, for him, vital for salvation. Man could, he argued, play an active role in his own redemption, and there was no assurance of salvation without good works. But, unlike the more extreme evangelicals, he remained convinced of the moral, as well as intellectual benefits to be derived from the study of classical literature. 'Pliny and Lucian', he wrote, 'both scorned the idea of the immortality of the soul, yet they are read by everyone for their learning, and rightly so'.[24] There was 'good learning' to be found in them, even in Juvenal's satires and in Suetonius's and Tacitus's histories. In that respect, Erasmus was as convinced and committed a classicist as any Italian contemporary. And it is not strictly true to claim that 'humanism in much of Northern Europe included little admiration of antique culture'.[25] Lessons were learnt and modes of artistic, architectural and literary expression were adopted from Greek and Roman antiquity. And it has been argued that the 'antique culture' which was admired in the North may have been rather more inclusive and wide ranging than that which was so lauded in Italy. The notion of a northern, Germanic and Netherlandish antiquity, its study and presentation, needs to be explored.

HUMANISM AND A NEW NORTHERN RENAISSANCE?

A recent thesis has advanced the view that Netherlandish scholars and writers of the later fifteenth and early sixteenth century 'sought to cultivate a renaissance on local soil, an ambition they shared with contemporary Netherlandish artists and patrons'.[26] This view entails a 'rejection of the long-held understanding of this period in Netherlandish art and intellectual history as defined by revelatory encounters with Italy and the rediscovered antiquities of Rome. Classical rhetoric, antique forms and antiquarian pursuits did not seep into Northern Europe passively and inevitably, like silt water after a deluge'.[27]

We can take the Netherlandish example as a test case. But a similar argument might be advanced for the German-speaking and Nordic lands, given that the impact of Albrecht Durer's and other Northern artists' Italian visits may have been exaggerated. England also presents another example of regional adaptation to the teachings and artistic and literary expressions of Renaissance humanism. A conscious and sustained effort, it is argued, was needed to create a 'Renaissance' culture in these regions, rather than merely a passive reception. And, as was the case with the reception and absorption of French, and French-derived styles and themes in other parts of Europe in the thirteenth century, those cultural forms could be adapted, altered and even transformed in the process.

A central figure in the introduction of the secular – and sensual – dimension of the culture of classical antiquity into Northern Europe was the artist Jan Gossart, from Hainaut, also known as Mabuse (*c.* 1478–1532). He had visited Italy in 1509 and to some extent followed in the steps of Durer, making drawings of classical monuments and antique sculptures while in Rome. Not only did he act as an early Northern exponent of the representation of mythological subject matter in visual art, he also contributed to the creation of an 'alternative "Netherlandish" antiquity'. This put him into the company of Netherlandish thinkers and writers who studied both the ancient and more recent past of their own regions and engaged in erudite antiquarian pursuits, thereby engendering something of a local renaissance. This was paralleled by other Northern European movements – in England and Scandinavia, for example. Humanist circles in different areas had their own agendas, as well as a common interest in the use and adaptation of classical and Italianate styles and models. Gossart, for instance, found some common ground with other Northern artists, such as Hans Baldung Grien and the Cranachs, father and son, in his realistic depiction of the nude.

His *Venus* of 1521 (Figure 23) provoked, and appealed to, the (male) viewer not only as a figure with symbolic and allusive meaning but as a living woman, rendered all the more engaging through the 'Eyckian' realism and naturalism of the image. Bartolomeo Fazio had seen a panel attributed to Jan van Eyck depicting a nude woman at her bath, with the scene reflected in a mirror, now lost but known to us only through its apparent survival in two copies – a panel of *c.* 1500 and a painting of 1628 by Willem van Haecht in which it forms part of a depiction

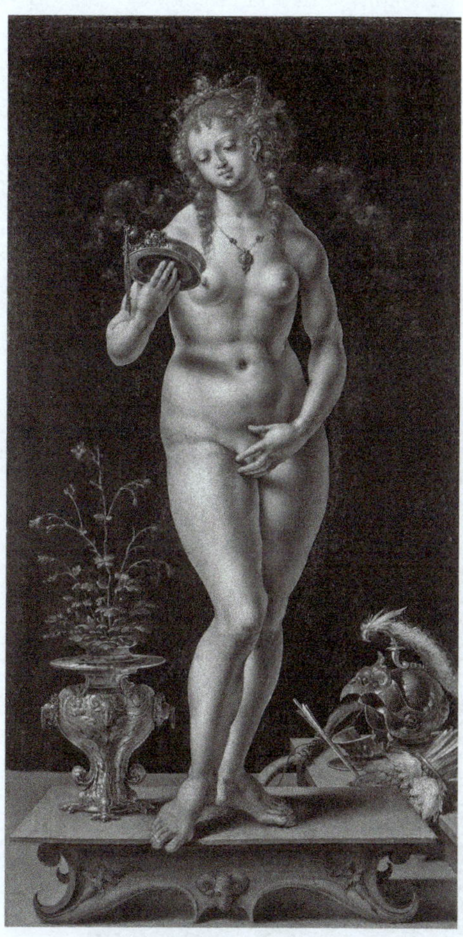

Figure 23 Jan Gossaert (Mabuse): *Vanitas* (Venus) (Rovigo).
(Fine Art Images/Heritage Images/Getty Images.)

of a contemporary picture collection. No evident biblical or classical allusion has yet been identified and the image appears to be of an entirely secular kind. It may have been in some way associated with the *Arnolfini Marriage* panel (1434), but there is no evidence that the panels were actually related, let alone joined, together. Whatever the case, the notion that fifteenth-century Netherlandish and German graphic art was devoid of representations of the nude, sometimes in deliberately erotic forms, is very wide of the mark (Figure 20). The evidence of woodcuts and engravings, as we shall see in a later chapter,[28] also gives the lie to that notion. Gossart's and Cranach's mythological nudes (Figures 23, 24, 25, 26) may therefore bear some relationship to previous Netherlandish and other Northern representations.

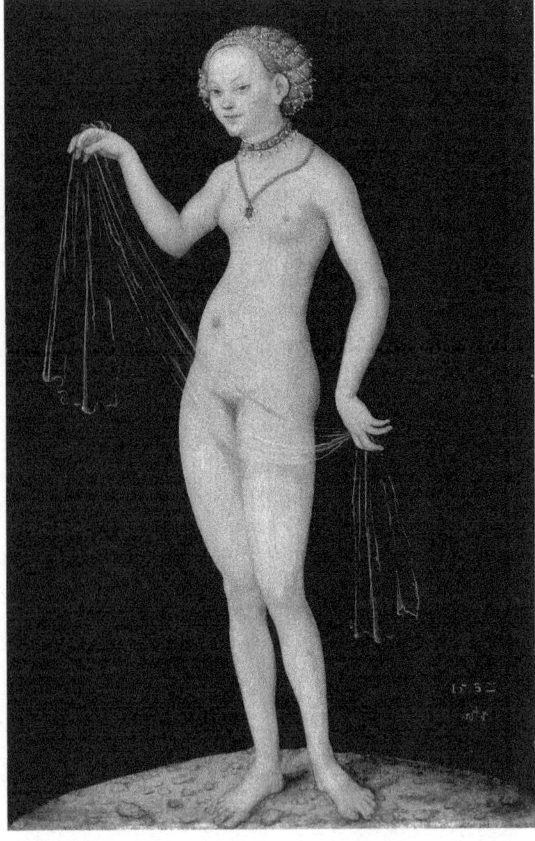

Figure 24 Lucas Cranach: *Venus* (1532) (Frankfurt). (Photo by DeAgostini/ Getty Images.)

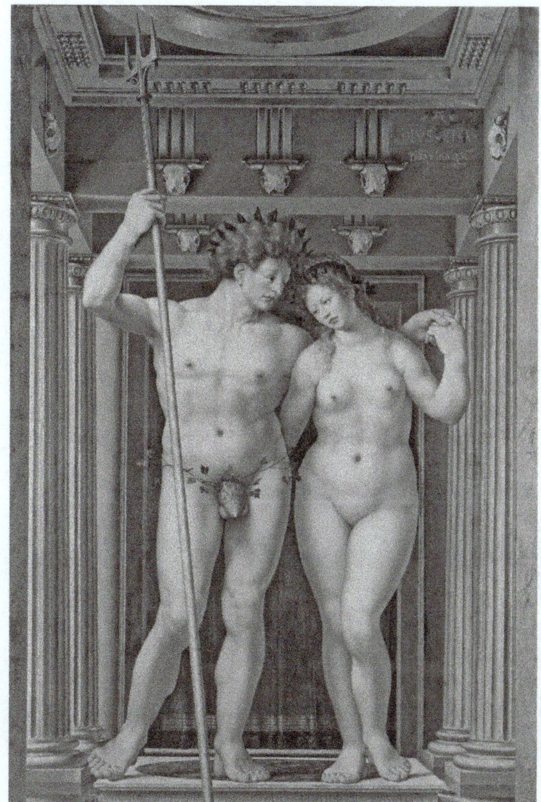

Figure 25 Jan Gossaert: *Neptune and Amphitrite* (Berlin). (Photo by VCG Wilson/Corbis/Getty Images.)

Humanism and the visual arts met in Gossart's *Neptune and Zeelandia (Amphitrite)* of 1516, where both a male and female nude are depicted in a classically monumental manner (Figure 25). It has been claimed that this was 'the first monumental depiction of classical nudes in the history of Netherlandish art'.[29] Collaboration between artist and humanist adviser can be posited here. The work was commissioned by Philip of Burgundy, admiral of the Netherlands, and bears his motto '*A Plus Sera*', rendered as a classical inscription. The painting was not only an erotic image but also a celebration of local antiquity, in which the female figure (Amphitrite) is a personification of the province of Zeeland. This followed the publication of the humanist Gerard Geldenhouwer's *Letter on Zeeland* (1514). This was the first work on the history, geography and topography of the watery province, reclaimed over the

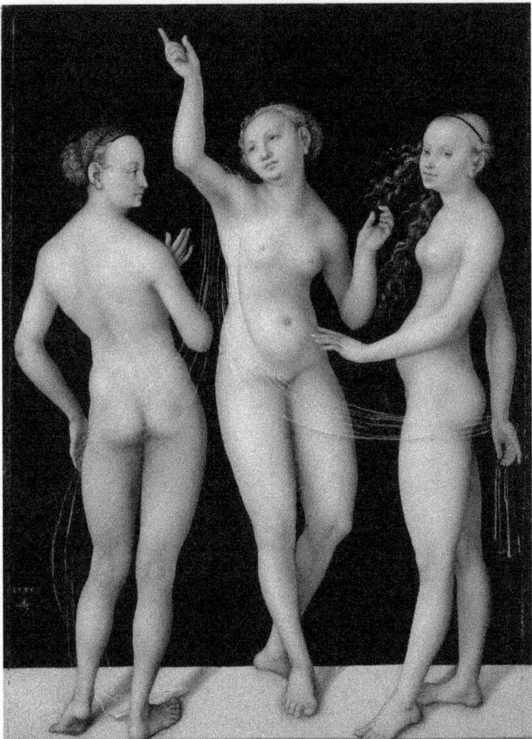

Figure 26 Lucas Cranach: *Three Graces* (1515) (Kansas City). (Photo by VCG Wilson/ Corbis/Getty Images.)

centuries, with great effort, from the sea. Geldenhouwer, from Nijmegen in Guelders, was secretary to Philip of Burgundy, and had a special interest in the Roman imperial peripheries, including the Netherlands. The development of antiquarian historical scholarship in Netherlandish humanist circles was also represented by Rudolph Agricola's defence of the North against Italian accusations of backwardness and barbarism. He went as far as to hope 'that his native shores might one day surpass Italy in civilisation and learning'.[30] Treatises on the ancient Batavi, the tribe inhabiting the Netherlands under the Roman Empire, began to appear, and even Erasmus, although no great lover of his native land, produced his *A Batavian Ear* (1508), praising Holland for its fertility, river-borne commerce and urban growth.[31] The rediscovery of Tacitus's *Germania* played a fundamental part in this recreation of Netherlandish past. And this interest in regional and local history received support and patronage from the highest authorities. Maximilian I and Charles V both emphasized the Netherlandish, as well as the Austrian and Spanish, dimensions of their imperial rule, and they and their clergy and nobilities collected coins, inscriptions, statuary, bronzes and medals from their northernmost dominions. There was therefore an ancient history of Northern Europe which, although strongly bound to that of the Roman Empire, did not always reflect the primacy of Italy and Rome itself in the classical and late antique world. There may well have been a 'triumphant classicism' in much of the art and literature of the Netherlands, especially after Charles V was crowned emperor in 1530, but it was always tempered by reference back to indigenous themes and styles, many of them of Burgundian origin. Northern humanists did not simply import Italian, or Italianate, versions of the culture of Greece and Rome, but devised their own interpretations of it. These could often lead to a very eclectic use of classical themes, images and motifs.

The distinctly hybrid quality which images of mythological and other classically inspired subjects displayed in Northern Europe was echoed in many areas of the arts. It has been argued that 'the influence of the Italian Renaissance' on, for example, England 'was not always immediate or direct; some stimuli, particularly those affecting literature and the fine arts, were at second hand, through the Low Countries above all'.[32] Although Italianate humanist rhetoric and learning entered England through men such as Humphrey, Duke of Gloucester; Robert Flemmyng, bishop of Lincoln; and Sir John Tiptoft,[33] hybrid styles were introduced into the visual and other arts. In architecture, the transmission of classical forms and styles resulted in a transposition of motifs, usually of a decorative kind, derived from antiquity, on to essentially indigenous building styles. The Italianate decorative motifs at Cardinal Wolsey's Hampton Court palace (1514–25), for example, provided evidence for the coexistence of borrowings from Roman antiquity beside the traditional vernacular brick-built architecture of southern and eastern England. Small numbers of Italian sculptors and craftsmen were recruited to work, in the first instance in collaboration with their Northern contemporaries, to produce examples of Italianate workmanship in an English or French setting. Giovanni da Maiano (*c.* 1486–*c.* 1542) was commissioned to create low-relief terracotta busts to set into the Tudor brickwork at Hampton Court. Normally identified as heads of Roman emperors, there may be grounds for believing that they were in fact intended to represent classical military heroes. They are framed in wreath-like circular *tondi* displaying military trophies of arms and armour. Other medallions celebrated the deeds of Hercules. Maiano, with Hans Holbein, also worked on decorations for Henry VIII at Greenwich palace. The popularity of the terracotta bust, imitating the commemorative sculptures of ancient Rome, was evident in England, where the Florentine Pietro Torrigiano (1472–1528), notorious for an alleged assault which broke Michelangelo's nose, produced polychromed terracotta images of Henry VII, the young Henry VIII and John Fisher, the austere humanist bishop of Rochester and university reformer. But his most striking achievements were the tombs and effigies of Lady Margaret Beaufort (1512), Henry VII's mother and Fisher's patroness, and of Henry VII himself with his wife Elizabeth of York (1512–17) in the king's great chantry chapel at the east end of Westminster Abbey. Lady Margaret's tomb 'exhibits an uneven visual tension between a northern late Gothic tabernacle and the new Italian-inspired tomb chest'.[34] The work for Henry VII, however, was more consistent in its Italianate character and has been described as the finest Renaissance-style tomb north of the Alps.

In contemporary France, the first signs of Italianate influence upon building styles were found at the royal castle of Amboise, rebuilt by Charles VIII (1483–98) from 1492 onwards. The earliest work there favoured late Gothic styles, and the interior was replete with fan-vaulting and fireplaces with traditional over-mantels. But some decorative detail of Italian origin was incorporated after Italian masons were recruited in 1495, and the castle received Leonardo da Vinci into French royal service between 1515 and his death there in 1519. The decorative elements at Amboise seem to have been independent of any humanist influence or intervention. A more consistent attempt to integrate Italianate and traditional features was made at the castle of Gaillon, in Normandy, built by the humanist Cardinal Georges d'Amboise, favoured counsellor of Louis XII (1498–1515), from 1502 onwards. It has been described as the 'earliest large-scale example of the Italian impact upon French ways of building'.[35] A fundamentally traditional Gothic structure was blended with Italianate elements in a Renaissance vocabulary. Gaillon stood at the beginning of a succession of French chateaux and hunting lodges, many of them in the Loire valley, such as Azay-le-Rideaux (1518–27), Chambord (1519–47) and Chenonceaux (1514–22) which, while retaining many of the fundamental, rectangular, turreted characteristics of the later medieval castle, incorporated Italianate features. Humanist influence in court and aristocratic circles pointed consistently in this direction. Yet the end result was still a hybrid mixture of styles, sometimes successfully blended, sometimes less so. Only with the rise of Palladianism at a later date did Northern Europe witness the introduction of a 'purer' version of the antique styles of what was perceived to be Roman temple and villa architecture. Palladio's (1508–80) *Four Books of Architecture* (1570) were to become extremely influential outside Italy but only in the seventeenth and, even more markedly, the eighteenth century.

The fifteenth century had witnessed the earliest, tentative attempts to introduce the classically derived styles of the early Florentine Renaissance into Northern Europe. The work of the French painter Jean Fouquet (*c.* 1420–81) had, for the first time, attempted to integrate Italianate architectural and decorative motifs into panel paintings and illuminated manuscripts commissioned largely by civil servants and lawyers at the court of Charles VII of France (1422–61) (Figure 27). His work for Guillaume Jouvenel des Ursins, chancellor of France (1400–72), and Etienne Chevalier, the treasurer of finances (*c.* 1410–74), alluded – in their backgrounds and settings – to the styles of the Florentine Renaissance. But his interpretation of classical forms in no way conformed to the canons and rules of ancient art and architecture. Above all, the rediscovery of the work of the Roman writer, architect and military engineer Vitruvius (d. 15 BC) by Poggio Bracciolini in 1414 was, in the long run, to prove seminal. Vitruvius's treatise *De architectura* was, over time, to become a fundamental sourcebook for humanist theories of architectural principles and proportions. But, until the early seventeenth century, its influence in Northern Europe was in the main derived from second-hand sources, such as the treatise on architecture (published between 1537 and 1554) by the Italian writer and architect Sebastiano Serlio. Many adoptions (and adaptations) of classical motifs in the North appear to have been derived from a somewhat free reading and loose interpretation of Serlio, whose accounts of the five classical Orders (with columns, pilasters, entablatures, friezes, etc.) were often used as templates on which to impose barely compatible decorative features and patterns at will. As in so many other areas, the Northern Renaissance possessed distinctive characteristics of its own.

The rediscovery of the past, both actual and mythical, was one of those features.[36] In the Low Countries, Netherlandish humanists such as Gerard Geldenhouwer and Cornelius Aurelius (1460–1531) traced the histories of prominent noble families, such as the Nassau and Egmont, back to Batavian origins. Aurelius's *Chronicle of Holland, Zeeland, Friesland, and of the Bishopric of Utrecht* (1517) was at pains to emphasize the antiquity of those provinces. With the onset of Habsburg

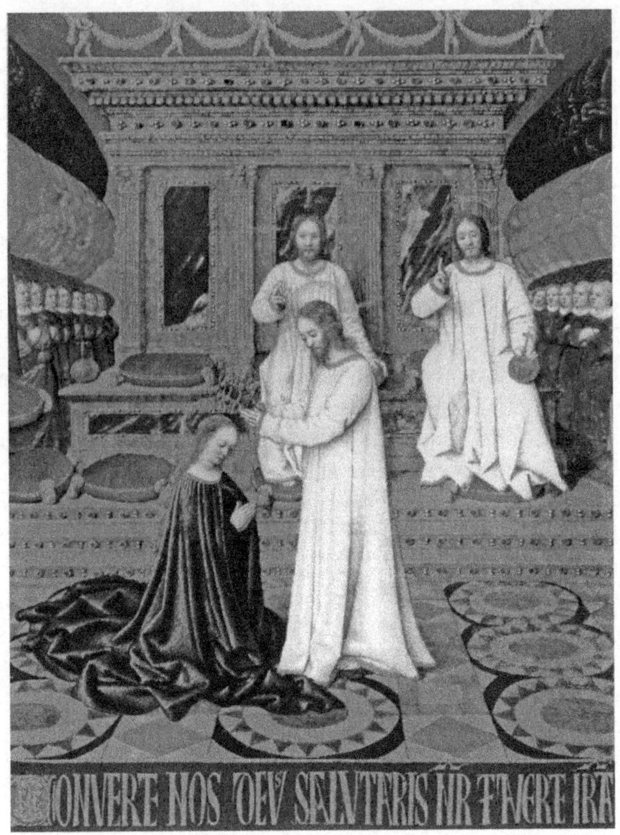

Figure 27 Jean Fouquet: *Coronation of the Virgin* (Chevalier Hours) (Chantilly, Musee Conde).
(Photo by Print Collector/Getty Images.)

rule, a growing cult of Hercules linked the emperors Maximilian I and Charles V, who adopted a Herculean emblem for himself, to the heroes of Greek and Roman antiquity. The poet and historian Jean Lemaire de Belges (*c.* 1473–*c.* 1515), working at the court of Margaret of Austria, regent of the Habsburg Netherlands, produced a French vernacular history of Gallic and Trojan antiquities (*Illustrations de Gaule et singularitez de Troye*, 1510–14). But many of these regional histories took much from the Burgundian Raoul Lefevre's *Trojan History* of 1464 and Lemaire de Belges was himself influenced by the Burgundian poet, chronicler and *grand rhetoriqueur* Jean Molinet (1435–1507). The ancestries of former Burgundian-ruled, then Habsburg-ruled, nobles were traced by their humanist advisers and tutors to the tribal chiefs in Tacitus's *Germania*, Caesar's *Commentaries* and other Roman sources. Their alleged Trojan origins were celebrated, as were those of the Polish and Hungarian nobilities of the time. But some aspects of the Greek and Roman past came under heavy attack in both Northern and Central Europe. Protestant iconoclasm had already appeared in the Low Countries by 1525, and the effects of the Reformation on at least some facets of the visual arts were to prove, literally, damaging and destructive. As in Hussite Bohemia at an earlier date, where the advances of Renaissance humanism were largely stopped in their tracks by proto-Puritanism, so in Germany and the Netherlands a concerted assault upon both religious imagery and the 'paganism' of some forms of Italian Renaissance art began. Sensuality, the unbridled depiction of elemental expressive force, and what Aby Warburg called the 'Dionysiac' in the visual and broader culture of antiquity, expressed through highly rhetorical gestures, were deemed incompatible with Christian doctrines and values by many reformers. Durer's early works, and those of other artists, which drew upon subjects associated with Dionysus, the god of intoxication, ecstasy and sensual abandon, reflected these tendencies. It may be no coincidence that after about 1520 Durer, who had been very much influenced by these Italian styles and modes of representation, began to react with 'indigenous Nordic calm'[37] against the excesses of Italian rhetoric and theatricality.

There were, therefore, essential differences between North and South in their treatment of the legacy of the classical tradition. Warburg thought that Durer 'countered the pagan vigour of Southern [Italian] art with an overtone … of robust composure'.[38] Durer derived much of his knowledge of the Antique through the filter of contemporary and near-contemporary Italian interpretations of classical themes and motifs. But in 1506, he claimed he was told by some Venetians, when in Venice, that his art 'was not in the antique manner and therefore no good'.[39] The movements within Italian culture, both artistic and literary, towards a more stylized mannerism and the subsequent flamboyance of baroque, were not universally admired or imitated in the North. Extremes of gesture and excessive rhetorical expression were not always applauded. The impact of humanism in Northern Europe was, if anything, more likely to exert a restraining influence upon the parallel excesses of exteriorized and theatrical devotional piety. To that extent it had something in common with Protestantism. Emotionalism, and the representation of pain and pathos, was certainly not absent from Northern art and literature. But they did not reflect what Warburg and others saw as 'the baroque language of gesture, towards which Italian art had been moving since the mid-fifteenth century'.[40] The sober monumentality of the early Italian – especially Florentine – Renaissance, found in the art of Masaccio or Piero della Francesca, was now giving way to depictions by Mantegna or Pollaiuolo of Bacchanalian and Dionysiac scenes, or titanic struggles between male nudes, full of emotive force.[41] The North had its own manner of depicting and describing similar and related subjects, which did not rely upon antique examples.[42] Some humanists, in both Italy and the North, showed very little interest in the visual arts. Humanism in the North was very much rooted in textual studies. It could be as pedantic and pedestrian as scholasticism. But, as Erasmus and Durer both demonstrated, it could introduce moderation and restraint into the polemics and histrionics of literary and artistic expression. And that, in an age of increasing religious turmoil and disorder, was perhaps no mean an achievement.

4

THE OLD AND THE NEW DEVOTION

Saying that we should have devotion, whether in prayer or in ceremony, while understanding nothing, is a great mockery. (Jean Calvin, *Preface to the Geneva Psalter*, 1551)[1]

RELIGION AND THE RENAISSANCE

It is incontestable that the civilization which produced the European Renaissance was rooted in Christian doctrines, beliefs and values. But the extent to which religious life and its structures fitted, if at all, into a 'Renaissance' culture and mindset can be questioned. For instance, incompatibilities and even contradictions between an admiration for pagan classical antiquity and the demands of Christian belief were spelt out by some of the greatest scholars of Renaissance culture, Burckhardt and Warburg among them. Was religious rebirth, renewal and revival ever part of a 'Renaissance' mentality? Can we speak, as some historians have done, of a 'Christian Renaissance', a 'monastic Renaissance', 'Christian humanism', or even 'biblical humanism' in Northern Europe? One historian has even combined these terms to produce the concept of a 'Renaissance of monastic humanism'.[2] In an age often characterized by the importance it accorded to the place and role of the individual, however those terms are defined, the other face, or *alter ego*, of secular Renaissance individualism – religious and devotional individualism – is worthy of closer study. It is no longer simply a question of the Burckhardtian 'discovery of the individual' in, and by, the Renaissance that demands our attention. Theses about that notion have dated it back to, at least, the twelfth century. The individualism which this chapter addresses is one which puts the individual, the soul and the self into a complex religious and devotional context, in which dramatic changes were taking place at many levels.

In a Christian context, the individual is defined essentially through his, or her, relationship with God. But the individual is also a member of the collective body, or congregation, of all believers, clerical and lay.[3] The anonymous author of the anticlerical and anti-papal tract known as *Antequam essent clerici* (*Before there were clergy*) wrote in 1296:

> Holy Mother Church, the bride of Christ, is not composed solely of the clergy; laymen are also part of it. ... Did Christ die and rise from the dead for the clergy alone? Not at all.[4]

One of the most significant issues in the religious life of this period was precisely that to which *Antequam* alluded – the position and role of the laity in the Church and in the living of the Christian life. There was an evident tension between two facets of the lay person's religious and devotional life. There was clearly, on the one hand, a need to establish a balance between an individual's personal devotion, expressed through private prayer and meditation (not only those prayers contained in Books of Hours) and, on the other, their participation in communal, collective worship. It can be argued that, during this period, balance shifted notably towards an emphasis on the private, personal devotional life and practice of the individual. For example, the appearance of individualized Books of Hours, often bearing clear marks of ownership and use, from the mid-thirteenth century onwards, reflected what were perceived to be the needs of an increasingly literate laity. These service books were made largely by lay people for lay people, in secular workshops rather than monastic *scriptoria* (writing offices). The core of a Book of Hours lay in the so-called Hours of the Virgin. These comprised the liturgical offices or services of the Church, as celebrated, originally in monasteries, at the eight canonical hours of the day: Matins (the 'night office' or watch, ending at dawn); Lauds (dawn prayer, or 3.00 am); Prime (the 'first hour', 6.00 am); Terce (the 'third hour', 9.00 am); Sext (the 'sixth hour', 12.00 pm); None (the 'ninth hour', 3.00 pm); Vespers (seasonal, 4.00–6.00 pm or sunset); and Compline (at bedtime). They first appeared in an entirely Latin text, standardized according to which 'Use' was common in a certain region – the Use of Rome, the Use of Sarum, the Use of Rouen, the Use of Utrecht and so on. But some Books of Hours began to include vernacular prayers, among them prayers requesting the intercession of personal patron saints and name-saints. Especially in the

Low Countries an increasing tendency for Books of Hours to contain many more vernacular translations and French and Dutch versions of the words of the Mass is discernible. An attempt was here being made to reconcile the demands of personal devotion with those of collective worship.[5] The Book of Hours could be easily portable, brought to the communal Mass or other office by the lay person so that the Latin words of the liturgy could be followed, if not fully understood. Yet it could also be read and recited in solitude, by the family in the home, or during the celebration of Masses in enclosed private chapels or oratories, where more elaborate and luxuriously decorated examples of the book might be kept. But the private/public balance in worship was never fully resolved. And if the Hours could be recited anywhere, however much that action brought the individual lay person into simultaneous remote communion with other believers, this was not collective worship within the fabric of the institutional Church. The extent, moreover, to which the Church ever fully met the individual needs of literate lay people was debatable and became more so as it underwent the crises and vicissitudes of the fourteenth and early fifteenth centuries.

The crises faced by the Western Church between *c.* 1290 and 1420 threw up fundamental challenges to its nature, structure and practices. Conflicts between the papacy and secular powers – the German empire and then, after the empire's post-Hohenstaufen decline in the second half of the thirteenth century, the kingdom of France – led to shifts in the balance of power relationships. The departure of the popes from Rome to Avignon (1309–78) was one reflection of those changed relationships. The effects of the series of epidemics which included and followed the outbreak of the Black Death in 1348–9 depleted the ranks of the clergy who bore much of the brunt of its onslaughts. Religious communities living together in close quarters were very vulnerable to the rapid spread of plague, and the pastoral duty of the priest in administering the last rites to plague victims meant that many fell prey to its ravages. The gaps in the clerical ranks had to be made good, and the need to fill benefices and meet the cure of souls could lead to the ordination and subsequent incumbency of less-than-ideal candidates. Rising levels of lay literacy, and greater lay understanding of doctrine and liturgy, had two main results: a higher level of lay expectation of the quality of the clergy, at monastic, diocesan and parish levels; and the emergence of doctrinal heresies which challenged the role of the priest, disputing his sacramental function in the mystery of the Mass when the miracle of transubstantiation was performed. The disciples, both clerical and lay, of Wycliffe and Hus laid great stress on the worthiness of the priest, often perceived to be lacking, and, especially in the Hussite case, argued for the admission of the laity to communion in both kinds, bread and wine, at the Eucharist. Matters were made worse by the outbreak of the Western schism in 1378, with rival popes at Rome and Avignon, which was not resolved until 1417. A dissident group, supporting an alternative pope, lingered on into the 1440s. The schism had been brought to an end by means of representative councils of the universal Church (Pisa, Constance, Basel), and the release of the papacy from the authority claimed by the councils became a hard-won fight which was not fully achieved until the mid-fifteenth century.

It was in this disturbed and turbulent ecclesiastical world that steps towards both structural reform and devotional renewal or revival were taken in the course of the later fourteenth century.[6] Among those tendencies, there emerged from the northern Low Countries, during the later fourteenth century, the so-called *devotio moderna* ('new' or 'modern' devotion). It has been claimed by a critical historian of the tendency and its exponents that 'their devotion was modern only in the manner in which they put it into practice'.[7] The justice of this conclusion remains to be assessed, and more recent scholarship has tended to modify this view.[8] But it remains the case that novelty or 'modernity' formed a fundamental element in the terms coined both at the time, and much later, to describe three important tendencies in Northern European culture: the so-called *ars nova* ('new art') in music, the *via moderna* ('modern way') which characterized the philosophical thought of William of Ockham and others and the *devotio moderna* ('new' or 'modern devotion') in religious life and practice.

The term *ars nova* ('new art') was, perhaps surprisingly, never applied by contemporaries to the visual art of the time. If anything could be called 'new', the art of the Van Eycks and their Netherlandish successors would surely have qualified for that title. The term was coined and adopted by early twentieth-century musicologists to describe a distinct period in the history of Western music. It was derived from the title of Philippe de Vitry's (1291–1361) treatise *Ars nova musicae* (*c.* 1322), as opposed to the *ars antiqua* ('ancient art'), setting out the novelties introduced into musical metre and harmony both by Vitry himself and Guillaume de Machaut in fourteenth-century France. The fourteenth century witnessed the birth of ecclesiastical choral polyphony in the Low Countries and Northern France, originating especially from the diocese of Cambrai, and the new part-writing for voices was a decidedly novel art form.[9] It never fully superseded plainsong (the unison singing of a single vocal line, which became known as Gregorian chant) but achieved a wide and popular currency throughout Europe. The Church's liturgical needs and demands, formulated by the higher clergy, patronized and supported by the upper laity, could thus initiate and shape stylistic and cultural patterns in a number of art forms. The Mass settings of Guillaume Dufay (*c.* 1400–74), John Dunstable (*c.* 1390–1453) or Johannes Ockeghem (*c.* 1420–95) demonstrated a superlative artistry in the interweaving of elaborate melodic lines, taking their starting point from the plainsong chant of the cantor, or sometimes from a popular song or refrain such as *L'homme arme* ('The Armed Man'). The effects of this kind of polyphony, mellifluous and sonorous as it was, could induce an almost mesmeric or trance-like state in the listener. Without employing later devices such as rising suspensions, beloved of romantic composers such as Wagner or Tchaikovsky, choral polyphony produced a stream of sound which took the words of the Ordinary of the Mass and other devotional texts to an elevated level of consciousness. The clear enunciation, and hence the meaning, of the words was, however, seemingly secondary to the quality of the sound, as a single syllable could often be set to a very large number of notes. Reformers, especially Protestant reformers, took grave exception to the practice and denounced choral polyphony from the pulpit and in their polemical writings. The Lutheran chorale, with its plainly heard words, stands near the opposite end of the musical and liturgical spectrum. But in terms of musical novelty, Netherlandish and Northern French choral writing stands comparison with other innovative art forms of the age. Polyphonic choral music, its composers and performers, was a major cultural export from the Low Countries to Southern Europe. The papal chapel at Rome, for example, by the 1420s and 1430s, was full of Netherlandish singers, and Italian princes such as the Malatesta of Rimini, or European monarchs such as the Aragonese kings of Naples and Sicily, recruited Flemish composers – such as Dufay – and musicians into their service. The origins of the retained *capella* (musical 'chapel'), and the *kapellmeister*, or music director, in princely service, performing both sacred and secular music, are to be found in this period. The increasing proximity of rulers' courts, as they itinerated, to the resources of the cities and greater towns of their domains, meant that there was a ready supply of musical talent to be drawn upon. Singers of the Burgundian ducal chapel, for instance, were often granted prebends (i.e. stipendiary positions) in the cathedral and collegiate churches of the duke's dominions.[10] The picture which emerges from studies of music at this time is one of innovation, vitality and creativity of a high order.

But the musical novelties of the age were merely one part of a much broader and deeper tendency within its devotional religion. The term 'modern devotion' was apparently first introduced by Henry Pomerius, early biographer of the great Flemish mystic Jan Ruysbroec (1293–1381) in his *Vita Beati Johannis Rusbrochii* (*Life of the Blessed Jan Ruysbroec*), written between 1414 and 1421. He was described by Geert Groote (1340–84), a leading disciple of Ruysbroec, as the '*fons et origo Modernae Devotionis*' ('The fount and origin of the Modern Devotion'). The term was therefore a contemporary usage rather than, as with so many other labels applied to movements in this period, a later coinage. The *devotio* has been defined as aiming for a 'dedicated inner life (*devotio*) ... in a suitably contemporary manner (*moderna*), striving to emulate the example of the first Christians for the renewal of an ailing Church '.[11] The earliest Latin-Dutch dictionary (Antwerp, 1488) defined the Latin word *devotio* as 'inwardness' (*innicheyt, innicheit*) in Middle Dutch. A *devotarius* was an 'inward person' (*een innich mensch*).[12] Latin *modernus* was rendered in Dutch as *novellus* (new). In this 'new devotion' the inner life was to be privileged over its external manifestations and expressions.[13]

The origins and development of the tendency can be briefly summarized. This chapter will devote a substantial portion of its content to the *devotio* because it was a product, exclusively, of Northern Europe and emerged from that region's particular forms of religious thought, preoccupations and practices.[14] It also had a significant influence, both directly and indirectly, over much of the rest of Europe. Emerging from the northern Low Countries, then comprising the counties of Holland, Zeeland, Friesland and Guelders, in the later fourteenth century, it formed a distinctive response to the more general, as well as local, problems of the contemporary Church. Schismatic, depleted in its ranks, accused (justly or unjustly) of increasing worldliness and corruption, and allegedly losing sight of the apostolic virtues, the Western Church of the later fourteenth century elicited various reactions, some more extreme than others, from its members. The *devotio* was thus a product of its times, sharing with other religious positions many of their features. But it also led the way towards a particular species of piety and personal spirituality that was to have wide- and far-reaching consequences. This applied to lay people as well as to the clergy. To some extent, the soil was well prepared for it by the emergence of forms of devotional and other literature which addressed themselves to the laity.

The English mystic and Augustinian canon regular Walter Hilton (*c.* 1340–96) had, between 1386 and 1390, identified the contemporary devotional climate and composed a treatise entitled *The Mixed Life* in which he argued that lay people can live a semblance of the contemplative life while fully engaged in the active life of the secular world. He applied this especially to the world of those holding and exercising secular authority – nobles, gentry, and the middle and upper ranks of urban dwellers – and his work has been described as advocating 'a complementarity of material and spiritual power'.[15] The *devotio* tended to broaden the base of the concept's appeal, extending it to a wider social range of lay people. Its teachings reached out well beyond the clergy. The notion, for example, that the writings of its major exponents were intended solely for monks has been discredited. There was an adaptability, even a malleability, about many of its teachings which could be embraced by people of many different persuasions, Protestants among them. Its first manifestations appeared as the result of the initiatives taken by Geert Groote (1340–84), from a wealthy family of Deventer, who had undergone a conversion experience during a serious illness in about 1373. He had studied at Paris, became a Carthusian novice, but abandoned that vocation, choosing to remain a deacon rather than becoming an ordained priest because he felt unworthy to assume that sacred office. Following to some extent in the footsteps of the earlier Netherlandish founders of houses of Beguines – pious lay women living in communities but taking no monastic vows – Groote established the first houses of Sisters, then Brothers, of the Common Life. Their means of support came from their own work, and from the endowments given to them by wealthy (and less wealthy) burghers, patricians and landholders. The houses were formed by groups of lay women, living in common at Deventer, Zwolle, Kampen and other small Netherlandish towns 'after the manner of the primitive Church'. The community at Deventer, established in 1374, became known as the 'new Beguines', and what Groote described as a 'little spark' was to kindle 'great fires'.

In origin, the *devotio* was therefore a product of urban life and, in part, of the particular conditions prevailing in the Netherlands at the time. This was a region, much of which had been arduously reclaimed from the sea, traversed by watercourses, subject to very adverse weather conditions and natural disasters. The threat of severe coastal storms, flooding to the point of near-total inundation, bitterly cold winters and recurrent epidemics, was ever-present. Chronicles written in the Low Countries are full of year-in, year-out laments for the adversity of the times. A degree of stoic acceptance of the hardships of this world characterized many of its inhabitants. Any religious tendency which put its major emphasis on the hope of release from such harsh material realities into another, better life was likely to have considerable traction in this region. Huizinga was to an extent right to emphasize escape and transcendence as two of the most prominent characteristics of the piety of the age. But the means by which that desirable afterlife might be achieved might vary – from the saying of Masses on an industrial scale, as promoted by the established Church, to a simple faith and trust in a loving, rather than a vengeful, God, a God made man in the person of Christ. The Church's stern admonitions to the laity about the consequences of unrepented sin – the pains of Purgatory and the fires of Hell – might be offset by a Gospel, not of fear, but one of love and hope. It was this latter course that the *devotio* advocated, although it did not spurn the offices and rituals of the Church nor the performance of 'good works' for the common welfare. It was also clear that in the urbanized economy of the region, in which a relatively high proportion of the inhabitants lived in towns, considerable wealth could certainly be made. The busy citizens of these small Dutch towns were likely to be attracted to a devotional cult, or cults, which were not incompatible with their business activities. Too severe a demand upon their time and resources, too strenuous a penitential regime of physical self-mortification, or even self-flagellation, was not conducive to active, rational, entrepreneurial and commercial pursuits. There may be an argument here for the notion that it was Catholicism, as well as Protestantism, that furthered the rise of capitalism. Arguments from material, let alone climatic, determinism must clearly be treated with extreme caution. But whatever the case, there were clearly more than sufficient reasons, given the harshness and uncertainty of everyday conditions, for an individual to retreat into a personal spiritual life, fostered by meditation, reflection and prayer. It was this well that was tapped by the *devotio moderna*.

Groote's early foundations for women were followed by the creation, in 1379, of so-called Brotherhouses for men. These were the work of Groote's disciple Florens Radewijns (*c.* 1350–1400). He had been a canon of St Peter's, Utrecht, but renounced his canonry after hearing one of Groote's sermons, and devoted himself to following Groote and furthering his principles. But the continued existence of religious communities consisting solely of lay people, observing no vows, was of some concern to the authorities of the Church. They could, among other risks, stray into error, becoming potential sources of heretical belief which might infect their surrounding communities. A move to integrate the *devotio* better into the existing monastic orders began with the foundation, at Windesheim, near Zwolle, in 1386–7, of a convent of six Augustinian Canons Regular, observing the Augustinian rule, but following the tenets of the *devotio*. This was to become a full-fledged monastic organization with the creation in 1395 of a Chapter of Windesheim, which then brought under its sway the daughter-houses of Syon, Venlo and Utrecht. The convent at Zwolle, known as that of Mount St Agnes (Sint-Agnietenburg) also formed part of Windesheim's congregation.

Yet the Brotherhouses and Sisterhouses survived as separate communities, the former owing their continued existence largely to the schools which they founded, usually in collaboration with civic authorities, and their work of copying and, in effect, publishing books. By 1470, there were eighty-two houses of Brothers; by 1500 a total of ninety houses of Sisters. Their 'manual' labour lay partly in manuscript book-copying, but they also embraced the new art of printing. Their house at Marienthal, near Mainz, the home of Gutenberg's first presses, became in 1474–5 a prolific liturgical book printer north of the Alps, followed by the house at Rostock in 1476.[16] Two parallel streams or currents had begun to run through the *devotio*. As the 'clericalization' of the movement gained ground, many – but not all – of the Brotherhouses and Sisterhouses adopted either the Augustinian or the tertiary Franciscan rule (especially for women). Their geographical range widened and, by 1511, there were 100 monastic houses, mainly of Augustinian canons, founded on *devotio* principles, stretching across the Low Countries, Northern France, Switzerland and the German-speaking lands. Their members observed the monastic vows of poverty, chastity and obedience, occupying their time with the writing, copying and illumination of books, preaching, ministering to the poor and sick, and taking responsibility for the affairs of the house. They also played some part, with their Observant contemporaries in the Dominican and Franciscan orders, in the reform of monasteries across the Dutch- and German-speaking areas. Their spiritual lives of individual, personal devotion were expressed by the commonplace books, or *rapiaria*, which they kept, filled with extracts from biblical and other texts, devotional treatises, prayers and observations on the good Christian life. One of these, the *rapiarium* of Gerlach Peters, was later worked up as a devotional treatise called the *Soliloquium* (literally the 'Speaking with Oneself') for use in private prayer and meditation. The Brethren were also noted for their schools, established throughout the northern, then the southern, Netherlands. They played an important and formative role in the education of many of their pupils, including Erasmus. Their school at Zwolle was especially famed for its alumni – priests, monks, magistrates, advocates, civil servants and other holders of secular offices from a wide area of the Low Countries and Germany. Master John Cele (d. 1417), master of the school there, who taught with 'fatherly care', encouraged musical talent among his pupils, being himself an organist, harpist, dancer and singer. The *devotio*, despite Thomas Kempis's strictures and Erasmus's criticisms, was thus not averse to employing the secular arts to further its work. Nor was it totally lacking, as some have claimed, in the creation of joy in this world of misery, despite the promise of incomparable joy in the next.

The tendency has been characterized as an 'intense, introspective and creatively imaginative mode of reaching out to God',[17] attuned to the laity as well as the clergy. It envisaged an essentially private, individualized form of spiritual and devotional life, based upon 'individual emotion and spiritual fulfilment'.[18] Its inherent quietism – later thought to be a typically Dutch trait – led to no reforming political or social agendas or actions. Sustenance of the poor, and working towards the common good, were part of its largely conventional emphasis on good works. Otherwise, educating the young and attempting to introduce improvements into the observances and lifestyles of monastic houses were its major contributions to reformist agendas. But in the context of a 'Renaissance' mindset, we might relate (or simply juxtapose) this consistent and intense emphasis upon personal spiritual development to broader movements of individualism, both religious and secular. Although emanating initially from a clerical background, the *devotio*'s cultivation of the skills of meditation, reflection and introspection was no longer to be confined to the monastic, mendicant and other orders within the Church.

KEMPIS AND THE NEW DEVOTION

The most significant and influential piece of writing to emerge from the *devotio* was the attributed work of the Augustinian canon Thomas Kempis, or Thomas van Kampen (*c.* 1379–1471) entitled *De Imitatione Christi* (*Concerning the Imitation of Christ*). 'Imitation' in this sense is normally understood to mean an attempt to live and act as Christ lived and acted as he walked upon the earth. So the 'Copying of Christ' offers an alternative translation. The work was composed entirely in Latin, in four books or parts, the first being completed by 1424, while the earliest manuscript of all four books dates from 1427. An autograph copy, attributed to Kempis's own hand, survives from 1441. Translations into many vernacular languages rapidly followed. The fact that there are 900 surviving manuscripts of it dating from between 1420 and 1500, and 100 printed editions before 1500, made it one of the most popular books in fifteenth- and sixteenth-century Northern Europe. It has subsequently become 'a classic of western spirituality'.[19] The *Imitation* became very influential among both Catholics and Protestants; for the latter, in part, because of its introspectiveness, its implicit puritanism and its essentially Bible-based message or what has been called its 'Biblicism'. The main qualities required of a good Christian life were the following: interiority (inwardness) whereby external actions were to be determined by inward thoughts, humility, simplicity, silence, contrition and patience – advocated for the laity as well as, especially, for the monastic clergy. The importance of self-examination and introspection was stressed, while – seemingly paradoxically – urging that, in the inner life, 'we must be dead to ourselves';[20] or 'the more completely we die to self, the more we begin to live to God'.[21] Here Kempis was to a large degree echoing the mystical thought of another Augustinian canon, Ruysbroec: the self is to be extinguished lest it detract from the promptings of a clear, clean and quiet conscience accompanied by reflection upon the amendment of life; a 'free and independent mind', uncluttered and unfettered by attachment to worldly things, is demanded. But there may here be an implied contrast between the inner and outer self; the outer self can be *in* the world but not necessarily *of* the world; the inner self was neither *in* nor *of* the world; and lay people, not merely the clergy, could attempt to aspire to this end.

The redemptive power of suffering, as experienced by the individual, with the possibility, or probability, of rejection by the world made Kempis's message especially reflective of the life of Christ. His title, 'Concerning the Imitation of Christ and Contempt for the Futilities of the World', was meant to convey the belief that there is little joy to be had in the earthly existence per se – that is largely reserved for the life to come. Even kings and popes, he says, are not exempt from the troubles and anxieties of the world; all worldly pleasures are essentially transient and ephemeral, and hence 'all the riches of this world are nothing'.[22] It may be indicative of the broader context from which he emerged that he singles out self-love and self-interest as especially prevalent among the *mercenarii* of the world – merchants, traders, financiers and many of the other lay people for whom the *Imitation* purported to offer a guide to the living of a good Christian life. Kempis warns them that 'there are not many who are so spiritual that they can be totally stripped of self-love'.[23] They are to 'put to good use the things of this world, but only to desire the things that are eternal'.[24] Riches may be gained, used well, but never desired. Behind the words may lie the shadow of the doctrine of good works, and the irreplaceable role of the rich and powerful in the endowment of the Church's mission and work in all their aspects. Without them, after all, no religious order would ever have survived. But Kempis stresses that inner possession of the 'Spirit of Christ' is all important; a place for Christ must be 'found in the heart' so the 'good life' can be lived. And it could, he apparently believed, be lived – within their limitations – by lay people, outside the world of the convent, the cathedral or the university. 'A humble peasant', he wrote, 'who serves God, is more pleasing to God than a conceited intellectual who knows the course of the stars but ignores the things of the spirit.'[25] Kempis's attacks on the uselessness of worldly learning was the other face of the humanists' onslaughts on scholasticism and its deficiencies. While humanist disdain for scholastic thought and its pedantry was to become a spur to the reform of university curricula, Kempis simply ruled out the value of advanced theological and philosophical studies altogether: merely serving Christ 'enables the humble-minded to understand more of the ways of everlasting truth in a single moment than in ten years' study at a university'.[26] And this sentiment, when applied to the knowledge of God, was to be echoed and shared by the greatest humanist scholar of his time, Erasmus. It may be a testimony to the strength of the *devotio's* influence, however grudgingly admitted, on his intellectual and spiritual formation.

There is a constant, if not relentless, reiteration in Kempis of the value of 'a good conscience and a holy life' as superior to a life of learning, outward devotion and observance, or theological and philosophical speculation. The contemporary Church, with what some critics regarded as its excessive external display and liturgical clutter, did not always nourish and sustain the devotional life. 'If we rely only on outward religious observances', declares Kempis, 'our devotion will rapidly fade away.'[27] Erasmus agreed, as did Luther and Calvin. Kempis reserves some of his severest strictures for the monastic life: 'having a tonsure and a habit are in themselves of little significance' as there must be a 'total transformation of your way of life and total mortification of the senses'.[28] Erasmus's disdain for contemporary monasticism, of which he had unwelcome personal experience, was an echo of this view. Kempis, with many others, clerical and lay, was especially critical of the monastic attitudes and behaviour of his time. With some honourable exceptions, the orders had departed from their rule, as laid down by the early church fathers and their own founders. Henry V of England (1413–22) thus accused the English Benedictines of straying far from the Rule of St Benedict. Kempis's censure of monastic 'negligence and coldness', 'sloth and lukewarmness', propensity for gossip, casual talk and 'aimless visits'[29] would have a sympathetic listener there.

Despite the privileged status accorded to the inner life that the *Imitation* endorsed, Kempis also cautioned monks and other members of religious orders about the neglect of collective worship. 'Do not', he wrote, 'become casual about the community observances, by putting your personal devotions as a priority' but use any 'left-over' time for your own prayer.[30] This evidently applied to the clergy but would be difficult to apply to the laity, who did not, as a whole, live in religious communities. They were, presumably, to bring their private reflections and meditations into the acts of collective worship they experienced in cathedral, collegiate and parish churches and perhaps in their confraternities and religious guilds. But this could also lead to an almost mechanical, mantra-like recitation or silent following of the words of the Latin Mass, which were not fully understood. Hence, the stress laid by contemporaries, including Luther, Calvin and Zwingli, on lay understanding of the sacraments and the Mass. Vehicles of instruction, apart from private reading and reflection, certainly existed, sanctioned by the Church, for the purpose. As we shall see, it became increasingly common to advocate the use of the so-called pulpit office, or service, of the 'Prone' and other means of preaching, edification and instruction. And the laity could take comfort from Kempis's observation that 'those who walk by inner insight, and are not unduly influenced by outward things, need no special time or place for prayer'.[31] As busy merchants and traders such as Francesco di Marco Datini of Prato (*c.* 1335–1410) demonstrated, pauses in the counting-house day to observe both the canonical hours and other times to pray for God's blessing on their activities, outside the fabric of any church or other sacred space, could become a recurrent routine. The preaching and teachings of that precursor of the *devotio*, the Dominican theologian and popular preacher Meister Eckhart (*c.* 1260–*c.* 1328), or of Ruysbroec and the Rhineland mystics, who argued that God could be found and worshipped anywhere, was exemplified by such behaviour. Ruysbroec communed with the divine, and experienced his mystical ecstasies on walks in the forest around his convent at Groenendaal, outside Brussels, of which he became the prior. The Neoplatonist Eckhart had preached that 'a man may go into the field and say his prayer and be aware of God', just as he might be aware of God in a church, as God was 'in all things and in all places'. Diderot's (1713–84) dictum *'Elargissez Dieu!'* ('Set God free!'), releasing God from the physical confines and ordered times of the Church, clearly had a long and distinguished, albeit controversial, pedigree in Christian thought. As Eckhart discovered to his cost, the risk of accusations of pantheism and prosecution for heresy was never far off. He died still under suspicion of heresy, with further trials pending.

A long tradition, both past and future, of evangelical Christian belief received its expression in the *Imitation*. The extreme Christo-centricity of Kempis's thought led him to privilege a believer's love of Jesus above everything else: the Lord Jesus Christ is the intimate friend, even the lover, and the believer is exhorted to 'love Him and keep Him as your friend', as He will 'help and protect you when all others fail you'.[32] Corporeal, quasi-sexual images are used by Kempis to describe the union of the individual soul with Christ: 'You in me and I in You, may we abide in one another for ever', as Christ is 'my Beloved'.[33] The desire for Christ is like a 'burning love' and the believer is to be 'on fire with devotion'. Once again, it is the individual, standing alone or even despised by the world, who is addressed here. He or she must bring this love to the Eucharist. For the literate lay person, attendance at the celebration of the Mass, and receipt of the Sacrament of Christ's body and blood in one kind only (the bread), on generally rare occasions, together with Bible reading and reflection, were, Kempis claims, to be their 'food and light'. The Eucharist provided spiritual food; the Scriptures were 'a lamp to my feet'.[34]

The *devotio's* emphasis on *meditatio* (meditation) and *ruminatio* (reflection) was to be echoed by many believers and, ultimately, by non-believers as well. It was soon to lead to the introduction and refinement of elaborate mind-focusing meditation techniques which can bear comparison with more modern practices. Spiritual exercises were among the ancestors of 'mindfulness' and other meditative and therapeutic techniques. In this respect, some practices cultivated by the *devotio* were truly 'modern' and outlasted their own time. Communion with the divine was to be achieved through prayer, meditation and also, as we shall see, through work. There was a Catholic, as well as a Protestant, work ethic, and it preceded the Protestant Reformation. It was, in part, a product of the doctrine of immanence, seeing the divine in all things, even in the meanest, most commonplace objects and most menial of occupations. Kempis expressed it perfectly: 'There is nothing created, however small and insignificant, that is not a reflection of the goodness of God.'[35] Such sentiments also applied to the performance of 'humble external tasks', and to the restorative power of work, even of the most menial kind, for the healthy cultivation of the life of the spirit. To be in a state of grace, the individual 'cannot be idle, but cheerfully welcomes work'.[36] Echoes of this notion are found in later Christian thought and its literature. George Herbert (1593–1633), Anglican priest and poet, put it well in his poem/hymn *The Elixir* (published in 1633):

> All may of Thee partake, / Nothing can be so mean / That with his tincture, *for Thy sake*, / Will not grow bright and clean / … A servant with this clause / Makes drudgery divine, / Who sweeps a room, as for Thy laws, / Makes that and th' action fine.

The practical application of these notions of the spiritual value of work is set out in the *Chronicle of the Canons Regular of Mount St Agnes* at Zwolle (1386–1477) attributed to Kempis, who was a Brother of the house. The chronicle contains what are in effect short biographies and brief obituary notices of both the regular canons and some of the lay brothers. Many of them were engaged in the work of transcribing, copying and, in a few cases, composing, devotional tracts and treatises, liturgical service books and music to be 'chanted in the choir'. They rivalled the Carthusians, also dedicated to book production, in the publication and dissemination of liturgical texts and devotional literature. Books produced by the *devotio* not only were made for their own use but also were sold, in relatively large quantities, on the open market to cathedral, collegiate and parish churches of the region and beyond. But other kinds of work – of a more laborious manual kind – were also mentioned and praised. In 1441 a lay brother, Jan Clotinc, died 'of the plague', having been 'very devout, and a pattern, for his long service in the brewery and the mill, and for his frequent prayers'.[37] In 1454, the death of Denis Valkenborch, a Donate (one who, often as a child, had been 'given' (*donatus*) to a religious house), aged seventy-three, was recorded. He had

> lived a humble and holy life with us for a great while … at first his tasks were to feed the swine and milk the cows, but when he grew old he was made the gatekeeper … ending his temporal life in a good old age he left a fair example to all.[38]

Another lay brother and servant, Gerard Hermannson, was a stonemason and 'a faithful worker so far as his powers did allow', for he suffered grievously, and died in 1455, from kidney stones; another Donate, Everard van Wetteren, had been a tailor, and made the habits in which the first four brothers of the house had been invested in 1398.[39] He then became chief cook to the house, for over thirty years, faithfully serving in that vital office. The mundane tasks performed by these men earned them a place in the annals of the house – but, as was reported of the gardener, Gerard Poelman, who died at the age of eighty-three, in return for their worldly labours they 'received a crown of life at the hands of the King of Glory'.[40] Some preferred to decline high office and instead served in lesser positions, as did Amilius the Priest from Guelders, who 'desired rather to have the tasks of the kitchen laid upon him than to be preferred to the honoured post of governing men' and he 'rejoiced in his servitude' there.[41] These mini-biographies of individuals are remarkable testimony to the workings of the *devotio moderna* when applied to the daily rounds and common tasks of conventual life. However menial their tasks, their lives were not to be forgotten, as the Emperor Maximilian I, albeit at a much more exalted level, said of himself, with the tolling of their funeral bell. The intense concentration of the *devotio* on the individual soul gave rise to what were in effect pen-portraits of some of the leading members of the tendency. Florens Radewijns, chief disciple of Groote, graduate of the University of Prague, co-founder of the Brethren of the Common Life, and vicar of Deventer, died in March 1400, and Kempis's obituary notice gave a description of his physical appearance which could have served as the basis for an artist's portrait. The *Chronicle* recorded that

> his garb was simple and grey in colour, his bearing was composed, his bodily presence full of grace, and his aspect lovable. His hair was black, but his beard was somewhat grey; his face was thin and had but little colour, his forehead was bald and his gait and bearing were full of dignity.[42]

As a result of the growing clericalization and 'monasticization' of the Brethren and Sisters of the Common Life, these biographies were increasingly confined to the members, whether they had taken monastic vows or remained lay brothers, of the Augustinian convents which now represented the aims and objectives of the *devotio*.

But the laity were also to be admitted to a share in employing and developing these forms of devotional piety. In some ways, Kempis's thought may seem to stand in contrast, almost in antithesis, to the Renaissance cults of individualism, self-realization and secular self-awareness. His 'Disciple' voice observes:

> A person's achievements are often discussed, but rarely the principles on which such a life is based. We enquire whether someone is brave, handsome, rich, clever,

a skilled writer, a fine singer or hard worker. But we seldom consider whether someone is humble-minded, patient and gentle, devout and spiritual. Nature looks at our outward characteristics. Grace considers our inner disposition.[43]

The cult of fame and worldly success seems to have no place in Kempis's catalogue of the virtues which should characterize the good Christian life. Yet a distinction is, again, here being made between inner and outer manifestations of the self. As with other strands in later medieval piety, it was an attempt to make those manifestations more congruent. It was yet another reminder to the rich and powerful that the Christian life now demanded an 'inwardness', an examination of the conscience and a conscious individual effort to contain, control and overcome natural instincts which might put the fate of the individual's soul in peril. It was a warning which confessors and spiritual advisers had addressed to those lay people who bore the burden of rule and governance at least since the later fourteenth century. It was the other side of the coin of Renaissance self-awareness and was designed to restrain the exuberance and excess of some forms of secular life. Its success, like all calls for moral reform from ranting preachers, hypocritical clerical moralists and other pious busybodies, was inevitably limited. The Church's culture of denial was not, and in many ways could not be, for the laity. The monastic virtues of poverty, chastity and obedience were not for them, especially – in the case of chastity or celibacy – if the reproduction of the human race was to be ensured. And Kempis was only too well aware of a common reaction of lay people to the Church's strictures about *their* behaviour: set your own house in order first.

THE PHYSICAL AND THE SPIRITUAL IN RELIGIOUS LIFE

There was a tactile, physical quality to much lay piety in the fourteenth, fifteenth and early sixteenth centuries. Its concentration on external features, attributes and practices could often appear to eclipse inner spirituality. Cults involving the touching and kissing of relics, sacred images and even books, or receiving holy water from sacred springs and wells, were to be found everywhere. The cults of the Name of Jesus, the Five Wounds of Christ or the Stations of the cross assumed a physicality which some, including many humanists such as Erasmus, found distasteful if not repellent. Reformers regarded lay people's fixation with the ritual elevation of the consecrated Host, to which they gave 'gestural assent', as a 'visible and corruptible thing'.[44] There was an overt theatricality about such practices, which could be exploited to render lay piety truly popular, if not populist. Representations of the saints, many of them utterly spurious, in both the drama and the visual arts, gave their lives and acts an immediacy which might exert a strong appeal to the laity. The *devotio* was not averse to the veneration of saints and their lives through images, but they were not to be worshipped. There was an incipient awareness, shared with reformers of the Church, that the cult of the saints and even of the Passion of Christ may have begun to get completely out of hand in Northern Europe by this time. Contemplation of both the physical and mental image of the wounds inflicted by his torturers and executioners on Christ's body, Kempis urged, should be no more than an aid to more profound reflection upon that ultimate sacrifice, made for the salvation of the world. But it was a means to an end, not an end in itself. As in the visual arts, there was a constant search for the inner meaning and significance of material objects and physical actions. The *devotio* had its own favoured saints, not only St Augustine, whose teachings had inspired the Augustinian rule. St Wilgefortis or Uncumber, for example, the legendary early Christian martyr, provided a perfect and literal example of the imitation of Christ. Her intense desire, after her conversion, to follow and seek the aid of Christ to keep her vow of virginity, had somewhat alarming consequences. She miraculously assumed physical features strikingly close to those of the Redeemer, thereby rendering her ineligible for the advantageous marriage that her father had planned for her. He had her put to death, and she died, as her Redeemer had died, by crucifixion. Memling's image of her on the Adriaan Reyns altarpiece at St John's hospital, Bruges (1480) duly depicts her with Christ-like features, including the beard, bearing the cross on which she was executed.

The *devotio* could be seen as a novel form of meeting between the learned and unlearned, between cleric and layman. Previous non-heretical devotional trends and movements had been largely confined to the clergy. This may have been what distinguished the *devotio* from earlier tendencies, such as the forms of intense devotional piety advocated by St Anselm or St Bernard for the clergy in the twelfth century, or by the Rhineland mystics, such as Meister Eckhart, in the early fourteenth century. The 'new' devotion shared many characteristics with earlier trends, among them the centrality of the Mass and the other sacraments for all believers, both clergy and laity. There was no question of Eucharistic heresy in its beliefs, unlike those of the followers of Wycliffe or Hus. Prayer and intercession had always been fundamental aspects of the Church's liturgy, but they now became more intensely personalized, especially in vernacular languages. The saying of Masses, and their endowment and sustenance, was regarded as one of the 'works', or 'good works' performed to gain God's grace and the ultimate salvation of the soul. But the mantra-like reiteration of the Latin words of the liturgy was not always conducive to inward spirituality, seeming often to represent only a superficial outward appearance of true devotion. Within the monastic and mendicant orders movements towards reform were already afoot – the Carthusians, Brigittines and members of Observant convents were setting examples which, through their wider influence, could lead to an enhancement of lay spirituality. The Benedictines had begun a process of reform, especially in Austria and the German-speaking regions, emanating from the congregations at Bursfelde and Melk. Historians have recently chosen to speak of this as a 'monastic Renaissance'. The foundation of Carthusian Charterhouses and Brigittine convents by lay princes and nobles was testimony to the respect in which their austere adherence to their rule was held by lay people. The great Carthusian houses at Champmol (1383) founded by Philip the Bold, Duke of Burgundy, and of Pavia (1396), founded by Galeazzo Maria Visconti of Milan, together with Henry V of England's establishment of the Brigittine and Carthusian convents of Syon and of Jesus of Bethlehem (1415), reflected this predilection for monastic austerity and a reformed observance of monastic discipline.

Such tendencies were not solely confined to Northern Europe. Italy experienced some similar and related movements. But there were clear differences between North and South. These revolved around the roles of the priest, the confessor and the sacraments. In Italy, it has been argued, the priest was cast in the role of a giver of absolution, and mediator of grace. In Northern Europe, he was conceived as an assessor and judge of a lay person's qualification for salvation through active good works and pious busy-ness. The performance of the works of mercy was thus seen as another form of imitation – that of God's, and thus of Christ's, mercy, as exemplified in the Sermon on the Mount (Mt. 5.3-12). The 'old' devotion therefore placed a very heavy emphasis on personal investment in salvation through the extensive endowment of Masses, works of mercy, pious foundations and other forms of reparation for sin. But this kind of active Christian life (the *vita activa*) was, for Ruysbroec and his subsequent followers in the *devotio*, merely the first few rungs of the spiritual ladder which the individual had to climb to achieve a higher spirituality. It was akin to the English mystic Walter Hilton's image of a Scale or Ladder of Perfection. The next rungs of Ruysbroec's ladder represented the inward life (the *vita interioris*), that essential goal of the *devotio*. Lastly, the summit of the ladder was to be reached in the contemplative life (the *vita contemplativa*). Yet, at those heights, the soul retained its individual, independent identity rather than merging with God in a mystical union. Northern emphasis on the active life of good works was given another dimension by the *devotio* and its proponents. It was a means to achieve a higher individual spiritual end, rather than part of a transaction between man and God whereby sin might be expiated, and salvation earned. Italian bankers and merchants, residing in both Northern and Southern Europe, Renaissance or no Renaissance, kept an account with God – they conceived of themselves as God's debtors. Cosimo de Medici (1389–1464) was careful to keep an account of, and publicize, the exact sums spent on his pious foundations. According to his biographer Vespasiano da Bisticci, Cosimo had spent the huge sum of 193,000 florins to settle his accounts with his Supreme Creditor. In 1448, or soon after, he commissioned a sumptuous tabernacle from his most favoured architect and sculptor Michelozzo (1396–1472) to be built over a miraculous image in the church of SS. Annunziata in Florence. But it was not customary, in Northern Europe, as Cosimo did in this case, to adorn a pious commission with the remarkable inscription: 'The marble alone cost 4,000 florins.'[45]

A further notable difference between Italy and the North lay in the place and significance accorded to Purgatory in religious thought and practice. The doctrine of Purgatory had been formally recognized and formulated by the Church in the thirteenth century. It encompassed the notion of a probationary, intermediate state between Heaven and Hell, in which purgatorial fire would inflict pain upon the soul but not consume it. The Church taught, however, that this posthumous ordeal could be mitigated by prayer on the deceased person's behalf proffered by the living, and by the performance of 'good works' of mercy during, and after, his or her lifetime. The lay person became aware that, given the inevitability of sinfulness, the sums accumulating on their purgatorial account must be steadily rising, and that this debt could only be fully offset and reduced by the prayers of ordained priests, above all through the celebration of Masses. The laity were thereby, in effect, trapped in the coils of a contractual arrangement whereby only the ministrations of the clergy could offer any real hope of salvation. Masses represented a high-value, high-return, investment in the purchase of paradise. Hence remission of time spent by souls in Purgatory was clearly central to the devotional life of later medieval Northern Europe. The sums invested by lay people in gaining the hope of that remission, and subsequent salvation, were formidable. Chantries, created exclusively for the saying and singing of Masses, and funerary churches, dedicated to that purpose and to the burial of the deceased, proliferated. Northern Europe's later medieval piety has been called a 'Purgatory-centred faith'.[46] No clear answer to the question of why this was the case has yet been given. It seems unlikely that it was a legacy of ancient pre-Christian practices of showing concern for the dead, or 'a by-product of the culture of mutual gifts that underpinned early medieval Germanic society'.[47] Nor can the 'commercialisation' of northern society in the thirteenth century be held responsible, as that would apply with perhaps even greater force to Northern Italy. But the evidence of thousands of personal wills and testaments from the North is unequivocal.

The 'purchase of paradise', as it has been styled, must have accounted, in toto, for a vast outlay of capital and assets on chantries, collegiate chapels and funerary churches, all celebrating thousands, if not millions, of commemorative Masses of many kinds, elaborate and less elaborate, according to the means of the testator. But their accompaniment, the discharge of the prescribed works of mercy, had at least one beneficial outcome – the alleviation of the lot of the poor and the sick through charitable giving. Penitence and penance was made to loom large in the collective psyche, and manuals for preachers and confessors laid heavy emphasis on the need for the repentance of sin and its expiation. To this concern the *devotio* brought a less material dimension. Hard cash for Masses was to be offset, if not entirely replaced, by hard reflection and introspective contemplation, leading to confession, or at least acknowledgement, of one's sinfulness. The road towards Protestantism was surely already beckoning. The lay person, under the 'old' devotion, piled up his or her reparations for sin so as to earn years of release from Purgatory. Unsurprisingly, this quasi-commercial, transactional doctrine became a prime target for Protestant reformers in the North – Luther, after 1517, waged war on the practice, telling the laity that the Purgatory industry and its associated devotions were simply confidence tricks by the clergy. In Italy and the Mediterranean lands, however, such ideas had less impact because, it seems, the Mass-saying industry was less well developed there. The Reformation in the South, when it came in the mid-sixteenth century, was a Catholic, not a Protestant one.

REFORM AND REVIVAL

The reform movements in the pre-Reformation Church of the fifteenth and early sixteenth centuries were the product of many, often disparate, tendencies.[48] Longer-term changes in religious sentiment and practice, as well as deep-seated doctrinal disputes, were accompanied by shorter-term and more localized issues. The marital problems of an English king, the condemnation of a radical thinker by the papacy, or the political aims of a German prince, in which the Church played significant parts – all contributed to the demands for change within the ecclesiastical hierarchy and for spiritual and pastoral renewal. In Northern Europe, there was an increasing tendency for sincerity and simplicity to become central to the beliefs and practices of reformers, critics and many ordinary believers. A revival, or renewal, of the beliefs and practices of the early Church, as they were understood at the time, was advocated. These were among the essential characteristics of the *devotio moderna*, but they also moved others, of more radical dispositions, to more extreme, root-and-branch denunciations of the established order. The German Peasants' War of 1525, for example, had a religious dimension. The underprivileged and unbeneficed lower clergy had always been a thorny problem to the Church but, from the later fourteenth century onwards, they figured more prominently in movements of social and economic protest and revolt. Lay reaction, fuelled by the preaching and writing of Luther, the Lutheran intellectual Philip Melanchthon (1497–1560) and their contemporaries, made its voice heard against what were deemed the abuses of the Mass-saying industry and the papal sale of indulgences.

A distinct lurch towards more extreme positions determined the fate of some of the more moderate attempts at reform and renewal within the Church. From 1520 or so onwards, the decline in the houses of the Brothers and Sisters of the Common Life demonstrated that, for the leading reformers of the Church and their followers, the sacramentally based, quietist faith practised by them and their monastic counterparts in the Augustinian and other orders was now unacceptable. Most of the houses and their schools were to all intents and purposes wiped out by Luther's and Calvin's Reformation. But within the much-criticized institutional Church itself, as we have seen, a move towards greater emphasis on individual, faith-based, personalized piety had been under way for some time. The balance between private devotion and collective, sacramentally centred worship was changing. Devotional self-awareness might be seen as an *alter ego* of 'Renaissance' individualism.[49]

The Church hierarchy had itself begun to take steps towards accommodating the needs of the laity in a series of liturgical innovations which were destined to lead to greater lay participation, as well as greater lay awareness and understanding of doctrine. The fourteenth century saw the introduction, or revival in a different form, of the pulpit office of the 'Prone' or 'pronaus'. It is not well documented and has therefore tended to be neglected by church historians. It was, as was the *devotio moderna*, a Northern European phenomenon. Liturgical practice may not seem, on the surface, to bear much relationship to movements of self-awareness and individualism. But in this period the content, as well as the form, of the liturgy was highly significant in moulding and shaping the devotional lives – if they had any – of both the literate and illiterate laity. The liturgical office of the Prone consisted of Sunday 'bidding' prayers, together with prayers for forgiveness and remission of an individual lay person's sins after the recitation of (admittedly generalized and not itemized) words of public confession. The Prone might also comprise the preaching of a homily, the giving out of 'notices' of papal, episcopal and sometimes royal edicts, calls for the celebration or commemoration of important events, the publishing of banns of marriage, and even the reading out of the Gospel in the vernacular. The term 'Prone' was derived from the Latin *proeconium* (proclamation). It formed part of a penitential rite performed before the consecration of the Eucharist, which included the later medieval equivalent of what was to become the Anglican and Lutheran Collect for Purity: 'Cleanse the thoughts of our hearts by the inspiration of Thy Holy Spirit, that we may perfectly love Thee, and worthily magnify Thy Holy Name' (*Book of Common Prayer*, 1662).

This had originally, in the eleventh century, been part of the priest's preparation for celebration of the Mass. But, by the later Middle Ages, it was also deemed appropriate for the laity as they prepared to witness the mystery of the Eucharist. The late fourteenth-century Middle English treatise *The Cloud of Unknowing* cited it verbatim, so its currency in a vernacular language was clearly evident by that date. The Prone became a common practice in later medieval England, South Germany, Switzerland and Sweden. It gave rise to changes in the choreography of the Mass and to the internal configuration of churches. The priest either came out of the chancel to the pulpit, placed in front of the chancel screen which divided the preserve of the clergy – the 'choir' – from the nave and aisles which housed the laity or would stand on the rood loft or screen platform. In Northern European churches this was a platform, or gallery, built onto the rood screen, surmounted by a sculpted representation of the Crucifixion, with the Virgin and St John the Evangelist at the foot of the cross. It was known as the *Lettner*, *jube* or *doksaal*, running along the top of the screen, from which the priest might also elevate the consecrated Host of the Eucharist in view of the people in the nave. The introduction of the rood screen was in part a product of Pope Innocent III's rulings at the Lateran Council of 1215 which formulated the doctrine of transubstantiation whereby, during the celebration of the Eucharist (Communion), the bread and wine became the body and blood of Christ. The copious and complex Eucharistic theology stemming from this doctrine led to the need to instil a greater reverence for the material elements of the Mass, which had to be protected from all harm and disrespect, and from acts of desecration and sacrilege. A tabernacle containing the reserved sacrament, housed in a ciborium, or covered vessel, was often installed in a reredos behind the altar. It was originally a central and fundamental feature of the Van Eycks' great *Ghent Altarpiece* (1432).[50]

The doctrine of transubstantiation could, and did, pose problems of comprehension and of over-literal interpretation, especially among the laity. It could assume an extreme physicality. Huizinga was right to identify this facet of later medieval piety, whereby the sacred assumed concrete physical form through the literal embodiment and incarnation of theological doctrines. It gave rise to mystical visions and implausibly miraculous occurrences such as the papally promoted and highly popular legend of St Gregory the Great. The belief among some lay people that the Crucifixion itself was literally and manifestly re-enacted during the Mass led to the depiction by fifteenth-century painters and engravers, such as Robert Campin, Simon Marmion, Geertgen Tot Sint Jans and Israel van Meckenem, of the crucified Christ as Man of Sorrows miraculously appearing in person above the altar as the pope-saint celebrated the Eucharist. Other lay people were more sceptical, and the currency of a doctrine which defied all reason and common sense led to more extreme reactions. The denial of transubstantiation by Wycliffe and Hus led to their beliefs being declared heretical, and Hus died for those beliefs. But there were also those among the orthodox clergy, especially at its higher and more intellectual levels, who had profound misgivings about the degree of physicality and materiality which now surrounded some of these doctrines. Post-Lateran sacramentalism had been furthered and enhanced by the inauguration of the Corpus Christi feast, originating at Liege, by Pope Urban IV in 1264. This merely gave added impetus to the need physically to conserve and protect the Sacrament. Further screening off of the chancel, sometimes by multiple series of screens, now took place. Kempis was uncompromising on the sacrality of the Sacrament. It was to be protected and revered. And it was to be administered only by holy and worthy priests, who must come to the celebration of the Mass with 'humility of heart and deep reverence, having examined their consciences carefully'.[51] Yet the role of the priest and his status and function in the Mass were now coming to be a subject for re-examination.

Parallel to the growth of private lay devotion, movements towards more public liturgical reform and renewal were also under way. A succession of vernacular expositions of the Mass for the laity were produced over the period from *c.* 1420 to 1500 by leading scholars and humanist theologians such as Jean Gerson, Jacques Lefevre d'Etaples and Guillaume Briconnet. Gerson had composed a manual for the laity entitled *Comment on se doit maintenir a la messe* (*How One Should Conduct Oneself at the Mass*) (*c.* 1400). Furthermore, one of the primary missions of Groote's *devotio* was directly aimed at improving the laity's understanding of the liturgy. As the Sint-Agnietenburg Chronicle tells us, he followed up Ruysbroec's vernacular writings in Middle Dutch with a series of vernacular translations of liturgical and other texts. These included the 'Hours of the Blessed Virgin' and 'certain other Hours' which he rendered into the 'Teutonic tongue' (i.e. Dutch).

> So that simple and unlearned Laics [lay people] might have in their mother tongue matter wherewith to occupy themselves in prayer on holy days ... and so that the faithful, reciting these Hours, or hearing them recited by other devout persons, might ... keep themselves from many vanities and from idle talking, and so, being assisted by these holy readings, might make progress in the love of God and in singing divine praises.[52]

Reformers of the Church and its liturgy at this time were particularly concerned by the behaviour of some lay people during the celebration of the Eucharist. Their 'idle talking' and signs of disengagement at Mass betokened a disrespect for an event, re-enacting the sacrifice of the Cross, of supreme importance to a fundamentally sacramental Church and its ordained clergy, castigated though they all-too-often were as unworthy of that high and sacred mission. If that irreverence could be countered by the provision of vernacular versions of the prayers and responses said at the canonical hours, then the non-Latinate laity might be less inclined to 'idle talking' and gossiping during a liturgy the words of which they did not understand. As with other aspects of the Church's practices, the miraculous transformation performed in the Eucharist was deemed by many reformers to be nothing but an elaborate clerical confidence trick. It was now all too easy for the laity to begin to believe that this was simply 'hocus-pocus' (*hoc est corpus meum*: 'This is my body'), as early Protestants were wont to mock the Latin words of the Ordinary of the Mass at the consecration of the Eucharistic bread and wine.

The need to instruct the laity led to the placing of a far greater emphasis on catechizing them in their vernacular language. This was to be done by the priest in the pulpit office of the Prone. It also promoted and enhanced the role of preaching in general. As Calvin admonished the clergy of his time,[53] understanding by the laity was now a prerequisite for devotion. The need to 'purify' the liturgy was felt by reformers and, in the 1520s and 1530s, movements of liturgical reform began at Zurich, with Zwingli, Strasbourg (Martin Bicer) and Geneva (Calvin). In 1506, Johann Ulrich Surgant published his *Manuale*, an influential treatise which printed German texts of the Lord's Prayer, the Ten Commandments, the Creed and so forth. It also concentrated on enhancing the understanding of the Mass by lay people. As a prelude to, and preparation for, the Eucharist, preaching should be directed to the congregation in the vernacular so that the words 'are understood and lead to the people's comprehension'.[54] Behind both Surgant's and Zwingli's proposed reforms lay the office of the Prone. The Prone had already become a vehicle for the preaching of repentance on an individual basis. It was sometimes accompanied by the singing of vernacular hymns and chorales, a practice which was to be much favoured by Luther and Lutherans. One example of the probable influence of the Prone on the laity was Joan of Arc's reply at her trial at Rouen in 1431: 'Asked if she knew whether she were in the state of God's grace, she answered: "if I am, may He keep me there."' This was taken directly from the office of the Prone, which beseeched God to 'preserve the just in a state of grace'. But the laity were not only coming to a better understanding of the faith, the Church and the liturgy through hearing the spoken word. The written word was just as significant. Lay literacy and the advent of the printed book, in multiple copies, gave the book a role in the religious lives of a larger number of believers on a very much greater scale than had ever been seen before.[55] The role of humanist textual studies of the Bible, especially of the New Testament, by Erasmus and Lefevre d'Etaples, was critical in this respect. The 'supreme humanist scholar',[56] a product of the schools of the *devotio*, Erasmus brought the textual rigour of humanist scholarship to bear on the sacred text.[57] But his spiritual and devotional life was very much a reflection of his upbringing and early experience, however much he might complain about its shortcomings. He was to that extent a product of the world of Groote and Kempis, a fifteenth-century man in a sixteenth-century context. He never embraced the Protestant cause. He advocated a 'quiet, austere devotion springing from inner contemplation'.[58] But he was just as much a 'Renaissance man' as Alberti or any of his Italian forbears and contemporaries. Self-expression and self-awareness run throughout his vast volume of letters.

What, if anything, did the Northern Renaissance contribute to the rise of Protestantism? Evidently it brought with it a more introspective piety, a desire to uncover the true, authentic and original meaning of the Bible, and a reconsideration of the role of the individual in his or her quest for salvation. The theatricality of the Mass was to be offset, if not replaced, by preaching, albeit with its own repertoires of histrionic rhetoric and gesture. That process had already begun by the fourteenth century. Reading, however, unlike preaching, did not require nor imply the use of gesture. Introspection was surely encouraged by reading and reflecting upon the written, and then the printed, word. Reading by lay people was a very largely, though not entirely, individualistic pursuit and practice.[59] It can be identified as a species of 'Renaissance' individualism. A religion of the Word – Christianity – contributed massively to the triumph of the word. Without lay literacy, and probably without the printing press, the Protestant Reformation, or Reformations, would have been far less likely an outcome of the crises of the later Middle Ages.

If the term 'Renaissance', defined as rebirth, is to mean anything at all in the context of Northern Europe at this time, then the idea of a 'Christian Renaissance' should not be too easily dismissed. A rebirth, or at least a reinvigoration, of a Christo-centric piety which was now no longer to be confined to the clergy but shared by the laity, both literate and illiterate, marked a significant departure from previous practices. The *devotio moderna* may not have been 'modern' in the sense that it introduced novel, or even radical, doctrinal concepts and beliefs into the existing body of later medieval devotional and pastoral theology. But its emphasis on the teachings of Christ in the New Testament, its concentration on the response of the individual to those teachings and its practical application of the doctrine of immanence – of God in all things – made it truly 'modern'. It both reflected and, to a certain extent, pointed the way forward to other contemporary tendencies and movements. Both clerical and lay communities felt its influence, an influence which had perhaps been underestimated until recent scholarship has tried to redress a tendency to undervalue it. The work of Erasmus and others of a humanist persuasion on the text of the New Testament may well have owed something to early experience of the *devotio's* practices, in its schools, through the preaching of men like Groote, and the writings of Kempis and others. Above all, the concern for the individual soul, and the intensity with which self-examination and introspection was advocated, opened the way to even more radical revisions of the Church's role in the business of salvation. It would be a largely unfounded, even gross, exaggeration to conclude that 'individual penance, and not the communal Eucharist, functioned as the primary sacrament for many people in the late Middle Ages'.[60] But such a statement may contain more than a grain of truth, given that an increasingly literate and knowledgeable laity, excluded as they were from receiving Communion in both kinds, felt a degree of exclusion from fully participatory worship. And a retreat from the Eucharist, in favour of prayer and preaching, was to become a primary characteristic of some Protestant sects and churches. The pulpit, rather than the altar, was to become, and remain, the focal point of many Protestant churches throughout Northern Europe.

Although never departing from the Church's sacramental teaching and rites, the *devotio moderna* nevertheless added its voice to contemporary criticism of the ordained clergy as unworthy of their mission. A 'Godly preaching ministry', advocated by Protestant reformers, may have not been so very far away from the kind of priesthood that was desired by Ruysbroec, Groote, Radewijns, Kempis and Erasmus. A desired rebirth, or regeneration, of the perceived characteristics of the early Christian Church in its alleged purity and simplicity linked, as well as divided, reformers of various persuasions. But the means by which that desired end was to be achieved produced many and varying views, some of them in direct conflict with each other. In the event, it was to lead to another schism, or rather a series of schisms, within Western Christendom which have lasted to this day.

5

THE IMPACT OF PRINT

In those days, in the city of Mainz, located in Germany on the banks of the Rhine – and thus not in Italy as some have falsely written – was invented and devised by the Mainz citizen Johannes Gutenberg that marvellous and hitherto unheard-of art of printing and impression of books. (Johannes Trithemius, *Annals of Hirsau abbey*, for the year 1450)[1]

Who dares to glorify the pen-made book? / When so much better brass-stamped letters look? (Wendelin of Speyer, printer, signing off his work in the colophon to his edition of Sallust (1470))[2]

RENAISSANCE, REFORMATION AND PRINT

The period which saw the advent and subsequent course of the Northern Renaissance witnessed a number of seminal discoveries and innovations. These, it is argued, were to carry a lasting significance for the history of both Europe and the wider world. Among them, the invention of the mariner's compass, the introduction and development of gunpowder, the discovery of Africa and the New World,[3] and the advent of printing with movable type have been singled out as especially seminal and far-reaching in their consequences. Together with the 'Eyckian revolution' in painting, the rise of polyphonic music, and the genesis of humanistic techniques of textual criticism, printing can be described as a true *ars nova* ('new art').[4] In origin, it was an exclusively Northern European innovation. Renaissance Italy very soon inherited, adapted and exploited what was essentially a German discovery. The 'Germans' (who at that time were thought to include the Netherlanders) could therefore not all be equated by contemporaries and later commentators with the 'barbarians' dear to Italian myth. A growing fifteenth-century cultural clash between

Germans and Italians came to a head with the advent, in the mid-century, of printing and the printing press. Not only had the Italian humanists constantly asserted their superiority over their Northern contemporaries in the revival and refinement of the Latin language but, they claimed, the Germans (and the Northerners in general) had left copies of precious classical texts to rot, neglected and unread, in monastic and diocesan libraries. But, as the German abbot Johannes Trithemius (1462–1516) wrote,[5] the Italians could not take the credit for all the best discoveries of the age. The inception and origins of Johann Gutenberg's (*c*. 1400–68) invention are obscure. He was a goldsmith, son of a goldsmith employed in the episcopal mint at Mainz, and appears to have conceived the idea of printing with movable type by the 1440s. It was apparently first put to use in *c*. 1450, when the Mainz press was said to have printed some schoolroom texts, including Latin grammars. But the firmest evidence comes from 1454–5, when we have the first surviving examples of its work. The new technique spread rapidly to Cologne, Strasbourg, Bamberg, Nuremberg, Augsburg and Basel. It was to have far-reaching consequences, some intended and others not. The printing press was an inanimate tool. A technological innovation of this kind is therefore necessarily dependent, for its application and impact, entirely upon human agency, and printing was no exception. It met both needs and demands, and it also created them.

In 1945, in a book rather misleadingly entitled *From Script to Print*, H. J. Chaytor wrote,

> No one is likely to contest the statement that the invention of printing and the development of that art mark a turning-point in the history of civilisation.[6]

It would be a gross exaggeration to say that nothing could be regarded as further from the truth today. But the notion that the invention and development of printing constituted a 'turning point' of that kind has most certainly been contested.[7] The very notion of a 'printing revolution' has been denied, on the grounds that the movement was evolutionary rather than revolutionary; that the commercial practices of printers had been anticipated by earlier manuscript book dealers; and that the copying of books by hand continued for a long time after the advent of printing.[8] For a long time, historians had shown very little concern to chart and assess the impact of printing, if any, on social, religious, economic and cultural changes in early modern, let alone later medieval, Europe. In 1957, however, the French cultural historian Lucien Febvre, founder (with Marc Bloch) of the *Annales*, published, with H.-J.

Martin, *L'apparition du livre*, translated into English as *The Coming of the Book: The Impact of Printing, 1450-1800* (1976). In that justly celebrated book, they argued that printing had 'altered the life of authors and readers, using the new, larger libraries of the age of print to chart transformations in the climate of opinion'.[9] A 'new history of the book' then arrived in France in the 1970s and 1980s, soon to be taken up with vigour and verve by North American historians, including a new phalanx of scholars, librarians and museum curators known as codicologists (students of codices, or manuscript books, and their interrelationships). A reaction inevitably set in, and a group of largely literary scholars, influenced by postmodernist ideas, set out to dispute virtually every aspect of the thesis that the impact of printing had had a transformative effect on Western culture. The subject is important enough, and the issues it raises sufficiently relevant, to warrant a brief treatment here of the academic debate.

For its later, modern critics, the impact of printing and the subsequent 'printing revolution' was 'inconsequential' (Johns) and could be dismissed as 'a minor episode' (Chartier).[10] Yet there was extensive evidence from the later fifteenth and early sixteenth centuries that the 'new art' was welcomed by contemporaries, and was deemed productive by them of significant changes in social, economic, cultural and religious life, despite criticism of the vagaries and abuses perpetrated by ignorant and incompetent printers on authors and their works. A false opposition between the allegedly pious, diligent scribe, working painstakingly in a monastic scriptorium, and the careless, feckless, strike-prone printer has been created, in part through the fantasies of nineteenth-century Romantics. Ruskin and Morris were sworn enemies of mechanical reproduction in any of the arts – though Morris, of course, had his own Kelmscott press set up and staffed on what he believed to be authentic fifteenth-century principles. And there was certainly a chorus of contemporary fifteenth- and sixteenth-century moralists and others who might welcome many aspects of the new medium, but who lamented the opportunities it gave for the wider dissemination of what they saw as potentially corrupting literature. The cheapness and availability of printed books, pamphlets and images meant that 'erotic fantasies' and even 'pagan myths' might be aroused and revived.[11] It was asserted that 'the virgin has a pen while the whore has print',[12] and some of the more extreme critics likened the printer's workshop to a brothel. But the more general consensus appears to have been favourable to the press and its products. Among others, Aeneas Sylvius Piccolomini (Pope Pius

II) (1405–64), Francois Rabelais (1494–1553), Polydore Vergil (1470–1555), Jean du Bellay (1494–1553), Desiderius Erasmus and John Foxe (1516–87), for their very different reasons, all praised and celebrated the invention of printing. But the force of what appears to be twentieth-century conceptual dogmatism tended to ignore, or at least undervalue, most of that evidence, and argue that the notion of a 'printing revolution' was simply a later construct, too closely associated with elitist eighteenth-century Enlightenment, and nineteenth-century liberal, thought to be tenable. As postmodernist literary criticism maintained that there are no truths, only interpretations; that the very idea of truth or objectivity in historical thought was to be profoundly distrusted; and that 'evidence' was the product of ideological, socially determined and hegemonic factors, the debate began to resemble a conversation, or rather a shouting match, between the deaf. Any idea that such a 'grand narrative' as a 'printing revolution' had any validity was therefore rejected out of hand by its critics. Postmodernist historical approaches and sensibilities can, as Elizabeth Eisenstein commented, sometimes seem 'tone deaf to the music of time'.[13] Context, chronology and the balanced assessment of evidence is not always evident in this approach.

Be that as it may, the scholarly controversy that has arisen about the impact of printing in this period has certainly raised some important issues. These, it could however be argued, have been largely concerned with methodology and terminology, sometimes expressed in highly polemical terms. Much of the argument has revolved around the meaning and implications of abstract constructs such as 'manuscript culture', 'print culture', 'image culture', 'word culture' or 'gulfs' between an 'age of script' and an 'age of print'. A more nuanced and less starkly polarized interpretation is surely possible. The impact of print, and the transition from script, can be charted and assessed from the available evidence, always bearing in mind its partial nature and the extent to which any conclusions have to be based only on such material as survives. But the recorded printing of about 500,000 books before 1501 provides a very substantial body of evidence. This chapter will therefore attempt to suggest that the coming of printing to Western Europe cannot be dismissed, as it has been by some, as a 'minor episode' in the continent's long-term history.

A traditional, formerly generally accepted standpoint maintains that the mid-fifteenth century witnessed the beginnings of what was to be an inexorable and irreversible process.[14] It arguably saw a transition from a world in which the fundamental medium of transmitting knowledge, information and ideas was the handwritten word to a world in which the mechanical reproduction of multiple copies of written texts, documents and images, on an unprecedented scale, was gradually to become far more common and, ultimately, the norm. Many factors enabled this process to take place, among them the greater availability of a suitable material upon which to produce clear and durable printed impressions, namely rag paper. But the replication of multiple copies of the written word was not the only innovation brought by the new art of printing. The contemporaneous, or near-contemporaneous, introduction of the techniques of woodblock cutting, engraving on metal plates with a stylus or burin and etching on metal, with the aid of acids, enabled multiple copies of *images* of all kinds to be made. 'However ancient the techniques of replication might be', it has been said, 'never before had images of such extraordinary intricacy and such astonishing density of detail been successfully multiplied'.[15] This innovation had profound effects on the multiplication and dissemination of visual images and the rise of a market for such products. Essential nuances have been introduced into the cruder 'script to print' arguments by some scholars, and the survival of handwritten material continues, of course, to this day. But, such was its arguable impact and influence, that it has been thought legitimate to describe the so-called printing revolution of the fifteenth and sixteenth centuries in terms similar to those used about the electronic and digital 'communications revolution' of our own time. Direct comparisons between the two phenomena have been made, sometimes in prophetic terms, from the 1960s onwards, by influential theorists and writers such as Marshall McLuhan (1911–80) or Walter J. Ong (1912–2003), who both claimed that the advent of printing 'transformed the Western psyche'.

Gutenberg's invention emerged from a background of technological experiment and change. Skills developed by the crafts and trades of the goldsmith, the metalworker, the striker of coins, the medal maker, the seal engraver, the paper-maker, and the designer and constructor of wine- and cider-presses all contributed to the conditions in which printing with movable metal type was enabled to make its impact. Printing had been known in China, but not in Europe, since the eleventh century and rag paper had been manufactured there since AD 300–400. In *c.* 1040, Bi Cheng had invented movable type, but it was produced from baked and hardened clay blocks and did not have an appreciable or long-lasting impact. An even older method of printing – with woodblocks – persisted in China for a long time. Gutenberg's invention was predicated upon the availability of a surface material for printing which was reasonably durable, yet absorbent enough to bear and retain the impression made by the hand-operated printing press. Rag paper, produced from the pulping of rags, especially linen rags, and other by-products and offshoots of textile processing, provided the answer. Paper manufacture had first been introduced into Western Europe via Muslim Spain by 1056, when a rag-pulping mill was set up in Xativa (San Felipe). The process spread through the Iberian Peninsula. But paper did not come into more general use in the rest of Western Europe until the second decade of the thirteenth century and its use was not widespread until the 1270s, when the first paper mills to be found in Italy, at Fabriano, were set up. Italian merchants soon adopted the cheaper material – paper rather than parchment – for their account books and, by the last quarter of the thirteenth century the Frescobaldi, Riccardi, Bardi, Peruzzi and other merchant and banking companies were using it in larger quantities than ever before.

In 1390, the first recorded German paper mill was established at Nuremberg, and others followed in Germany, Austria and the Low Countries over the next century. It was no longer necessary to rely upon imported Italian paper, and this was a key issue in creating the necessary conditions for the advent of printing. But the process of printing on paper, in its earliest stages, had been undertaken in the West (as previously in China) with woodblocks, in which each page of a text was set up in its immutable entirety from one separately carved wooden panel. The first examples that we have of woodcut prints stem from the late fourteenth and early fifteenth centuries. One of the earliest surviving examples is a Bavarian image of St Dorothy (*c.* 1410) and others survive from Austria, South Germany, France and Bohemia. But many of these early examples were in effect separate and discrete images, which could also be used as book illustrations, sometimes with a woodblock-printed text or caption attached to explain them. They were then pasted or bound into texts which were produced either in manuscript, by scribes, or by woodblock printing. There was therefore a prehistory of printing, especially in Northern Europe, before the appearance of Gutenberg's radical invention in the 1450s. But his movable metal type, in which each character was separately punched and cast in molten metal, enabled the texts of books to be assembled line by line and page by page. Once assembled, a 'run' of pages could be printed, and complete books could be produced in this way. But the movability of the type meant that it could be dis-assembled and reused to compose other texts once a sufficient number of copies of a given work had been printed. As we shall see, the gains and economies in terms of labour productivity, speed and volume of production, fixity, uniformity and standardization of texts and, in general terms, potentially greater textual accuracy, were very significant indeed. They could not be matched by scribal production methods.

As we have seen, European paper mills (outside the earlier examples in Spain) began to be established in the later thirteenth century, so that the ideal material for printing became both cheaper and much more widely available. In 1492, however, although he was a great admirer and exploiter of Gutenberg's invention and its subsequent applications, the abbot Johannes Trithemius was sceptical about the likely longevity of works printed on paper. He thought that while paper might last for 200 years, parchment had a natural life of 1,000 years. He was to be proved totally wrong. Rag paper, kept in suitable environments, and dating from the earliest period in the history of paper-making, has survived to this day, much of it in near-perfect condition. The relative cheapness of paper made it an ideal instrument for the printing of items of which hundreds, if not thousands, of copies, were demanded. Some of the very earliest surviving examples of printing with movable type in Western Europe are not books, nor are they products of secular or humanistic culture. They are papal indulgences, mass-produced in print, in multiple identical copies, to serve as pro formas on which the seller of the indulgence would insert by hand the name of the payer, the amount paid, and the date on which it was granted. An indulgence, as Luther reminded his audience, was an unashamedly mercenary means by which the Church attempted to finance a stated project or purpose, granting a period of absolution in return for a money payment. The first printed batch of these contentious documents was apparently issued at Mainz in 1454, and the first surviving copies are dated, by hand, to 27 February and 7 March 1455. Archbishop Dieter von Isenburg of Mainz had resolved to put Gutenberg's very recent invention, stemming from his own diocese, to good use. He issued these printed documents as receipts, or quittances, for payments made to further a proposed papal campaign to defend Cyprus against the infidel Ottoman Turks. The printed indulgences simply imitated and reproduced scribal manuscript copies, but in greater numbers and at lesser expense. Gutenberg's famous 42-line Latin Bible was thus not the first item to come off his press, although it is the first known complete printed book (1455) to survive. The Church was an early and, perhaps surprisingly enthusiastic, patron of printing, and the Benedictine order appears to have supported and encouraged the production of Gutenberg's Bible. A close association between monastic houses, some of whom had their own presses, and nearby commercial printers soon developed at Mainz, Augsburg and Strasbourg as the new invention spread across the German-speaking lands. The presence of a bishopric, a monastery or a university in or near a German town offered stimuli and opportunities to the new printing industry, promptly taken up by the Fust and Schoeffer families at Mainz, and the Pfister at Bamberg.

During this period of 'first impressions', which we can date from 1455 to about 1500, the immediate impact of the new art of printing is hard to assess.[16] It is incontrovertible that, as Eisenstein pointed out, printers' workshops appeared 'in every important municipal center' across Northern and some parts of Southern Europe, during that period.[17] A current research project, using digital technology and statistical analysis, has established that between 1450 and 1500, 30,000 editions of books were printed in 450,000 surviving copies.[18] This was the era of 'incunabula', that is, of the earliest printed books dating from before 1501. Printing had spread well beyond its Rhineland homeland by 1500. But figures for the rate and speed of production from these early presses are hard to come by for this early period. In the 1470s, it is, however, known that three printers working for three months were able to produce 300 copies of a 366-folio (i.e. 732 numbered pages) edition of the works of Pope Gregory the Great.[19] That worked out at an average of twenty-five copies per week. This would have been quite impossible to achieve with a similar number of scribes. The organizations and structures of the printer's workshop and the scribal *atelier* were quite different, enabling a far greater volume, speed, accuracy and degree of mass production than was ever possible even in the largest of monastic *scriptoria* or secular scribal workshops. Between May and December 1477, for instance, the print shop of the German printer Pieter Maufer, then working in Padua, produced a 1,000-page edition of a commentary on the works of the Islamic medical and scientific thinker Avicenna (980–1037), employing 6,800,000 pieces of type.[20] Four presses were engaged on the task and it was completed within seven months, despite strikes on the printing floor. The average print run at this early period seems to have been about 300 to 400 copies per edition, increasing to as many as 1,000 copies by 1500. The effects of such mass production on the dissemination of knowledge and ideas, and on the availability of texts, was nothing if not significant, even perhaps potentially revolutionary. By *c.* 1500, no less than 30,000 editions of printed books had come off Western European presses. And the new process had moved across Europe at phenomenal speed.

From the 1460s onwards, some Mainz printers had moved their businesses to Cologne. Printing tended to follow the main trade-routes, gravitating towards major commercial hubs and markets, some of them already long established as trading posts of the Hanseatic League. It was indicative of broader economic trends, including an evident shift away from Italy towards the North, in the economic configuration of Western Europe. Yet Italian production of printed books was widely spread by 1500: Venetian books, for example, enjoyed a wide distribution throughout Europe, especially in Germany. The patterns of book production in Western Europe as a whole accordingly began to change. Although, as we shall see, the Low Countries still provided a major source of texts for printed reproduction, the towns and cities of the German-speaking regions, soon followed by Italian cities and towns, now began to lead the field as centres of book production. By the 1460s, printing had reached Bamberg (1460), Cologne (1465), Basel (1468) and Nuremberg (1469). The first surviving examples of printed books in a vernacular language come from Bamberg, seat of an important bishopric, in *c.* 1461–2. In *c.* 1461, Albrecht Pfister printed three editions of the highly popular *Biblia pauperum* (*Bible of the Poor*), two in German and one in Latin, combining woodcuts with printed typeface. These had been preceded, in February 1461, by a book of fables, in the German vernacular, entitled *Der Edelstein (The Jewel)*, by the Dominican friar Ulrich Boner (*c.* 1349), illustrated with 101 woodcuts, which makes it one of the very earliest surviving volumes to be printed in a vernacular language. In 1462, Pfister also produced a series of small-format volumes, in the vernacular, again illustrated with woodcuts, containing Old Testament 'Histories'. These recounted the stories of Daniel, Joseph, Judith and Esther. Printing was once again being brought into the service of devotional religion. They were intended for lay readers as 'we (the laity) don't all know Latin'.[21] Many of these early printed books were in effect hybrids, combining the arts and skills of the printer with those of the woodcut carver, manuscript draughtsman and illuminator. Penwork had not yet been banished from the printed page and, from *c.* 1460 to *c.* 1480, some editions printed in Mainz and elsewhere left spaces in their texts for hand-drawn and hand-painted decorated initials and half- or full-page illuminations. But this was soon to become a thing of the past as, by the 1490s, the level and pace of demand for printed books meant that woodcut initials and illustrations were replacing hand-finished work on a large scale.

The Church seems to have grasped the advantageous potential of the new art at an early stage. It was to play a significant part in the so-called

Christian Renaissance, as well as the later Protestant Reformation, of the age. In 1476, the prologue to an edition of vernacular sermons, printed by the Brethren of the Common Life on their press at Rostock, expressed satisfaction that 'this admirable book, … lurking in the hands of a few in their cells, should be published abroad by the printing art, chief of all the arts for the advantage of the holy Church'.[22] A major function of the printing press and the printing industry at this time was the replication and dissemination of liturgical books and manuals. As we saw in Chapter 4,[23] one of the functions of the communities dedicated to the principles and rules of the *devotio moderna* was to copy service books and liturgical texts and sell them on the market. From 1475 onwards, some of these houses began themselves to adopt the printing press, and between that date and 1530 they owned six presses. Of these, five were employed by houses of the Brethren of the Common Life, and one by a convent of Augustinian Canons Regular. Their motives were in large part to procure and produce 'standardised texts for the liturgy … to underscore homogeneous monastic observance'.[24] Similarly, the commercial printing house of Fust and Schoeffer at Mainz had been producing large-format altar books, especially psalters, as early as 1457 and 1459. In October 1459, they also produced copies of Guillaume Durand's (*c.* 1230–96) *Rationale divinorum officium*, a handbook and manual for priests which set out the texts of all the services of the liturgical year, in a new, clear and simplified typeface, not modelled on the more ornate and elaborate hands of episcopal chanceries and manuscript workshops. Such initiatives stemmed essentially from the monastic reform movements, such as the Melk reform (begun 1418–25) of the Benedictine order, which had emerged just before the advent of printing. The desire to standardize and render the texts of the Bible, the works of the Church fathers and the service books of the liturgy more uniform, and to confer a fixity of form upon them, was far easier to realize in print than in manuscript. In 1485, a newly printed text of the missal was authenticated by a German bishop and was said to be 'through God's grace, identical in every copy, sentence by sentence, word by word, and letter by letter, and to correspond precisely with the diocesan exemplar [in manuscript] provided to the printer'.[25] A premium was here put on the art of proofreading and checking of the printed text, a relatively new skill which soon became part of the apparatus of the printer-publisher's workshop. Cardinal-bishop Nicholas of Cusa became almost obsessive in his concern that in his diocese of Brixen-Bolzano, where he ruled from 1450 to 1464, the 'liturgies … be centrally corrected'.[26] Printers were supplied with corrected manuscript or earlier printed copies of a given text, as recorded in the preface to a commentary (*c.* 1465) on preaching by St Augustine. This asserted that the book was produced in multiple copies during the mid-1460s by Johann Mentelin's (*c.* 1410–78) press at Strasbourg, with the 'corrected copy before his eyes'. Printing could, and did, of course multiply erroneous as well as correct versions of a text, and Francois Rabelais set out the potentially extreme consequences of this when he observed that an uncorrected error in a printed medical treatise could potentially cost the lives of thousands of patients. Pages of errata (lists of errors) began to be distributed by printers by about 1500, and these would be bound or pasted into earlier editions of a given work. But, with relatively large numbers of identical printed texts in circulation, comparison, checking and the consequent correction of errors could be more easily made.

Many of the practices outlined above had been established at a relatively early stage in the development of printing, especially in its place of origin, the city of Mainz. But it was to Cologne, an important commercial centre, also frequented by crowds of pilgrims to the shrine of the Magi (Three Kings) and the church of St Ursula and her 11,000 virgin martyrs, seat of a great prince-archbishopric, that much of the subsequent activity and enterprise in early printing began to gravitate. The origins of printing by Englishmen, for instance, can be traced to the presses of Cologne in the 1470s. In 1471–2, William Caxton (*c.* 1422–*c.* 1491), a London mercer with strong continental contacts and connections, was in exile (for political reasons) at Cologne. There was a continental European prehistory of printing in the English language before Caxton created his press in the almonry at Westminster Abbey in 1476. He had served, between 1462 and 1471, as governor of the English 'nation', or merchant community, of Merchant Adventurers at Bruges, tasked with representing English commercial and other interests at the court of Burgundy. He enjoyed the patronage of Margaret of York, Duchess of Burgundy and sister of Edward IV of England. Caxton's entrepreneurial instincts led him to put some faith in the new medium of printing and, in 1471–2, he commissioned three Latin books from Cologne printers, all of them well-tried-and-tested works which had already enjoyed a steady market demand. In doing this, he was following a pattern already set by other printers, who produced volumes such as the *Facta et Dicta memorabilia* of Valerius Maximus, illustrated with hand-drawn and coloured illuminations.[27] One of these favoured works, the *Lives and Deeds of the Philosophers*, led to Caxton being described by its later English translator (1496) as 'the first printer of this book in Laten tonge at Coleyn' (Cologne). But Caxton's truly innovatory role was to produce the first book ever to be printed in the English language. Although reflecting a more general European tendency, Caxton's edition of an English translation, from the French, of the Burgundian court chaplain and writer Raoul Lefevre's *Recuyell of the Histories of Troye* (1464) was soon to bring the art of printing, for the first time, to England. The story of the ancient city of Troy was a popular late medieval classical theme, in which the deeds of such Greek and Trojan heroes as Hector and Agamemnon were deemed by Caxton and many others to be 'worthy ... of great memory'.[28] The appearance of the *Recuyell* (Fr. *Recueil*) marked not only a significant turning point in the history of English book production but also a demonstration of how the old was combined with the new in the world of early printing. Caxton himself tells us, in his preface to the volume, that it had been 'translated and drawn out of French into English' by him. In this instance, the old mechanisms of princely and aristocratic patronage operated for the early history of the printed book just as they had functioned for manuscript books in the past. Caxton had been 'commanded' to translate Lefevre's book by the Duchess Margaret, and he had begun the work at Bruges in March 1468. It was finished on 19 September 1471 'in the holy city of Cologne'. Caxton then explained how and why he had decided to commit his translation to print. The wearisome travails of the scribe were first of all set out when he wrote,

> In the wrytyng of the same my penne is worn, myn hande wery [weary] and not stedfast, myn eyen [eyes] dimmed with overmoche lokyng on the whit[e] paper, and my corage not so prone and redy to laboure as hit hath ben, and that age crepeth on me dayly and febleth alle the bodye.[29]

In order to both please his patroness and fulfil a promise made to various 'gentlemen and friends' to whom he had vouchsafed copies, he tells us that

> I have practysed and lerned at my grete charge and dispense [expense] to ordeyne this said book *in prynte* after the maner and forme as ye may here see, and is not wreten with penne and ynke [ink] as other bokes ben, to the ende that *every man may have them att ones [at once]*; for alle the bookes of this storye ... thus emprynted, as ye here see, were begonne [begun] in oon [one] day, and also fynyshed in oon day, which book I have presented to my sayd redoubtid lady [Margaret of York] as afore is sayd.[30]

Caxton's boast about the speed of production must be deemed something of an exaggeration, yet the point that so many more copies of a book could be produced and distributed relatively quickly than was ever possible through the use of scribes certainly stood. Old systems of commissioning and patronage were still in place, but methods of book production were clearly beginning to change almost beyond recognition. The organization of the book trade also underwent significant changes: the rise of the printer-editor-publisher, often with their own bookshops as well as printing floors, together with the continuation of book fairs (which had formerly displayed and marketed manuscript books) as vehicles for their wares, had begun. There can be no question that the volume of books produced, whether as commissioned works, speculative publishing ventures or initiatives taken in response to market demand, increased rapidly between 1460 and 1500.

The spread of printing outside the German-speaking lands was almost as rapid. A first wave of German and French printers entered Italy in the 1470s and 1480s, soon to be followed by many indigenous Italian printers by *c.* 1490. The personnel of the printing houses, however, in these earliest stages, remained very largely German. Printers, like artists and masons, were migrants. France witnessed its first printing presses at Paris and Lyon in the 1470s. In Paris, the university led the way. A press was sponsored at the College of the Sorbonne by two of its professors, Jean Heynlin de Lapide and Guillaume Fichet, in 1470–2, producing about twenty works, some of them authored by its humanist founders and their colleagues. In the Low Countries, Caxton had set up a press in Bruges by 1474, once again relying for his titles on the contents of the Burgundian ducal library and of the collections of Netherlandish nobles. Oxford received its first printing press in 1478, operated by Gerard ten Raem, who brought it from Cologne. Its first book was a text by the fourth-century writer Rufinus on the Creed. But the press ceased to operate in 1481 and ten Raem was replaced by another Cologne printer, Theodoricus Rood. It was geared entirely to the needs of scholars and students, producing a dozen editions for the university and for Magdalen College School, including a commentary on Aristotle. But it came to an end in 1483, after which date the university imported its printed books from elsewhere.

Perhaps the most significant impact of the new art on the culture and commerce of a wider Europe at this time was the establishment of a printing press at Venice in 1469.[31] Once again, German printers brought their skills into Italy, and Johann and Wendelin of Speyer set up their press there, using a newly designed 'Roman' typeface, derived from humanistic script. Their Venetian press specialized in the production of academic texts on classical literature, theology and law, directed mainly to the scholarly and student market. The new typeface was a radical departure from the letterpress formerly used by German printers, which was either derived from a formal Gothic 'chancery' hand, or from the cursive script of Burgundian and other scribes. The Old German type font, known as *Fraktur*, or *Gebrochene Schrift* (Broken Script), was derived from Gothic book hand, exemplified at its most elaborate by the inscriptions in the Emperor Maximilian I's woodcut *Triumphal Arch* of 1515. Wendelin's new 'Roman' typeface was cut by the Parisian coin and medal maker Nicholas Jenson, who had come to Mainz from the Paris royal mint in 1458. Well versed in the punch-cutting of matrices and the creation of moulds, Jenson brought the techniques of coin and medal making to the new art of printing. His setting in type of the *Natural History* of Pliny (1472) was universally acclaimed for the fineness of the edition, set up as it was in the newly invented Roman fount. The origins of many later typefaces, such as the various italic and roman founts, and such common variants as Times New Roman, lie in these innovations. But a Gothic fount, known as Blackletter, remained the norm in much of Northern Europe for a very long time, surviving in Germany well into the twentieth century. The Renaissance was not a one-way process, and the coming of the German art of printing to Venice, and also to Rome, was one indication of that North-South movement. By 1500, about 15 per cent of all European printed works had emanated from Venice, with its 200 or so printing houses. In total, about one-third (10,000) of all known editions before *c.* 1500 were printed in Italy. Similar, if not higher, levels of output were to be maintained in the early years of the next century, in part by the printing and publishing house of Aldus Manutius, who for a time was Erasmus's printer of choice.[32]

The first half-century (*c.* 1455–*c.* 1500) in the history of printing in Northern Europe witnessed the beginnings of a movement whose technical, commercial and organizational features spread rapidly across Germany and Northern Italy. It led to important changes in the structure and composition of craft and trade guilds, as printer-publishers and associated workers were either integrated into existing bodies or formed new organizations consisting of new combinations of crafts and trades. Its effect on the intellectual and cultural life of the age was less clear at that early stage and took some time to make its full effects felt. An increase in the sheer volume of books, texts and documents in circulation clearly made the written (or rather printed) word more readily available and affordable. To measure its impact, much might depend upon the nature of the market and the demands of various institutions and individuals. But the advent of the printed book had a transformative effect on, for example, the contents and composition of both institutional and private libraries. In 1482, the library at abbot Trithemius's Benedictine monastery at Sponheim, near Mainz, contained 40 works; by 1500 it held 2,000 volumes, most of them in print, not manuscript.[33] The much smaller, reformed Benedictine house at Scheyern, in upper Bavaria, had seventy volumes in its library in 1500. Of these, 25 per cent were in manuscript and 75 per cent in print.[34] At this period, no hard-and-fast distinction had yet been made by librarians or readers between the printed and manuscript book. They were shelved together, and the two kinds of text were sometimes bound up together so that some books were hybrid examples of both manuscript and print, especially in the composite popular miscellanies of the time. Binding, it has been said, was 'a great equaliser'.[35] But times were changing and the free-standing, independently produced printed book was already making its appearance in ever-increasing quantities. Opportunities to consult and compare identical, or near-identical, texts and to make use of more of them, increased. Elizabeth Eisenstein observed that it has often been suggested that 'something like a knowledge explosion was experienced in the sixteenth century … in connection with the Northern Renaissance if not with the advent of printing'.[36] But to separate the 'printing revolution' from the Northern Renaissance would tend to lie at variance with the facts.

It has recently been said that 'print was the offspring of the Renaissance, a technology born of an era intrigued by, even obsessed with, texts'.[37] If so, then it was in the first instance an offspring of the *Northern* Renaissance. It presupposed the existence of a literate class of readers substantial enough to create sufficient demand for multiple, replicated copies of the same text. The needs of the Church, of university scholars and students bulked large, of course, in creating and sustaining that demand. But there was also a market for books among the laity. Lay literacy rates at this time are notoriously difficult to estimate. Recent studies have suggested that in sixteenth-century German towns a male literacy rate of approximately 30–40 per cent was not uncommon, while the estimated average over the German-speaking lands as a whole was around 5 per cent. So the printing press was also the offspring of the town and its culture. It is to the urban world of German imperial, episcopal and other cities, as well as to their Italian equivalents, that we have to go to chart the contribution of printing to the Renaissance and of the Renaissance to the introduction and spread of the art of printing. Perhaps, as has been argued, the 'knowledge explosion' of the early sixteenth century – if such it was – went hand in hand with the rise of print.

The sheer volume and number of texts produced, especially in the 1520s, might bear that conclusion out. It has been established that the printing and publication of books rose in the German lands from 416 editions in 1517 to 1,331 in 1524. Of these, vernacular German works accounted for about 25 per cent of the total in 1517 and for about 80 per cent in 1524. It has been claimed that 'the years 1518 to 1526 were the powerhouse of the European Reformation and Luther's printed writings lay at their heart'.[38] Besides books, the number of printed pamphlets and short vernacular treatises also jumped very suddenly over the same period, rising to a total figure of approximately 6.5 million copies. This clearly represented an unprecedented increase in the production and circulation of largely polemical religious literature. Martin Luther was responsible for about 20 per cent of the total. The scale of the pamphlet wars which both stimulated and accompanied the Protestant Reformation would undoubtedly have been much smaller, less influential and confined to a far narrower elite of Protestant reformers and Catholic anti-reformers, without the printing press and without the availability of relatively cheap paper. Yet the impact of print was not confined to the replication of written texts and documents. Side by side with the emergence and spread of the printed word, the printed image also began to appear, thereby creating a series of new forms of more widely available visual representations.

THE PRINTED IMAGE

Three techniques were adopted to achieve the creation of this new species of reproduced image: woodcutting, engraving and etching. As we have seen, the first independent woodcuts emerged in the late fourteenth and early fifteenth centuries. The earliest of them tended to depict religious and devotional subjects, but there was also a growing market for woodcut-printed playing cards, and for prints showing secular subjects. This was to be taken up and exploited by the next generation of printmakers, by means of engraving and etching. Many woodblock cutters remain anonymous, but we know that they included both men and women. A large number of family firms evolved, employing women as painters for the hand-colouring of woodblock prints, and sometimes as cutters. In 1531, for example, a Katherina Hetwighe was described as a *Formschneiderin* (block-cutter) at Nuremberg.[39] Durer, Burgkmair and others brought the art to a peak with their prints, including the largest woodcut ever produced, the *Triumphal Arch of Maximilian I* (1515) which measured 12 × 10 feet (3.57 × 2.95 metres). The emperor's contribution to literature and the arts throughout his dominions was both substantial and idiosyncratic, but they offered employment to the leading artists and engravers of his time (Figure 28).

By the 1430s, however, a further technique had emerged from South-West Germany and the Rhineland. What has been defined as 'intaglio printing', as opposed to 'relief printing', was created by the use of incised metal plates. Printing from engravings had been born, although

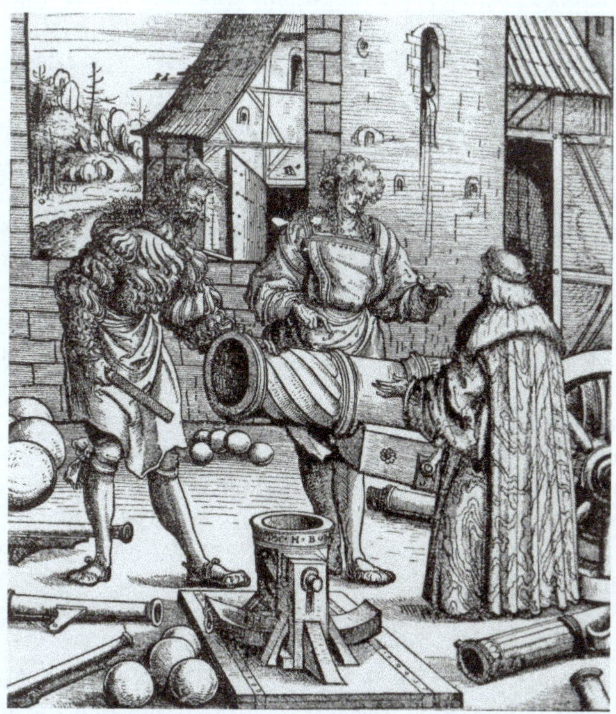

Figure 28 Maximilian I: *Military Consultation* engraving from Weisskunig. (Photo by ullstein bild/ullstein bild/Getty Images.)

the technique of engraving on metal had been known to, and used by, goldsmiths for some long time already. Some of the earliest surviving examples are to be found on playing cards, including the *King of Wildmen* from a pack of cards dating from *c.* 1435–40. These early engravings were produced either by using the burin, a sharpened hand-held steel tool, or by the drypoint stylus, the engraver's main tools, on copper plates. Initially printed by hand, a cylinder press was then introduced, enabling greater speed and accuracy of reproduction. A final stage in the advance of intaglio, or incised plate printmaking, was reached when the art of etching was devised, in Augsburg, around 1500. Daniel Hopfer invented the practice of etching on iron, whereby acid was used to incise lines and create contrasting areas of light and shade. The technique was taken up by Durer, Burgkmair and, in the Netherlands, Lucas van Leyden, using copper, not iron, plates and thereby achieving a finer, subtler effect. Behind its emergence as an artistic technique lay the practice of decorative etching on armour. Augsburg had become famous for armour-making during the fifteenth century, rivalling and in some instances surpassing Italian armourers such as the Missaglia of Milan, long famed for their products on the European market.

A further significant change in printmaking had taken place by the 1470s, when a class of engravers known later as *peintre-graveurs* (painter-engravers) emerged. Printmaking became elevated in status to rival the art of the painter, and the autonomous engraved print now came to be considered a work of art in itself. The first great, named master of the medium was Martin Schongauer (1448–91) whose *Large Procession to Calvary* (*c.* 1475) set a new standard for printmaking (Figure 21). Schongauer, from Colmar, was perhaps the most 'painterly' of the early engravers before Durer. A direct comparison has been made between his work and that of Andrea Mantegna in Italy, who also combined painting and printmaking. A stress on tonal gradation, density and volume is a hallmark of Schongauer's compositions. Profoundly influenced by the great Netherlandish masters – especially Van Eyck, Van der Weyden, Memling and Bouts – Schongauer epitomized the interaction and integration of the graphic arts and painting. His engraving of the *Death of the Virgin* bred a large number of copies and adaptations by others, and his art was a major influence on Durer.

What has been described as a vigorous, robust artistic vernacular was cultivated by Northern printmakers such as 'Master E. S.' (*c.* 1420–68), working in the Rhineland.[40] His art benefited from the development of techniques whereby large numbers of high-quality images could be printed from long-lasting plates. Master E. S. met and exploited the demand of a ready market for such images. In 1466, he was commissioned by the Swiss monastery at Einsiedeln to produce a series of three prints commemorating the 500th anniversary of the miraculous appearance there of the Virgin and a host of angels in 966. They were bought in large quantities by pilgrims attracted to the monastery by the event. The prints were impressions of fine quality, signed or monogrammed with the artist's initials. This set a pattern for subsequent masters including, most famously, Durer's 'AD' monogram. Their work became collectable items, ranking not far below paintings. One of the first such collectors was Hartmann Schedel, humanist, doctor and author of the great illustrated Nuremberg *Weltcronik* (World Chronicle) of 1493. Between 1500 and 1514, he amassed a collection of 500 prints, most of which he pasted into books. By the 1490s, Nuremberg had become the centre of the largest European printing enterprise, largely under the management of Anton Koberger. Widely distributed across Europe, these Nuremberg products set very high standards of printmaking. A new kind of integrated book production developed there, in which the printed text and engraved image were presented with a 'strong sense of graphic layout',[41] designed by book illustrators such as Michael Wolgemut (1434–1519), Durer's mentor, working in Koberger's employment. What has been described as a 'Northern style', quite independent of Italian forms, was developed by them. In this respect, the Northern Renaissance, as with other art forms, made the woodcut and the engraving 'no longer merely a form of vernacular art but rather a medium capable of aspiring to the highest level of excellence'.[42] They were now sought after by very high-status purchasers and patrons, as well as discerning and discriminating collectors. Above all, the Emperor Maximilian I himself chose to have his own semi-autobiographical and self-promotional literary works – the *Weisskunig* (1505–16), his great tournament book *Freydal* (1515) and *Theuerdank* (1517) – illustrated by the best woodcut printers and engravers of his time[43] (Figure 28).

A market for prints of all kinds, which was larger and more socially wide ranging than that for the painted or sculpted image had clearly developed by the end of the fifteenth century. Printing on demand became a standard market practice, as well as the fulfilment of specific commissions in both book production and the creation of independent prints. One of the most prolific of printmakers was the goldsmith Israhel van Meckenem (d. 1503). He was not only a producer of his own, often highly inventive designs, but a shameless exploiter of the work of others. He has been described as a pirate, copyist and plagiarist as well as an

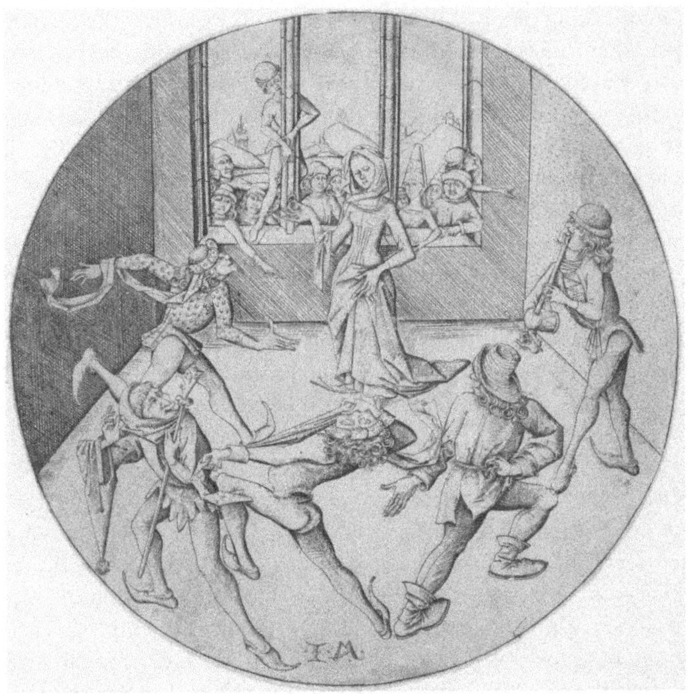

Figure 29 Israhel van Meckenem: *The Morris Dancers*: Art Institute Chicago, Clarence Buckingham Collection, 1936.174.

astute entrepreneur. His work was much influenced by that of Master E. S., by whom he was probably trained, and contemporaries were lavish in their praise of him. Initially rather harsh and angular, his style had become more refined, under Holbein the Elder's influence, by his later years. Although capitalizing on the popularity of devotional images, he also produced work of a satirical, ironic nature, making great play with the folly, absurdity and hypocrisy of priests, scholars, doctors and lawyers among others.[44] His representation of a *Morris Dance (Moresca)* could be taken as a characteristic example of secular subject matter, with an erotic content, which was clearly so popular at the time (Figure 29). His work survives in larger quantities than that of any other printmaker of his age. Of the 3,000 or so engraved images surviving from fifteenth-century Europe, van Meckenem produced 620, while Master E. S. created 300, and Schongauer 116, making 33 per cent of the total European print production the work of just 3 masters.[45]

It has been claimed that the rise of printmaking contributed to what has been seen as a Renaissance redefinition of the arts. Prints have been viewed as a catalyst in the process whereby the visual arts were to become defined 'according to the conceptual nature of their endeavour'.[46] The techniques and the specific kinds of materials used in the creation of works of art were no longer crucial to that definition. The integration of printmakers into painters' guilds in many major European towns linked print to drawing and thence to painting. At Augsburg, Paris, Louvain, Leiden, Haarlem, Amsterdam, Antwerp and Strasbourg, the printmakers joined the painters, sculptors, mapmakers and book printers, often gathered together by the civic authorities in the painter-led Guilds of St Luke. Visual artists were now grouped together institutionally and, in some cases, the same individual could, like Schongauer or Durer, be an exponent of a number of different arts and their related crafts. The often-noted rise in the status not only of the Renaissance painter and sculptor but also of the woodblock printer, engraver and printmaker, as well as of the book producer, was surely indicative of a changing artistic and aesthetic world. Northern Europe, as well as Italy, certainly experienced that tendency.

The mere fact that, between *c.* 1500 and *c.* 1540, the number of prints and books produced by the new techniques showed a tenfold increase over the total produced between *c.* 1455 and *c.* 1490 points to something not far short of a revolution. But that revolution was firmly rooted in the fifteenth century. The contribution of printing, from the mid-fifteenth century onwards, to the creation of what Erasmus called 'a library without walls' was critical. Its distribution and dissemination networks were unprecedented. Never reticent in the art of self-promotion, Erasmus at least recognized that much of the celebrity he enjoyed during his lifetime was due to the new invention. He disparaged his clerical contemporaries by claiming, with supreme Renaissance self-assurance, that 'they preach obscure sermons; I write what will live for eternity; they … are listened to in a few churches; my books will be read everywhere in the world'.[47] Much of that wider and greater readership must have been owed to the availability of the printed word. In sum, the evidence points to the conclusion that, as Elizabeth Eisenstein observed, 'intellectual and spiritual life, far from remaining unaffected, were profoundly transformed by the multiplication of new tools for duplicating books in fifteenth-century Europe'.[48] It was perhaps the greatest contribution of the Northern Renaissance to the subsequent history of Europe and the world beyond its frontiers.

6

WISDOM, FOLLY AND THE DARKER VISION

WISDOM, PASSION AND THE CONCEPT OF FOLLY

> By stoic definition, wisdom means nothing else but being ruled by reason; and folly … is being swayed by the dictates of the passions. So Jupiter, not wanting man's life to be wholly gloomy and grim, has bestowed far more passion than reason. (Erasmus, *Praise of Folly*)[1]

So Erasmus, in classicizing mode, muses on wisdom and folly, reason and passion. Such themes were to be found, whether celebrated or disparaged, in much of the literature and some of the visual art of the age. The causes, symptoms and consequences of human folly were painstakingly set out by him and others, in both literature and art, where folly often seemed to have gained the upper hand.[2] Humanists and moralists pointed to the eternal conflict between the wise and the foolish, epitomized by the two most famous and popular Renaissance satires: Erasmus's *Praise of Folly* (1509, 1514) and Sebastian Brant's (1458–1521) *Narrenschiff* (*Ship of Fools*, 1494). Both works shared some common themes and displayed some important differences, but had serious purposes. Erasmus attempted to disarm critics by stressing that his *Praise of Folly* was full of jokes, but jokes nevertheless 'which aim at doing good rather than giving a display of learning and wit' as other humanists tended to do.[3] Brant, though a translator of the jest books *Facetus* (*Der Deutsche Facetus*, 1496) and *Moretus* (1499) from Latin into German, was adamant that

his German vernacular verse *Ship of Fools* had a clear didactic purpose.
He concluded:

> Of fools such tidings I did tell / So that all men would know them well; / But if
> you're prudent through and through, / Read Virgil's works, they're meant for
> you. / A good, wise man of prudence rare, / As one can find scarce anywhere / In
> all the world is Socrates – Apollo gave him gifts like these.[4]

Models of wisdom, Brant claimed, could be found among the ancients
– Pythagoras, Plato and Socrates 'who through their creed / Won lasting
fame and honour's meed'[5] despite their ignorance of Christian teaching.
Wisdom, he wrote, led inexorably to enlightenment:

> To darkness wisdom puts an end / If but to wisdom we attend, / It shows us too
> the difference / 'Twixt folly's course and prudent sense.[6]

But even the greatest and wisest of philosophers, not least Aristotle, could
(it was claimed) be so distracted by love and passion, and so deceived by
the subjects of their affections, that they could behave like fools.[7]

These didactic and satirical themes, as well as even darker ones,
were also illustrated and more widely disseminated to a larger audience
through the graphic work of many woodcut-makers, engravers, etchers,
book illustrators and the paintings of, among others, Hieronymus Bosch
(*c.* 1450–1516), Quentin Matsys (1466–1530), Matthias Grunewald (*c.*
1470–1528) and, in the next generation, Pieter Bruegel the Elder (1525–
69). As we shall see,[8] they were treated with varying degrees of skill and
inventiveness between *c.* 1450 and 1500 in the works of printmakers
and engravers such as Israhel van Meckenem (1445–1503), the Master
of the Housebook or Amsterdam Cabinet (*c.* 1450–*c.*1500), Master B+G
(*c.* 1440–*c.* 1500), Master E. S. (*c.* 1420–*c.* 1468) and the Master of the
Playing Cards (*c.* 1420–*c.* 1465).[9] A major characteristic of many printed
satirical works of the age was the provision of copious illustration by
means of the relatively new media of woodcuts and engravings. Holbein
illustrated the 1514 edition of the *Praise of Folly*, and the many editions
of the *Ship of Fools* printed between 1494 and 1548 in Latin, Low
German, English, French, Flemish and Dutch contained images from the
hands of a range of different artists, the vernacular versions being clearly
intended for a wider market among the urban populace. They depicted
ships crowded to capacity (and beyond) with fools, with their caps, staves
and bells, captained by the satanic Doctor Griff (Figure 30). They are on
their way, without compass or rudder, to Narragon (*Ad Narragoniam*,
the Land of Fools) via *Schluraffenland* (the Land of Cockaigne, where the

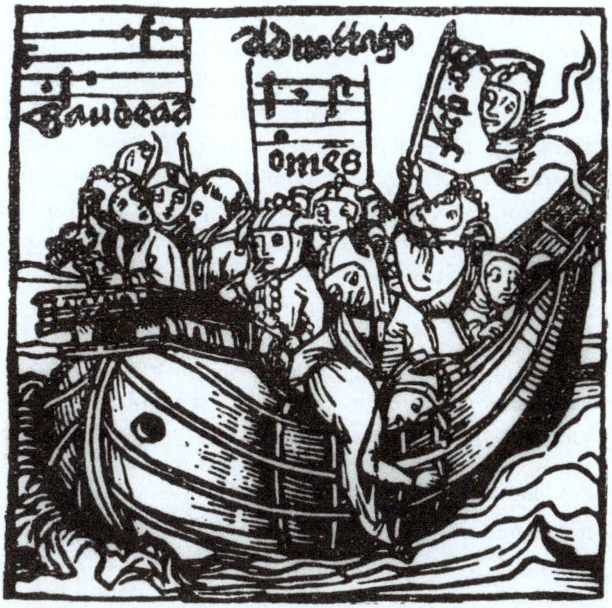

Figure 30 Sebastian Brant: *Ship of Fools* engraving (1494).
(Photo by DeAgostini/Getty Images.)

Schluraffen, or 'lazy apes' dwell), singing *Gaudeamus omnes* (*Let us all be joyful!*) like a crowd of rowdy, drunken students with their *Gaudeamus igitur* song. Their place of transit, the utopian Land of Cockaigne, had come on to the scene in the twelfth century and was celebrated in the Latin Goliardic verse of the Northern French cathedral schools and their clerical alumni. This was an imagined land of luxury and licence, ease and plenty, overflowing with sensual pleasures and delights.[10] It was at the opposite end of the spectrum to the life of hardship and privation which most people lived in the 'real' world and represented a source of imaginative escapism for the lower orders of society. The higher, more affluent orders may have felt less need for it and found their routes of escape elsewhere. Some aspects of their worlds could come a little closer than those of the majority to the Land of Cockaigne. Hedonistic pleasures were thought to be instantly available in this land of luxury and liberty, including ready-to-eat cooked food, sex on demand and unlimited supplies of drink. In moralistic literature, it became known as a 'fool's paradise' where the sins of sloth and gluttony reigned supreme.

In some versions, entry to Cockaigne demanded a heavy price, such as the seven-year penance mockingly prescribed in an Irish manuscript of *c.* 1330–40 whereby the penitent was required to 'wade through pigshit to his chin'.[11] Rabelais took up some of these themes in his Panurge and Pantagruel tales. In 1567, Pieter Bruegel the Elder produced his painting of *Luilekkerland* ('nice, luscious land'), adopting some motifs which Hieronymus Bosch had also used, such as an egg running about on a pair of legs (Figure 31). Bruegel's depiction of a sated and inebriated peasant, soldier and clerk, incapacitated by their excesses, also appears in an engraving of *c.* 1570, copying Bruegel. It has a Dutch inscription reading: 'The slothful and gluttonous peasants, soldiers and clerks get there [to the Land of Cockaigne] and taste all for nothing.' It was yet another visualization of folly, its causes and consequences.

At the most 'popular' level, the theme of folly was taken up by the carnival plays (*Fastnachtspielen*) staged indoors in taverns, burghers' houses and halls, and by the performances given on waggons and platform stages during pre-Lenten festivities and the Feast of Fools, celebrated around 1 January since the later twelfth century. The *Fastnachtspielen* – secular, Shrovetide plays, performed during the period before Lent, in large cities such as Strasbourg, Nuremberg and Augsburg, and smaller

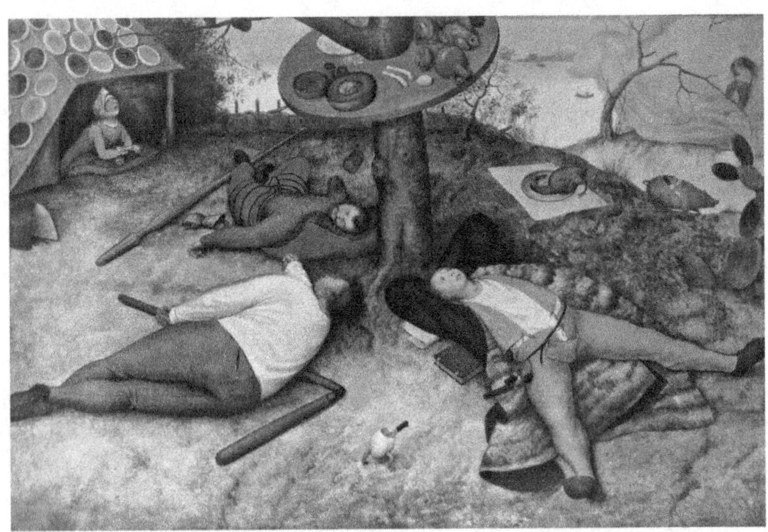

Figure 31 Pieter Bruegel the Elder: *The Land of Cockayne* (1567).
(Photo by Universal History Archive/Universal Images Group/Getty Images.)

towns such as Ulm or Freiburg-in-Breisgau – from at least the early fifteenth century onwards, also took up the theme of the fools' sea voyage. Many of these plays were in effect farces, some replete with ribald and ingenious (and less ingenious) references to various sexual and other bodily functions. Unlike the contemporary French farces (*soties*) they were performed indoors and there was virtually no physical separation between audience and players. In North German towns such as Lubeck, the plays appear to have been staged by members of the patrician and upper burgher classes, and the actors were generally young men from the middle and upper ranks of that class. They performed a far greater number of religiously centred 'morality' plays there than was the case in South Germany and the Rhineland. In Nuremberg, the plays seem to have been managed, produced and performed by guildsmen, craftsmen and apprentices. They were idealized, represented by the cobbler-poet Hans Sachs (1494–1576) – whose fictitious *alter ego* proclaims the need to preserve and defend 'holy German art' (*'heil'ge deutsche Kunst'*) – in Richard Wagner's opera *Die Meistersinger von Nurnberg* (1868). There was also, however, clearly some input into the Nuremberg plays from the patrician class who, after all, as representatives of the civic authorities, were prepared to allow their performance. Potentially subversive though they were of the political and social order, it has been argued (by Bakhtin and others) that the Shrovetide and carnival plays acted as a form of safety mechanism or pressure valve, releasing and satisfying all kinds of repressed impulses, as well as class and other tensions.[12] They could – paradoxically – in effect sustain and reinforce the existing order. There may well be some element of agitation and propaganda in them, advocating social and political change, not least in their often virulent anti-Jewish sentiments.[13] The plays were therefore taken up by later anti-Semitic movements for their depiction of Jews which was uncompromisingly hostile and denigratory.

But, like other forms of satire at this time, much of their mocking sexual and scatological humour spared no class of society, nor any status-group, profession or community. They may well have had the social function of 'relieving class tensions and intra-group hostilities'[14] and provided an outlet for aggression, but the objects of their ridicule were widely spread and broadly based. Their urban audiences clearly hugely enjoyed their representations of the rural peasantry as stereotypes of vulgar stupidity and sensual folly, and this prejudice was also vividly illustrated by the woodcut-makers and engravers. The *Fastnachtspielen* often satirized the very same targets as Brant's and Erasmus's more elevated works.

But Erasmus himself, in his self-justificatory letter to Maarten van Dorp (1515), to some extent identified, however disdainfully, with the sentiments and satirical jibes of such popular plays. 'Can't we at least', he wrote, 'allow my little book (the *Praise of Folly*) what even the ignorant crowd permits popular comedies? How many taunts are freely thrown out there against monarchs, priests, monks, wives, husbands – against anyone in fact?'[15] The distinguished humanist was thus not averse, when the occasion required it, to seeking justification for his masterpiece in much lower forms of literary and theatrical life.

It has been suggested that one possible origin for Brant's choice of the theme of a ship of fools may have lain in popular drama and what was in effect street and tavern theatre. The idea of a ship, whether of folly or of penitence, had stemmed from the legend of St Ursula and her ships full of 11,000 virgins destined for martyrdom at Cologne. Brant's *Ship of Fools* became, in turn, an influence upon other published genres. In 1497, a book of exemplars from the St Ursula legend was compiled by Alsatian Carthusians for the use of the laity. Entitled the *St Ursula Schifflein* (*St Ursula's little ship*) it became the subject of sermons delivered in Strasbourg Cathedral in 1498–9 and was printed in 1510.[16] Confraternities bearing that title also began to emerge in the German-speaking lands at that time. By what seems to be an inversion or distortion of the hagiographical story, the ships of Ursula's holy martyrs became ships of fools. A vernacular sermon preached in *c.* 1470 tells us that 'this is a pretty preaching given on St Ursula's day, which speaks of the spiritual [or unworldly] ship of fools' (*dem geistlichen Narrenschiff*).[17] The preacher spoke of a ship carrying twenty-one fools, with Christ himself as the twenty-second passenger, urging them to abandon their vessel and board a ship following Him as he walked on the waters. There may have been a conflation here between the Ursula legend and the contemporary practice of dispatching the mentally ill, epileptic and those deemed to be possessed, as pilgrims to the Irish saint St Dymphna's shrine at Geel, near Antwerp.[18] The city of Nuremberg sent its mentally troubled inhabitants there, as did other German and Netherlandish towns. The saint became patroness of the mentally ill, and the town a place of sanctuary and care for them. It may be no coincidence that, in the legend, one of her companions on her journey to escape the potentially incestuous clutches of her father was a court fool. By the 1480s her shrine had become a major place of pilgrimage. Ships of fools, conveying the mentally afflicted, were thus a reality, as well as a fiction, as they voyaged to and from Geel, during the period.

For Erasmus and Brant, in satirical mode, folly was everywhere, and played a dominant, if not *the* dominant, role in human affairs. But the paradox that folly was true wisdom (Erasmus), and that only fools were truly wise, also emerged from the debates of humanists, moralists (both clerical and secular) and the polemical literature of the age. The moral was to some extent exemplified in the story of a debate between King Solomon and the court fool and jester Marcolf. A fifteenth-century Latin *Dialogus Salomonis et Marcolfi (Dialogue of Solomon and Marcolf)*, of which several German vernacular versions also survive, represented an encounter between 'higher' wisdom (Solomon, biblical) and worldly clear-sightedness and practical sense (Marcolf, secular). A fool could therefore possess a degree of worldly wisdom denied even to the great sages of the past. Even the most learned of men could be distracted not only by their passions but also by their pretentious and often rigid dogmatism, which needed to be exposed for the idiocy that it was. There was little doubt that Erasmus's target here was the scholastic theologians and philosophers with whom he took such issue. He observed that while wise men and grave advisers only offered misery to a prince, their court fools spoke the truth to power, even to tyrants: they 'can speak truth and even open insults and be heard with positive pleasure',[19] wrote Erasmus. Fools, he contended, enjoyed a degree of happiness – and indeed licence – denied to others. Whereas, he continued, the wise man, whose youth had been lost through the acquisition of learning, was

> thrifty, impoverished, miserable, grumpy, harsh and unjust to himself, disagreeable and unpopular with his fellows, pale and thin, sickly and blear-eyed, prematurely white-haired and senile, worn-out and dying before his time.[20]

There may have been some element of self-parody, if not self-pity, in all this but Erasmus proceeded to list the follies of all those who enjoyed a reputation for wisdom in uncompromisingly critical terms. They included schoolmasters (whose establishments were 'treadmills and torture chambers'), rhetoricians (trivial word-mongers), writers (self-torturers), lawyers (self-satisfied pontificators), sophists, dialecticians and philosophers (garrulous windbags), theologians (supercilious and prickly) and, above all, scholastics (peddlers of tortuous obscurities, more interested in idle speculations than in issues of genuine moral and religious experience).

Erasmus pursued the notion of the greater happiness of the fool further by using the analogy of Plato's views on the 'madness of lovers'. Like the pious, who become 'beside themselves' in their zealous fervour, lovers are taken out of themselves by a kind of madness.[21] This led him to formulate the idea of the 'Christian fool'. Erasmus claimed that this condition – some form of pious ecstasy – gave man a foretaste of paradise. He was taken out of himself 'and happy for no reason except that he is so outside himself' so that 'he will enjoy some ineffable share in the supreme good which draws everything into itself'.[22] He went on to argue that the truly pious few, as a result of this transformative, transcendental experience, in which the body and its needs was left far behind, 'know that they were happiest when they were out of their senses in this way, and they lament their return to reason, for all they want is to be mad for ever with this kind of madness. And it is only the merest taste of the happiness [in paradise] to come.'[23] Plato here in effect met Christ, and Erasmus had, at least to his own satisfaction, succeeded in reconciling ancient philosophy with Christian teaching. Nicholas of Cusa (1401–64) had in his *Idiota de sapientia et de mente* (1450), earlier spoken of the 'folly', innocence and simplicity of the true believer, as Christ himself had taught.[24] As St Paul had written, 'God chose what is foolish in the world to shame the wise' (1 Cor. 1.27). Cusa argued that wisdom was to be found in lay people and was not confined to a clerical elite, learned in theology or philosophy. There was a clear connection here with the thought of the *devotio moderna*, rather than with Erasmian Neoplatonism, in this aspect of Cusa's writings. The influence of Meister Eckhardt, the Rhineland mystics, and the ideas expressed in German vernacular texts such as *Der Ackermann aus Bohmen*, in which a pious ploughman debates with death, were also evident. Cusa argued, against the humanists, that eloquence was not an essential adjunct to wisdom. But he also rejected scholastic notions of wisdom based upon human rationality. There was therefore a kind of 'spiritual folly' or 'learned ignorance' (*docta ignorantia*) which lay beyond mere human reason, and was an essential path to spiritual fulfilment through evangelical humanism. The concept had originated and developed in Northern Europe during the fourteenth century, subsequently influencing Kempis, Erasmus and many others. And although they were not the most compatible of bedfellows, there were some signs that Italian Neoplatonists such as Giovanni Pico della Mirandola (1463–94) were not entirely unaffected by such ideas. As with other concepts of the age, the notion of holy foolishness or spiritual folly had many interwoven and sometimes entangled strands within it.

The nature of wisdom, and its antithesis folly, had long been debated in medieval thought. A biblical exemplar of wisdom was presented in the figure of King Solomon although, as we have seen, it was claimed that he was not entirely immune from folly and unreason. Another was to be found in the story of the wise and foolish virgins. Wisdom and justice often went hand in hand, and there was constant reference to Solomon's judgements in medieval didactic treatises, sermons and 'mirrors for princes'. But the literary and artistic representation of the folly of wise men swayed by passion, and hence abandoning reason, had established itself since at least the early thirteenth century. As with so many other subjects, the rise of representational realism during the Northern Renaissance gave a new immediacy and vividness to their depiction in visual art. The foremost examples were the stories of Solomon 'the Wise' worshipping a strange and *false* god, and of Aristotle ridden by Phyllis. The story of Solomon and the false god that he, in old age, idolatrously worshipped at the behest of his foreign concubines and of Aristotle's humiliation at Phyllis's hands, both pointed to the baleful power of women over men otherwise renowned for their wisdom and sagacity. Both narratives were not without a substantial element of misogyny embedded within them. The Aristotle theme was an early-thirteenth-century invention and may have been used to discredit the scholars or 'Thomists' who followed the Aristotelian teachings of Thomas Aquinas at the University of Paris. It has been argued that the theme's appearance in an arresting engraving by the Housebook Master (*c.* 1485) (Figure 32) was directly inspired by an attack by a faction of Heidelberg scholars and students on their Thomist contemporaries. The University of Heidelberg and the humanistic court of the Rhenish count Palatine Philip the Sincere (1442–1508) may well have harboured a group of Ockhamist and humanist proponents of the academic *via moderna*, anxious to enjoy 'an exquisite joke at the expense of the neo-Thomist *Via Antiqua*'.[25]

But there were more popular, less elevated sources for the theme. The Housebook Master and Master E. S., between 1485 and 1490, and Hans Baldung Grien, in 1515, all produced engravings derived from the tale of Aristotle ridden by Alexander the Great's young mistress or concubine wife Phyllis. Aristotle had warned his pupil Alexander about her wily ways but had then himself fallen in love with her. As a punishment she rode on his back, bridling and whipping him like a horse. Baldung Grien represents both protagonists naked, and the sexual overtones of the whipped and bridled Aristotle's humiliation by a dominatrix-like Phyllis are hardly disguised (Figure 33). The Housebook Master's source for *his* highly realistic and lively version of the scene may, however, have been a popular fifteenth-century vernacular *Fastnachtspiel* entitled *Ain*

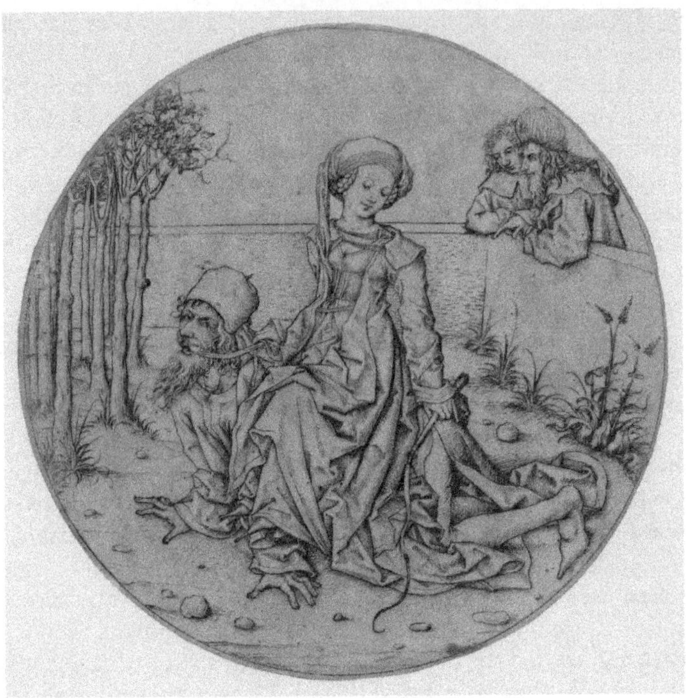

Figure 32 Master of the Housebook: Aristotle and Phyllis engraving
(*c.* 1485): (Rijksmuseum, Amsterdam).

Spiel van Maister Aristotiles (*A Play of Master Aristotle*).[26] The link
between the engraver's art and the popular theatre may be quite close in
this case, as in others. In Nuremberg, Hans Folz, playwright and master
barber-surgeon (*c.* 1437–1513), produced *A Play about Fools* and *A
Carnival Play Concerning Those Who Allow Themselves to Be Made
Fools of by Women*. Dame Venus was shown there hearing tales of sexual
adventures and mishaps in which foolish male lovers were wrong-footed,
outwitted and humiliated. Both the Housebook Master and Israhel van
Meckenem also depicted the theme, also often represented in popular
plays, of the hen-pecked or dominated husband, usually a peasant. The
mocking reversal of conventionally accepted roles was illustrated by
their engravings of a topsy-turvy world in which peasants stand on their
heads; husbands (like Aristotle) are ridden by distaff-wielding wives;
hideously ugly peasants pull or push their hideously ugly wives along
in wheelbarrows; and heraldic shields bear absurd devices such as garlic

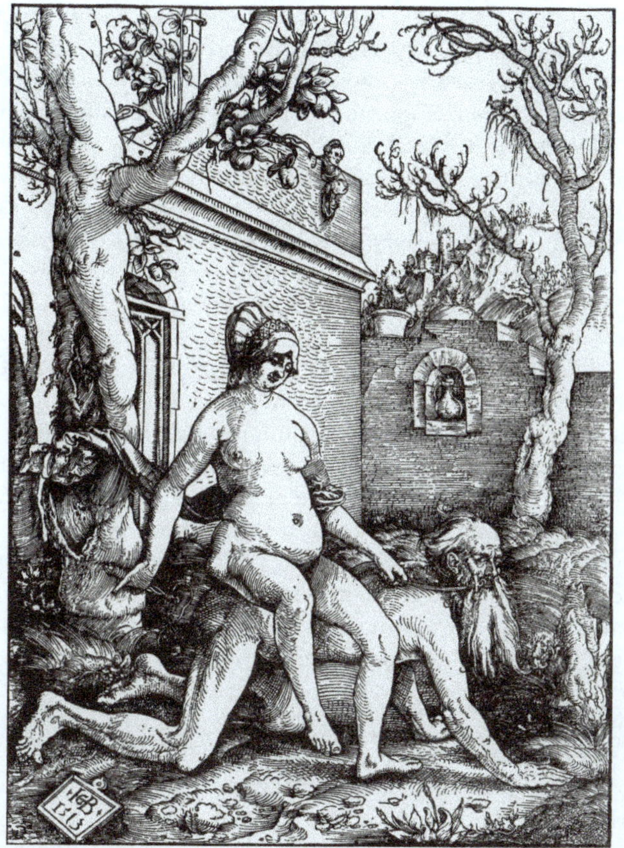

Figure 33 Hans Baldung Grien: Aristotle and Phyllis engraving (1513).
(Photo by The Print Collector/Print Collector/Getty Images.)

or radishes. The extent to which misogyny drove such images can be disputed but it is certainly there.

The wisest, as well as the most stupid, of men could thus be led astray by their passions. To overcome those passions, reason and moderation had to play their part. If they did, then passion might be transformed into virtue especially when directed towards worthy ends which might serve the common good. The advocacy of what was perceived to be a good cause demanded a forceful, effective and even passionate mode of persuasion. It has been argued that, besides the medieval alliance between wisdom and justice, a 'Renaissance' revival of the union between wisdom and eloquence, as advocated by Cicero, took place, largely in Italy, and more specifically in Florence, in the later fourteenth and early fifteenth centuries. Cicero, the great Roman orator, had written that 'wisdom without eloquence leads to very little of value for civic bodies (*civitatibus*), while eloquence without wisdom for the most part performs in an excessive fashion and leads to nothing' (*De Inventione*).[27] But that union between philosophical and rhetorical modes of thought, between rhetoric, philosophy, wisdom and eloquence of speech had never been absent from the minds of many medieval thinkers, including John of Paris (1255–1306) and Marsiglio of Padua (1275–1342). Much hung upon the person and capabilities of the orator, whose wise and persuasive speech played a vital role in the conduct of public affairs. Far from there being a radical break between 'medieval' and 'Renaissance' thought in this respect, their continuity has been emphasized. In Northern as well as Southern Europe, the eloquent counsellor, envoy or diplomatic representative, often described as an 'orator', bridged the purely artificial divide which has subsequently been constructed between 'medieval' and 'Renaissance' thought, politics and culture. And it was the medieval papal chancery that produced some of the best examples of Ciceronian written prose, with its rhetorical devices and grandiloquent phrases, during the thirteenth and early fourteenth centuries. Yet the idea of wisdom (*sapientia*) was not immune from all changes during the following period.

It is claimed, not without justification, that the concept of wisdom, like so much else, experienced a degree of secularization during the Renaissance.[28] Wisdom which was derived from the exercise of piety could also, it was argued, be reached by more secular paths. Revelation and divine grace were not its only sources. Erasmus, Sir Thomas More (1478–1535), Sir Thomas Elyot (1490–1546) and Guillaume Bude (1467–1540), perpetuated ideas about wisdom previously found, at an earlier date, in the writings of Florentine humanists, with a firm emphasis upon the deployment of wisdom in the active political and religious life, rather than in the contemplative or speculative sphere. Wisdom became 'transformed from contemplation into action, and from knowledge to virtue'.[29] Erasmus followed Kempis in arguing that learning was not an inevitable nor a necessary companion of wisdom, and that it could produce pedantry, arrogance and a singular lack of judgement in the affairs of the world. Yet, even among the most secular-minded of thinkers, Bible-based and revelation-based wisdom was never, and could never, be excluded from the argument. And the devotional trends of the age also moved in the direction of the active rather than the contemplative Christian life. Moral action, to both the exponents of the *devotio moderna* and some Protestant reformers, stemmed from the exercise of wisdom inspired by biblical and devotional precept. But the non-Christian Cicero – infused, it was thought, with a Christian spirit before the advent of Christianity – was admired by many of them, including Calvin, rejecting the *otium* (idleness or inactivity) of some forms of study, and seeking the exercise of virtue by way of an active engagement in political and civic, as well as religious, life.

To this was added the study not of philosophy, but of history which, as it had been in the past, was a major source to be tapped for evidence of wise behaviour in human affairs of all kinds. One of the Flemish nobleman Philippe de Commynes's (*c.* 1447–1511) unsolicited pieces of advice to princes in his *Memoirs* was that they should learn from history, especially from ancient history. Wisdom was to be derived from the example of ancestors, and history opened up ranges of experience which could never be encompassed by a single individual in his or her lifetime.[30] Much of the advocacy of history as a source of wisdom did not depart from the long-established medieval tradition of following the precepts of classical – above all Roman – rhetoric in fulfilling the essential requirements of both history and rhetoric 'to teach, to move and to give pleasure'. Such novelty as there was stemmed from the mid-fifteenth-century rediscoveries of the works of Polybius and Tacitus, and from the reception in the West of the Greek, as well as the Roman, historical tradition.[31] As we have seen, advances in the criticism of historical texts and documents, by Petrarch, Lorenzo Valla and Nicholas of Cusa, were also innovatory.[32] In the harsh world of politics, those in power and those who advised them looked to historical precedent and example. Practical, rather than theoretical, wisdom, exemplified by cunning calculation and a readiness to listen to wise counsel and advice, was a quality essential to the success of the properly educated prince. Louis XI of France's (1461–83) avoidance of pitched battles, because of their unpredictable and highly risky nature, was instanced by the clear-eyed and sceptical Commynes – described by the French writer and critic Sainte-Beuve (1804–69) as 'our Machiavelli' – as a practical example of such princely wisdom.[33] If his ends could be achieved by other means, such as sowing discord among dissident subjects, or outwitting opponents by diplomatic means, then there was little or no need for a prince to put his cause to God's judgement in battle. There were plenty of good examples of this from ancient history. And as we have seen,[34] in France, the German lands and the Netherlands, histories by humanist writers such as Gaguin, Geldenhouwer and others sought to portray, and draw examples from, the deeds of earlier rulers, military commanders and their advisers.[35] The rediscovery of the works of Tacitus contributed substantially to this redirection of historical writing. Francia, Germania and Batavia (part of the greater Netherlands, originally the land of the Germanic tribe of Batavi) were now seen as former provinces of the Roman Empire which had become independent polities with their own distinct identities. They were now deemed, beside imperial Rome itself, to be worthy subjects of historical inquiry.

SATIRE: VERBAL AND VISUAL

As we have seen, wisdom and folly had for long been the subject of much medieval theological, philosophical and didactic writing.[36] They were also among the objects of medieval satire. In the *Roman de Fauvel* (1310–14), Gervais du Bus had held up all classes of society to ridicule for their folly. The theme of *Fauvel*, the horse petted by all and who ends up ruling a kingdom, was taken up by Brant in the *Ship of Fools*. As part of his diatribe against courtiers, he denounced those who 'stroked the fallow stallion', declaring,

> Who now strokes the fallow steed / And dotes upon a scurvy deed/Deserves a haughty courtier's meed. I wish I had a covered ship / Wherein all courtiers I would slip.[37]

There was thus a certain degree of continuity in the world of later medieval and Renaissance satire. There was also a long and enduring tradition of satirical literature in the form of *fabliaux* (fictional tales) from the later twelfth century onwards. Some of Chaucer's *Canterbury Tales* were a late example of the genre. A common theme carried over from the past was the story, in its many variants, of unequal and mismatched lovers. Historical reality lay to some extent behind the object of the satire here. A common later medieval tendency for older men, especially of the upper and propertied classes, to marry much younger women, and for older women, widows and dowagers, to marry younger men, was visually expressed by double portraits of such couples. A good and particularly fine example is Robert Campin's pair of portraits (*c.* 1430) showing such a couple, probably from Tournai, widely separated by age. But the theme became one for jibe and satirical treatment both verbally and visually.

The Housebook Master, subsequently copied by Israhel van Meckenem, produced two prints (*c.* 1470–80) depicting the folly of unequal lovers, one showing a young man with an old woman and another an old man with a younger woman (Figure 35). In both cases a loaded bag of coins is fondly stroked by the younger partners. Money, not love, was clearly thought to be at the root of these relationships, and the folly of the lust displayed by the older lovers, which would not satisfy their younger partners, is also made plain. The theme was taken up by other artists, including Lucas Cranach the Elder, Hans Baldung Grien and Dürer.

In so many of these engraved images of secular subjects an underlying, and sometimes overt, sexuality is omnipresent (Figure 34). Pairs of lovers make clearly physical overtures and advances to each other, however

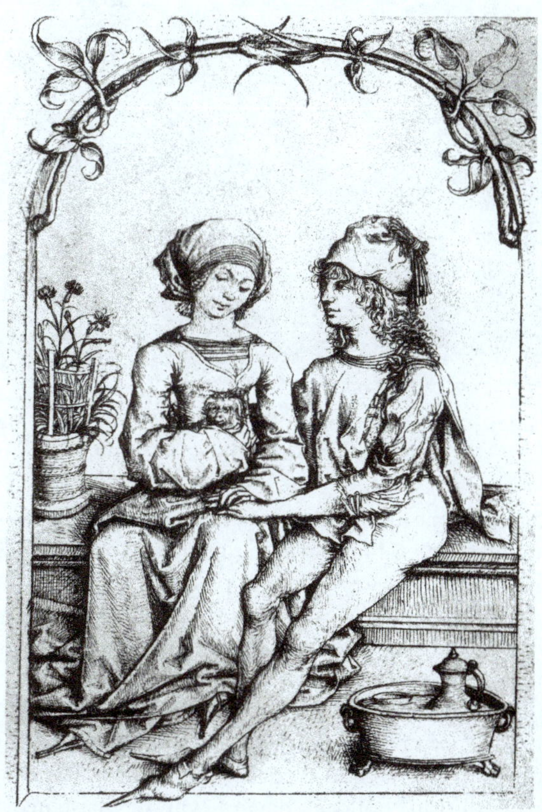

Figure 34 Master of the Housebook: Love couple engraving.
(Photo by ullstein bild/ullstein bild/Getty Images.)

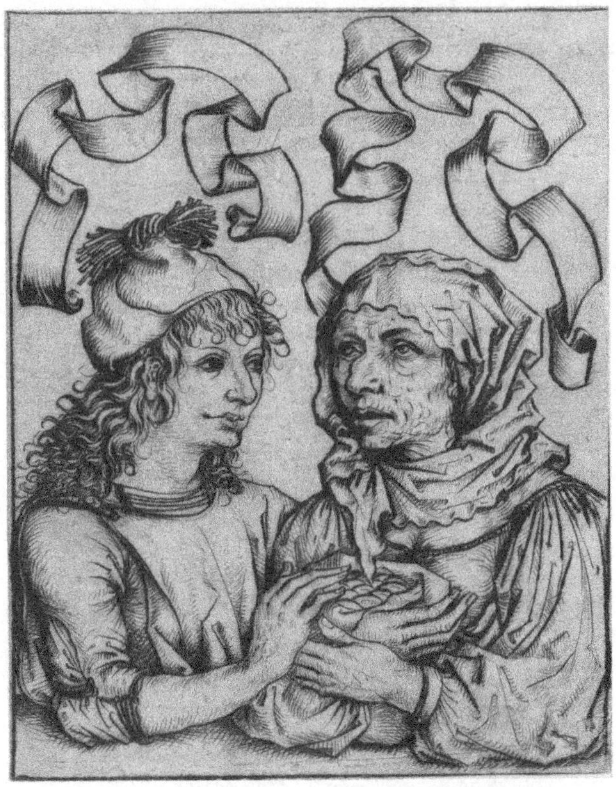

Figure 35 Master of the Housebook: *Ill-matched Couple: Young Man and Old Woman* (Rijksmuseum, Amsterdam).

elegant and refined the ambient setting, such as a 'garden of love', appears to be. Young men, often finely attired, display swords and daggers hung in poses which cannot be anything but phallically suggestive (Figure 36). In one of the Housebook Master's prints of *A Young Man and Death* (*c.* 1485–90) a handsome, elegantly dressed young man, with elongated pointed shoes, carries a provocatively hung dagger at his belt, made all the more suggestive by its so-called 'ballock' or 'bollock'-shaped handguard.[38] The two rounded lobes between the hilt and the blade had clear sexual connotations and were seen as such at the time, hence the name. The phalliform 'bollock' dagger was re-christened the 'kidney' dagger, and thus made more acceptable to their more prudish audiences, by nineteenth-century antiquarian students of armour and weaponry.

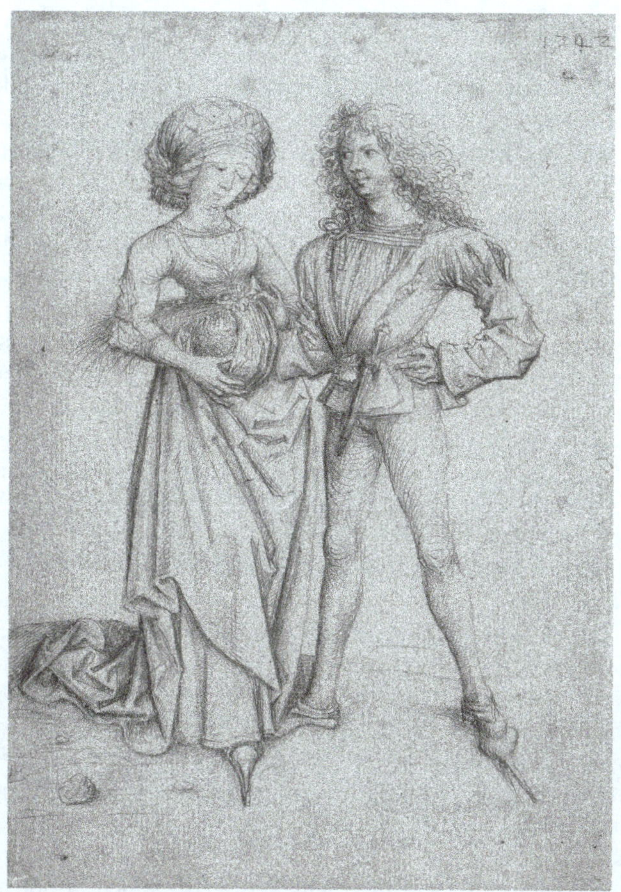

Figure 36 Master of the Housebook: *Standing Couple* (Berlin): (bpk/
Kupferstichkabinett, SMB/Jörg P. Anders (00040651)).

The Housebook Master's powerful image leaves no doubt as to its
allusion. But the presence in the print of a snake and a toad, as well as a
skeletal and menacing figure of death, tells us that all this elegance, poise,
fashionable style and potent life-force are transient, mortal and destined
to decay.[39]

A less moralizing attitude towards sexuality is found in some of the
more ribald comic texts and images of the time. Sexual metaphors and
double entendres abound in both written and visual sources of this
kind. In many of these, one partner – or both – in a sexual relationship

175

is discomfited, mocked and derided. There was a long tradition of such satire and imagery, much of it stemming from the various editions of the *Roman de la Rose* by Guilaume de Loris (*c.* 1200–*c.* 1240) and Jean de Meun (*c.* 1240–1305). But the later Middle Ages witnessed an escalation of such texts and images, in part enabled and furthered by the production of multiple printed copies. The early fifteenth century had also witnessed something of a reaction against the apparently misogynistic character of the *Roman* in the form of an epistolary debate between the female author Christine de Pisan (1364–*c.* 1430), Jean Gerson and other Parisian scholars known as the *Querelle de la Rose* (1401–3).[40] The literature accordingly began to change its character and widen the terms of the discussion and defence of the place and value of women. As in other areas, the heightened polemicism and increased realism with which these themes, both for and against, were treated could only add to their immediacy and impact. In the satirical texts, the use of double entendre or *double sens* was a common feature, found in what has been called 'a large family of texts [of this kind] … which flourished from the fifteenth to the seventeenth centuries'.[41] A classical dimension was injected, in texts such as the verse *Debat de Mars et du Cul* (*c.* 1465–80), into a series of combative dialogues and encounters between Mars, the bellicose god of war, and Cul, the goddess of eroticism and scatology. Wordplay, punning and innuendo give the dialogues and debates an ambiguous, ambivalent and equivocal meaning throughout. These exchanges have a strong dramatic, theatrical element, and although the single surviving manuscript of the *Debat* was owned by the family of Cleves-Ravenstein, from the high Burgundian nobility, the influence of the popular theatre and of popular songs is clearly apparent in it.

An analogous example is to be found in a series of six elegant colour-washed drawings of Flemish origin (*c.* 1470), which adopt a similar approach and technique in their rendering of both text and image.[42] An armoured 'galant', equipped as a foot soldier rather than a knight or esquire, armed with a spear and revealing a prominent codpiece, is about to mount an assault on a lady's castle. A banderole, or label, tells us that he said to her:[43]

> Gently-born and honest *damoiselle* / I must conquer your tower; / sooner or later, at least, / I'll enter into the Lower Court.

Standing at the top of the gatehouse tower, the *chatelaine* replies:

> Gallant, I'm not worried about your assault; / I've a castle which is very strong and well defended; / And it can't be beaten down by any [siege] engine / except by a battering ram.

Another drawing makes play with the image of the key and the lock. A courtly lady stands in front of a fashionably dressed prospective lover, holding a large chest before her, and says to him:

Friend, please feel free to open my coffer / which to you I deliver, give and offer.

The prospective lover replies:

Lady, the coffer pleases me greatly, / but the lock doesn't; / Because my key isn't big enough / to fit into the keyhole.

A third drawing continues the theme along similar lines. A finely dressed lady stands holding a shield in front of her, as a mounted lover, armed with a strangely bent lance, approaches her. He tells her:

How is it that, whatever I do, / my thrusts don't hit your shield / As they ought to do; / they're always too high or too low.

The lady replies:

My dear, it's not my fault, / but it's because your lance is drooping; / You can't hit the right spot / unless the wood is harder.

The setting is clearly a courtly one; the humour is scarcely very sophisticated, yet effective. There is clearly a parody of the 'courtly' pursuit of love and sex here. But the visual double entendres and verbal innuendos are precisely the same as those found not only in the *Debat de Mars et du Cul* but also in such texts as the *Cent Nouvelles Nouvelles* [*The Hundred New Tales*] attributed to, and told by, members of the court of Burgundy (in the 1460s), which could hardly be more 'courtly' in their origins. If there is any hint of folly in these verse quatrains, with visual images to match, it is implicit in the puzzlement of the male partners about their apparent lack of potency and virility. Perhaps, as we shall see later, charms and talismans of a sexual nature, to bring good fortune, were needed after all. This body of literature has often been deemed entirely misogynistic. Although males are held up to a certain degree of ridicule, it was of course the very existence of women, productive of adverse male perceptions as to their nature, which was deemed responsible for their discomfiture.

THE IMAGE OF THE COURT FOOL OR JESTER

The figure of that epitome of folly, the fool, or court jester, underwent some significant changes during the period of the Northern Renaissance.

As we have seen, his 'folly' could sometimes be portrayed as a form of wisdom. He is not seen as in any way mentally unbalanced or deranged. But the presence of the court fool, interestingly often tonsured, with his cap, staff and bells, also carried other connotations. He became a figure linked to the idea that lust was a species of folly. Previously associated with the Psalms of David which spoke of the fool who 'says in his heart there is no God' (Ps. 14.1, 53.1), and often depicted as a ragged or half-naked madman, the fool in his courtly incarnation gained unprecedented popularity in the fifteenth century as a symbol of unbridled sexuality, often depicted as such by engravers in scenes of 'gardens of love'. The degree of licence permitted to the court fool to speak truth to those in power and to indulge in playful insult of their often sycophantic entourages could be seen not to end there. The uninhibited nature of his behaviour could lead to a suggested association with licence of other kinds, including sexual ones. The fool's presence, in poses of an erotic and suggestive nature, brought him into the essentially courtly genre of 'love garden' scenes, where he provided a foil to offset the elegant young men and women who disport themselves there. In Master E. S.'s *Large Love Garden* engraving (*c.* 1460–70), the fool, aided and abetted by a woman, exposes his genitals, while his pipe and tabor (drum) – both sexual symbols – lie on the ground (Figure 37). In another engraving, the *Small Love Garden*, Master E. S.'s figures are seen in provocative poses, including a fool playing bagpipes, another sexual allusion, taken up also in the paintings of Hieronymus Bosch.[44] Early decks of playing cards, first introduced into Western Europe in the late 1370s, showed bagpipe-playing fools, usually carrying the lowest value in the suit, with other figures representing the hierarchy of a princely court. The even more robust themes of fools urinating, defecating or exposing their backsides graced the cards of knaves in the suits of bells, cups, acorns and shields. These were the German equivalents of the French (and modern) suits of hearts, clubs, diamonds and spades. Although many of the players of card games were from the middle and upper ranks of German society, the images on their cards came straight out of 'popular' culture, street theatre and the *Fastnachtspielen.*

It seems that sheer comic effect, rather than the more abstruse allusions proposed by some iconographers, might explain the eruption of some of these images into the world of 'high' culture. The line dividing those cultures was, in any case, a thin, often blurred and artificial one. But the representation in these engravings of fools, often in the company of young lovers, prostitutes or hideous old women, with

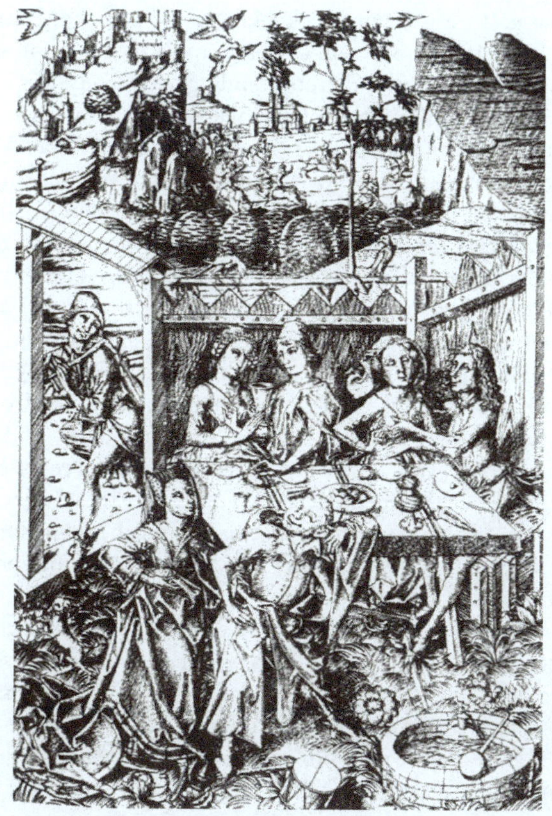

Figure 37 Master E. S.: *Large Love Garden* (Wikimedia Commons).

owls (creatures of the night and portrayed as decoys for the unwary in their sexual exploits); chalices and beakers of wine (Brant, in the *Ship of Fools*, declared that 'drinking leads to fornication')[45]; and jars, spoons and ladles (referring to male and female genitalia) *can* provide the iconographer with a feast of sexual, erotic and obscene imagery. In one engraving, by Master B+G, of *c.* 1475–80, a fool plays a lute and sticks out his tongue in the company of an old woman who holds a jar and a spoon or ladle. In fifteenth-century German, *Loffel* (ladle or spoon) could also mean 'fool'. Two prints, by Israhel van Meckenem and Master E. S., both show a *Morischkentanz* (Morris dance or *Moresca*) (Figure 29). Here the participants in this popular and evidently frenzied dance, represented as court fools, encircle a young woman who makes a suggestive gesture (in van Meckenem's work), or holds an apple (in Master E. S.'s version). She will give the apple to the 'fool' who makes the most sacrifices for her, thereby tending to parody the conventions of courtly love whereby potential lovers made vows to attract the woman's attention and undergo privations in her service. Among such parodic vows were those involving mid-winter bathing in icy water, self-mutilation or self-soiling. The winner in one farcical Nuremberg *Fastnachtspiel* was the fool who permitted his beloved to defecate on his head. In so many scenes of this kind, the court fool is there, as an accomplice colluding in, and often provoking, the sexual advances in which the other actors, both male and female, engage. The jury is still out on the meaning and purpose of such images. Were they the product of essentially moralizing tendencies pointing to the folly of licence in sexual behaviour? Or were they a secular, 'joyful and exuberant expression of sexuality',[46] and of erotic and emotional release, stemming from the context of the *Fastnachtspiel* and carnival? Whatever the case, the images produced in Southern Germany and the Rhineland between *c.* 1450 and 1500 breathed new life into older themes and poured some distinctly new wine into old bottles.

Visual satire depended upon a wide range of sources and influences, written, acted and spoken. In the literary sphere, satirical verse and prose were taken up, classicized, made more topical, relevant and perhaps even more biting by, among others, Erasmus and Brant. In the *Ship of Fools* (1494), Brant set wisdom against folly, saying of the Teaching of Wisdom: 'Who harks to Wisdom e'er and learns / And every day to wisdom turns / Eternal honour richly earns'.[47] Yet the wisdom which Brant praised was not the secular wisdom of the world, untouched by either man's conscience or God's grace. Moreover, God's wisdom, like God's purpose, was set apart from all human agency, and was accessible only through simple belief in, and reliance on, Christ. The aimless voyaging of the fools on Brant's ship means that they can never 'hasten to wisdom's shore'.[48] The *Narrenschiff* (*Ship of Fools*) intends to set sail on a futile search for the land of 'Narragonia' or 'Narragon', populated entirely by fools (*Narren*). Both Erasmus and Brant were writing satire, both making allusions to the classical past, and their work was compared by contemporary humanists to the satires and diatribes of Lucian of Samosata, Horace and Juvenal.[49] Erasmus's *Praise of Folly* has been called 'the first and in its way the finest example of a new form of Renaissance satire'.[50] The debate between wisdom and folly was now being conducted within parameters laid down by the satires of antiquity.

While Erasmus wrote in classical Latin emulating Roman satirists such as Lucian, mainly satirizing the attitudes and behaviour of the elites of his day both ecclesiastical and lay Brant, writing in German, cast his net wider and took aim at the lower orders and their follies, including the peasantry. Writing on 'Peasants' Squandering', he declared:

> My mind had almost made a slip / Since I procured no extra ship / When on to peasants' vice I skip ... / They want no jackets cheap and plain, / From Leyden, Mechlin [Malines] they export / Clothes cut away and slit and short ... / Who burger, peasant used to be, / Now he'd profess nobility.[51]

Another manifestation of folly among the peasantry was their desire to have a priest within their family. Brant complained:

> For every peasant wants a priest / Among his clan, to dodge and shirk / And play the lord, but never work; / ... They want a high-placed relative / On whom the other kin may live.[52]

The follies of all social classes were thus set out and denounced. Class prejudice, if not hatred, was certainly rife among these Renaissance elites, and the depiction of peasant and lower-order life in the visual arts displayed little sympathy with their lot. As butts of humour, disdain and derision, the common people took their place in the art of the age. Representations, however, of the Adoration of the Shepherds at the Nativity generally proved an exception to this rule as, in literature, did the ideal type of the pious and God-fearing ploughman. In Hugo van der Goes's *Portinari Altarpiece* the three Flemish shepherds, praying in wonder, awe and evident delight at the appearance of the Christ child, make an immediate claim on our sympathy and respect. And Erasmus himself, normally no friend of the common herd, wished that 'the ploughman would [be able to] sing a text of the Scripture at his plough'.[53] The figure of the humble tiller of the earth soon became a chosen vehicle for Protestant polemics urging vernacular translation of the Bible and the 'democratization' of lay piety. But the inhabitants of the contemporary countryside normally elicited little empathy in artistic or literary representation. A fantasy countryside was, however, another matter. Its inhabitants, peopling a mythical and imagined past, could be seen to embody forms of uninhibited behaviour in which the passions enjoyed a freer rein than that permitted to more 'civilized' societies. And the depiction of human passions and the fantastical, bizarre and surreal made its appearance in the work of some of the great masters of the time.

THE IMAGERY OF PASSION, FANTASY AND THE IRRATIONAL

One purpose of this book has been to explore the extent to which novelty and innovation characterized a 'Renaissance' in Northern Europe. The life of the imagination has always offered a fertile soil for the re-imagining and expression of highly charged emotion and the creation of mythical themes and invented beings, some innocuous and benign, but others sinister and malevolent. A classic image of the Renaissance, however, especially in its Italian and Italianate forms, saw its quintessence represented in and by an art of serenity, rationality, balance, harmony, beauty and 'stillness'. Raphael (d. 1520) was often regarded as the finest example of those qualities, followed by Perugino (d. 1523). They were to some extent both preceded and paralleled in Northern Europe by Memling (d. 1494), described by the art historian and critic Sir Martin Conway as 'the Perugino of the North'.[54] But, once again, it was Aby Warburg who first broke through the mould and began to concentrate on the 'images of passion and suffering' which Italian artists also derived from the literature, art and above all the sculpture, of classical antiquity.[55] In addition, he stressed the significance of what he called the 'Dionysiac' element in both Greco-Roman and Renaissance art, whereby images of violent movement and elemental energy, as well as hedonistic, intoxicated and other forms of excess, were depicted. Much of the prevailing attitude towards the arts of classical antiquity had been moulded by the views of the eighteenth-century German art historian and archaeologist J. J. Winckelmann (1717–68).[56] Winckelmann saw ancient art as possessing a 'noble simplicity and calm grandeur' which it passed on to the Renaissance. Warburg, on the contrary, while accepting that nobility and grandeur certainly characterized some examples of both classical art and its Renaissance successors, thought that the 'passionate and destructive menace' of the Dionysian could not be disregarded.[57] Warburg cited Durer's drawing of the violent *Death of Orpheus* (1494), derived from a lost original by Andrea Mantegna (1431–1506) to illustrate his argument. Subjects chosen by Mantegna and Antonio del Pollaiuolo (1433–98) often displayed the 'emotive force of gesture' rather than the 'tranquil classical ideal'.[58] Although it could be argued that the two elements – the serene and noble 'Apollonian' and the ecstatic and violent 'Dionysian' – might complement each other, Warburg was never able to fully reconcile them in either ancient or Renaissance art.

Durer, while deriving inspiration from Italian examples, brought a characteristically Northern explicit realism to his depictions of violent actions such as his engraving of nude *Men Abducting Women* (1495) or of *Cain Slaying Abel* (1511) (Figure 38). But such gestural images, in the North, were by no means all derived from antiquity. There was also a strong, indigenous current flowing from popular Northern European and Nordic folklore, legend and erotic fantasy, as well as exceptionally vivid and graphic representations and descriptions of the sufferings of Christian saints and martyrs, and of the Passion of Christ.[59] There was a Northern equivalent to the emotive power of Italian art in the depiction of what Huizinga called *'s'levens felheid'* or the 'intensity of life' by

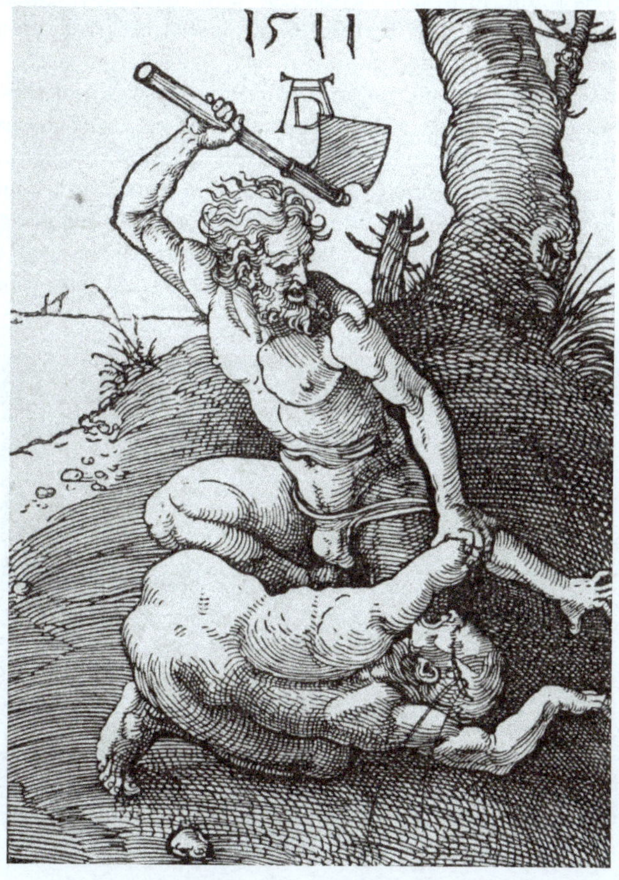

Figure 38 Albrecht Durer: *Cain Slaying Abel* (1511).
(Photo by The Print Collector/Getty Images.)

Northern artists and engravers. These tendencies reached a climax in depictions such as the image of the crucified Christ on Matthias Grunewald's (*c.* 1470–1528) *Isenheim Altarpiece* (1512–16) (Figure 39). This representation of Christ's twisted, distorted body, hideously pock-marked and punctured by scars and weals from scourging, merged a vivid, heightened realism with something approaching later German Expressionism and can still shock the spectator. Its distortions and exaggerations of reality express an inner world of turbulent emotion, rejecting any idea of harmony or beauty. There is no transfiguration or transcendence in this stark and brutal image of terrible suffering. A similar tendency is found in Martin Schongauer's (*c.* 1445–91) *Temptation of St Anthony* (1470) where the saint is tormented by grotesque demons. There is not a hint of idealization in such images, nor any attempt to render the expression of pain and suffering, physical and mental, in a stylized or classically restrained manner, as was often the case in Italian artists' depictions of the martyrdom of saints or the Crucifixion.

Representation of human passions in the visual arts could often lead artists to portray them as products of fantasy and symptoms of the irrational. The meaning of the word 'fantasy' changed over the centuries. The Old French *fantasie* (Lat: *phantasia*) meant 'illusion',

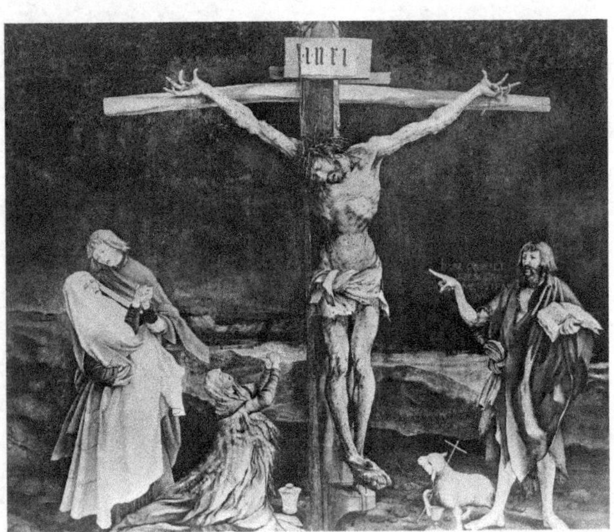

Figure 39 Matthias Grunewald: Crucifixion from Isenheim Altarpiece (Colmar): (Bettmann/Getty).

'illusory appearance' or simply 'imagination'. By the 1530s, the word had acquired a meaning closer to 'overheated' or 'inflamed imagination', and 'phantasy' came to mean 'hallucination'. The diagnosis of patients prone to fantasy and afflicted with phrenitis, that is, an inflammation of the brain, listed its symptoms as fever, frenzy and delirium. The term thus came to acquire overtones of a more sinister, if not dangerous, kind in the fifteenth and early sixteenth centuries. At that time a patient could be said to have 'incurred a wondrous disease of the phantasy' (*mirabilum fantasialem morbum incurrit*).[60] There was also a visual dimension to the 'phantastical', in which the imagination pictured images and visions to itself and began to 'fantasize' in a more modern sense. The period thus saw the creation of new mental pictures of imagined, idealized and sometimes menacing and feared worlds. Some of them made their appearance in the visual arts. The sources for those images were disparate, lying in literature, both classical and vernacular, Northern European folklore and superstition, and in popular culture. Their visual expression was increasingly found in multiple prints made from woodcuts and engraved plates, as well as on panel and wall paintings, and in the applied arts, from domestic gold and silver plate, jewellery, biscuit moulds and waffle irons, to heraldic emblems and playing cards. As we have seen, the engraved, printed image was now forming a new genre, meeting the demands of a wider market, and employing some of the greatest, as well as the less great, artistic talents of the time. Besides the fantasy subjects of painters such as Bosch, the Cranachs, Hans Baldung Grien and Holbein, a whole new body of images and imagery was emerging in mass-produced prints which both reflected and shaped the demands of their audiences.

Who, if anyone, inhabited these fantasy worlds? A secular mindset could argue that both Heaven and Hell represented fantasy worlds, peopled on the one hand by angels and saved souls, on the other by devils and damned souls. As we have seen,[61] these supernatural realms provided rich and abundant material for the visual arts. But there were other imaginative worlds which more closely resembled terrestrial reality. And they did not all take the form of Hieronymus Bosch's *Garden of Earthly Delights* (Figure 40) or the many idealized versions of Gardens of Love and Fountains of Youth. The idyllic was contrasted with the sinister and threatening. In the real world, darker forces were embodied, both imaginatively and in practice, by the personifications of evil spirits and vices, expressed at their most potent and destructive in the fear and persecution of women deemed to be witches and men who practised necromancy. The Northern Renaissance added little to the body of superstition and myth already surrounding these themes. It adapted them, and perhaps made them more immediate and threatening, in part by means of the extreme realism with which they were now depicted in the visual arts. But such fears and traumas had a very long ancestry.

THE WILD PEOPLE OF THE FOREST

One of the most common themes of fantasy stemmed from the myth of the 'wild man' and 'wild woman'. These mythical, entirely fictitious creatures of the imagination were described and depicted as feral beings covered with dense growths of their own hair or clothed in leafy foliage. Pictured as black, bear-like creatures, the original wild men, as described in twelfth-century sources, were ogre-like figures of violence and aggression. They were shown carrying a club or tree trunk which, with their enormous strength, they had uprooted. They were thought to inhabit forest and mountainous regions, set apart from all human society. Analogies for them are found in the mythology of Hellenic and Roman antiquity. The figures of Silvanus, the tree-god, or Silenus, the god of mountains and forests, often carried uprooted trees and were sometimes depicted coated and covered

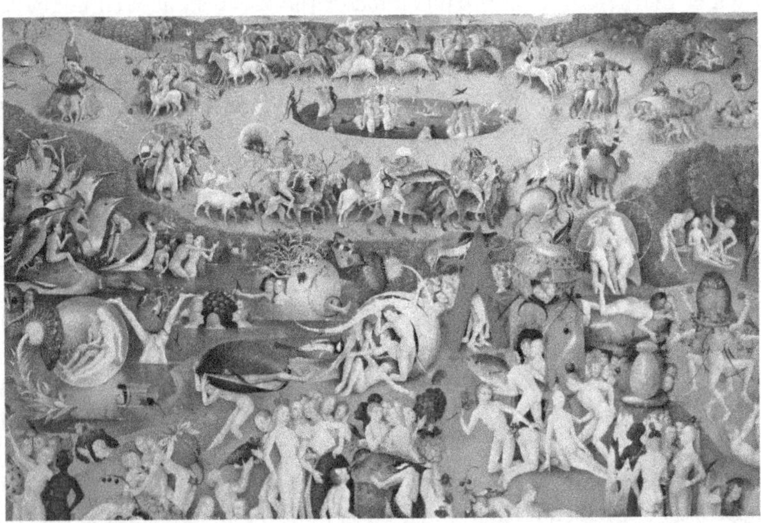

Figure 40 Hieronymus Bosch: *The Garden of Earthly Delights* (Madrid, Prado). (Photo by Joe Sohm/Visions of America/Universal Images Group/Getty Images.)

in hair. Other forest deities and demons, such as fauns, satyrs and centaurs also shared some common attributes with the wild people of the North. But Northern Europe had its own versions of the theme of the primitive, irrational, instinct-driven creature. The wild man and wild woman were manifestations and incarnations of the 'other'. They represented the forces of insanity and chaos, innately irrational and a threat to human society, especially to its children, who they were thought to abduct and cannibalize. This species of hunter-gatherers did not interact with others except for acts of procreation, expressed by their insatiable sexual appetites. They reflected the darker side of human nature, sublimating 'chaos, insanity and ungodliness'.[62] Thirteenth-century literature introduced the figure of Hellekin (or Hellequin) and his *Mesnie* (retinue), a rampaging band of wild men, erupting out of the forest to terrorize the inhabitants of the countryside, and staging tournaments in which they jousted using uprooted trees as their lances. Their violence became proverbial.

But, by the later fourteenth and early fifteenth century, a shift took place in the depiction of the wild man and, especially, of the wild woman, primarily in the woodcuts and engravings of the time. A more sympathetic attitude can be seen emerging towards them, as they were thought to live in complete harmony with nature, as free and uninhibited creatures unbound and unburdened by the conventions and constraints of human society. They began to move away from myth and into fiction. The explorations and discoveries of the fifteenth century, in Africa, the Far East and the New World, began to dispel existing notions of distant continents inhabited by monstrous creatures resembling the wild men and wild women of myth and legend. Inherent contradictions certainly remained, and the wild people never completely lost their connection with violence, aggression and unbridled sexuality. But it was tempered and lessened by the early Renaissance's re-invention of them in a far less repugnant and threatening light. The notion of the 'noble savage', living in some past Golden, or even Silver Age, may have been born at this time. A form of primitive gender equality was thought to have prevailed among them. An elegantly drawn print by Master E. S. shows a wild man and a wild woman mounted on male and female unicorns, jousting together, the man armed with a rake for a lance, the woman with a distaff. Engravings by the Housebook Master, Master E. S., Master B+G, the Master of the Playing Cards and others injected a dimension of quasi-domesticity into the mythical world of the wild people, and showed wild men, their wives and children, all clothed in their own hair or covered in leaves, living apparently carefree and contented lives. Their harmony with the natural world was expressed in what appeared to be their rapport with animals, restraining and controlling the violent impulses of their unicorn or equine mounts. A kind of woodland idyll was depicted, and the Germanic forest, so full of dark and sinister associations, became (in the folkloric imagination, at least) a little less threatening and dangerous. Although it was in the depiction of the wild woman that the most significant changes took place,[63] the character of the wild man also underwent some shifts of emphasis. In external appearance, these hirsute primeval beings retained a 'brutish' character, but some images now showed them in a more tamed and domesticated role, as fathers defending and caring for their children. Master B+G's print of *A Wild Family* (c. 1475) pictures the father in just such a role. But wild men still carried an identification with violence with them. In Durer's print of *A Wild Man Abducting a Woman* (1516), the man rides a powerful unicorn stallion, carrying the woman off forcibly, slung across him in a pose suggestive of rape. Conversely, one of Master E. S.'s prints depicts a wild woman restraining a unicorn and another shows her seated in perfect harmony with a tamed unicorn stallion.

Sources other than woodcuts and engravings suggest a similar trend. The sermons and tracts of Johann Geiler von Kayserberg, priest, humanist, preacher and educator (1445–1510) offered a new view and treatment of the wild woman. Geiler was a friend and contemporary of Sebastian Brant at Basel University and, like Brant, lived for much of his life in Strasbourg. In 1511 a series of lectures on Brant's *Ship of Fools* given by him at Strasbourg was posthumously published. His sermons became celebrated in Renaissance Germany. In one of them, he categorized the wild women of myth together with ascetic, anchorite saints, such as St Mary of Egypt, often represented – as in Memling's *Adriaan Reyns Altarpiece* (1480) – partially draped in her own hair. An even closer analogy was to be found in depictions of St Mary Magdalene, described in the thirteenth-century *Golden Legend* as a penitent anchorite in later life, living apart from society, as a penance for the sins of her alleged former life as a prostitute. A striking print of the *Magdalene in Ecstasy*, in the *Nuremberg Chronicle* (1493), by Wilhelm Pleydenwurff, represents her miraculous levitation from her desert cave, supported by angels, towards Heaven where she received celestial food every day, entirely sufficient for all her bodily and spiritual needs, in the form of angelic choir music. The extraordinary print shows her clothed entirely in her own luxuriant hair and, just as in representations of wild women, with only her hairless breasts exposed. In his tracts, Geiler von Kayserberg saw hairy wild women as akin to anchorite saints and martyrs, such as the Magdalene, claiming that the first wild people were not brutishly savage, but holy men and women, clothed in their hair or in palm leaves.

This identification with some aspects of the primitive sanctity of hermits, anchorites and recluses may have helped to render the image of the wild woman, in particular, more acceptable to a society which was placing greater and increasing emphasis on simplicity and 'primitivism'. Wild women were now largely excluded from the demonized company of other figures of fantasy who lay outside 'civilized' society. In the prints and engravings, they exuded not only erotic, sensual appeal and youthful physical beauty but also maternal care and concern for their children. It would be hard to see this as an example of the influence of contemporary ideas and ideals of bourgeois domesticity, as some have argued. It is by no means certain that these prints were produced for an exclusively 'bourgeois' audience and, in any case, the social composition of the patrician and upper burgher groups in German and Netherlandish towns included members of an urban-dwelling nobility. The *Book of Hours of Katherine of Cleves* (*c.* 1440), for instance, contained illuminations showing scenes of the Holy Family's 'bourgeois' domestic life commissioned and owned by a member of the very highest nobility of the Netherlandish and German-speaking lands. It is more likely that the 'domestication' of the wild people owed more to contemporary (and indeed older) conceptions of a better, simpler, enviably guilt-free and carefree society, exempt from the ills and evils of so-called civilization. It may also tell us something about shifts in attitudes towards women at this time, represented by their defenders such Christine de Pisan and some male humanists such Cornelius Agrippa of Nettesheim.[64] But the existence of the mythical wild people in some kind of woodland idyll, or dwelling in a fantasy countryside, evidently proved alluring to the imaginative lives of the urban inhabitants of Northern Europe. In 1545, Hans Sachs produced, in collaboration with the Nuremberg engraver Hans Schaufelein, their *Klag der wilden Holtzleut uber die ungetrewen Welt* (*The Lament of the Wild Forest Folk over the Perfidious World*). The bucolic, rustic, forest life of the 'wild' folk was compared, satirically, with that of 'civilized' society. Nature was here contrasted with culture.

THE DARKER VISION IN THE NORTHERN RENAISSANCE

Neither Erasmus nor Brant ever really considered the problem of folly as a mental illness or disability, let alone the social and other issues posed by madmen or mad women, but by the stupid and the deluded. The 'darker vision', of which mental trauma and its related afflictions were often symptoms, demands some attention. What has been called the 'night side of life' and the 'dark side of the Renaissance psyche' has received considerable recent study.[65] It has been claimed that reason itself was under attack, exemplified by a retreat from rationality into 'blind faith', advocated not only by Luther and other Protestant reformers but by more moderate thinkers. Both Kempis and Erasmus, as we have seen, stressed the deficiencies and inadequacies of reason for the understanding of the invisible God. Sincere Christian simplicity or 'Christian folly' (Erasmus) required at least a suspension of reason, for the nature of God could only be known through revelation. This emphasis on the all-powerful nature of faith led, it is argued, to the death – or at least the sleep – of reason for Christian believers. In the world of daily reality, the 'darker vision' made its presence felt in high levels of criminal behaviour, spiritual trauma and popular superstition. There were also more obviously constructed categories of profound and disturbing concern such as demonic possession, witchcraft, necromancy and some forms of satire. Above all, there was an increased concentration on the irrational nature of man. In literature and the arts, the scope for vivid, realistic and graphic description of such themes was wide and far-reaching. Each of these themes would be, and have been, a topic for a book in themselves, and some of them lie outside the chosen range of this study.

Evidence for spiritual and mental trauma, and the significance of the irrational, non-rational and supra-rational, has been put forward to counteract the common notion of the Renaissance, both Italian and Northern, as a kind of proto-Enlightenment. The idea that the period saw a universal dawning of enlightened innovation and rationality has long been discredited, although it still holds sway in the popular imagination. The creative intellects and talents of the age were by no means immune from traumas. We have at least one piece of striking evidence for the mental illness of an artist during the period. In 1480 or 1481, while returning from a visit to Cologne, the Flemish painter Hugo van der Goes (*c.* 1440–82) was taken ill.[66] In 1477–8, he had renounced his previous worldly life and entered an Augustinian convent (of the congregation of Windesheim), known as the Rood Klooster (Red Cloister), at Oudergem in the forest of Soignes, near Brussels, as a lay brother. While there he had continued to paint, he became increasingly plagued by some form of depression. His fellow-monk Gaspar Ofhuys, the house *infirmarius* (keeper of the infirmary), left a description and diagnosis of his illness, written between 1509 and 1519. Hugo's condition, Ofhuys wrote, took the form of extreme mental disturbance, marked by what appears to have been paranoia, raving, self-harm and attempted suicide. On his return from Cologne to Brussels, the prior of Hugo's convent had musical and dramatic performances played to him as a form of therapy, among other attempted cures, which secured a temporary remission. The therapy was imaginatively depicted during the nineteenth-century revival of interest in the lives of early Netherlandish artists by Emile Wauters's painting of *Hugo van der Goes Undergoing Treatment at the Roode Klooster* (1872). A distinctly deranged-looking Hugo is there shown with a choir of boys and singing men, conducted by the cantor of the house. But the historical Hugo soon relapsed and died, believing himself to be cursed as a 'son of perdition' (*filius perditionis*).[67] According to another near-contemporary, the Nuremberg physician and humanist Hieronymus Muenzer, writing in 1495, Hugo had suffered a crisis of confidence in his art, becoming unable to finish his paintings, and had lapsed into melancholy and lassitude. He felt that he could never equal the art of the Van Eycks, as displayed in the *Ghent Altarpiece*. It is notable that, although demonic possession was certainly not ruled out, these diagnoses also suggested alternative explanations, which were the product of what looks more like rational clinical analysis. Whatever the case, it was thought that Hugo had lost his reason, resulting in acute mental breakdown. Ofhuys thought that 'there is close to the brain an extremely small and tender vein ... vested with power over the imagination and fantasy' which had been ruptured.[68] Too lively an imaginative and fantasy life, it was thought, upset the balance of the mind. And the darker forces which fuelled those fantasies and traumas showed no sign of abating.

It has been argued that the period 1300–1650 was an age of a spiritual trauma, both predating and postdating the Northern Renaissance.[69] Europe's inner demons, as they have been called, lay close to the surface, emerging at times of crisis, as they have always done. Notions of demonic possession became, if anything, more prevalent, resulting in outbreaks of persecution of witches, heretics, Jews and other outsiders and outcasts.[70] The sixteenth and early seventeenth centuries witnessed such acts of persecution on a far greater scale than the fourteenth and fifteenth centuries had ever known. A darker vision of the Renaissance itself has accordingly emerged in more recent historical scholarship, put at its most extreme in such statements as:

> The vast creativity of the Renaissance, and its unrivalled talent for innovations, its instinct for beauty and intellectual adventure, are glorious blossoms rooted

in a slime stinking far worse than anything that can be identified in the earlier centuries of the Middle Ages or in more modern times.[71]

There was clearly a dark underside to the enlightened rationality claimed for the Renaissance, Northern and Southern, and the omnipresence of death,[72] coupled with an acute awareness (and suspicion) of evil forces at work, could give rise to obsessions and nightmarish visions taken up by the visual arts.

Sebastian Brant had confined his deluded fools to a ship. In the world of reality, provisions were certainly made, in more institutionalized settings, for the unsound of mind. These included relatively small-scale, localized hospices and the facilities offered to the mentally ill and their carers in places such as the town of Geel.[73] The mad, however, remained essentially marginalized by society and many, rather like the passengers and crew of the Ship of Fools, simply wandered from place to place. And it was often merely the physical symptoms of such illness, rather than the causes, which were addressed and for which attempts were made to relieve and mitigate. The creation of more centralized, large-scale establishments specifically devoted to the confinement of the mentally ill, however, belongs to a later period. It has been claimed that, with the foundation of the Hopital General in Paris (1656), 'the great threat that dawned on the horizon of the fifteenth century subsides, the disturbing powers that inhabit Bosch's paintings have lost their violence. ... Oblivion falls on the world navigated by the free slaves of the Ship of Fools'.[74] 'Disturbing powers' may well be found in the works of Hieronymus Bosch, but their exact nature, origins, purpose and form of representation have been the subject of intense art-historical controversy. Bosch (*c.* 1450–1516) is probably the most enigmatic figure among all Netherlandish artists of the fifteenth and sixteenth centuries.[75] So little is known of his life and background that his art and the influences upon it have provided a fertile field for speculation. Known as Jeroen van Aken (Aachen) 'called Bosch', he was a citizen of s'-Hertogenbosch, the Dutch town in North Brabant from which he took his name. It was undergoing something of an economic boom and surge of prosperity during his lifetime. He was a prominent member of a religious guild there, the Brotherhood of Our Lady in the church of St John, and Bosch's patrons included members of the highest nobility of the Burgundian-Habsburg lands, members of the Brotherhood of Our Lady itself, officials in the central and local administration, and wealthy burghers of the region. He was commissioned by Philip the Fair, son of Maximilian

I, to produce a *Last Judgement* (1504) and a *Temptation of St Anthony* (1505). A further high-status commission probably came from either Engelbert II of Nassau-Breda (1451–1504) or his nephew Henry III (1483–1538) in the shape of the celebrated *Garden of Earthly Delights* (*c.* 1495–1503) (Figures 40, 41). But, as far as we know, nothing in these typical and conventional acts of patronage prepared his audiences for the extraordinary inventiveness and unconventional iconography of his paintings.

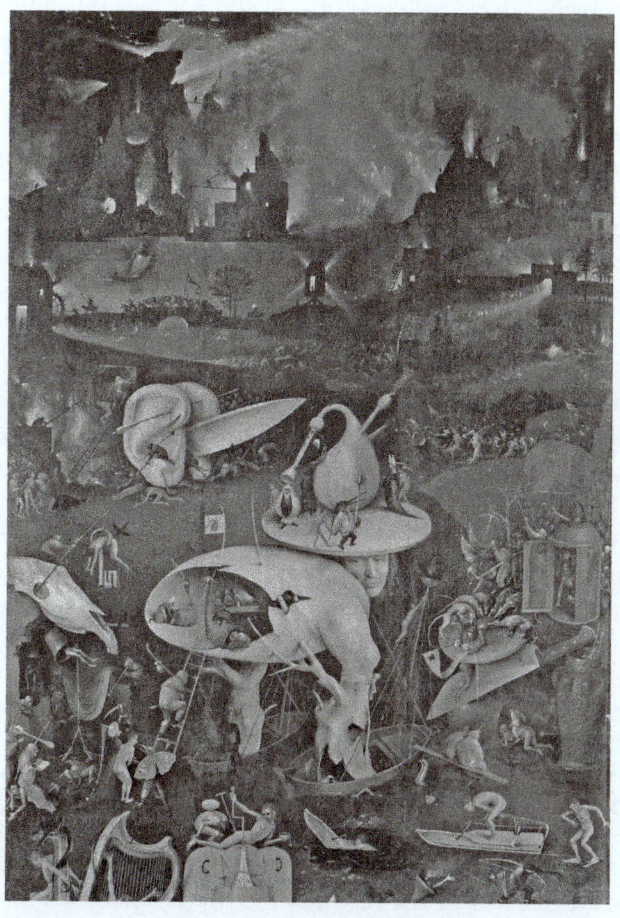

Figure 41 Hieronymus Bosch: *Garden of Earthly Delights* (detail). (Photo by Imagno/Getty Images.)

Max J. Friedlander said of Bosch: 'To paint or to draw always meant, to him to invent.'[76] Although not totally unprecedented, Bosch's paintings and drawings (and those of his many imitators) introduced novelty into Netherlandish art by their depiction of obscene, farcical and demonic motifs on a very large scale. An iconology of the absurd, the profane and the bizarre was in effect created by him. The degree of popularity that this body of themes and motifs enjoyed was exemplified by the vast array of copies and imitations of his work. By the 1530s a so-called school of painters, working mainly in Antwerp, were producing 'Boschian' images. For every known genuine work by Bosch there are at least ten or fifteen copies or close imitations. Pieter Bruegel the Elder was a major contributor to them. They served to promote Bosch's reputation among contemporaries and later commentators solely as a purveyor of 'monsters and chimeras', 'wondrous and strange fantasies', 'absurdities', 'spooks and monsters of Hell' and all kinds of highly inventive and original grotesqueries. But some early commentators leapt to his defence, arguing that he was fundamentally a God-fearing devotional painter, producing many panels and altarpieces of a thoroughly orthodox and conventionally pious nature. In *c.* 1560, the Spanish humanist, writer and art patron Felipe de Guevara (d. 1563), in his *Commentarios de la Pintura*, wrote,

> I dare to maintain that Bosch never in his life painted anything unnatural except in terms of Hell or Purgatory ... he endeavoured to find for his fantastic pictures the rarest objects, but they were always true to nature ... and [any] with a monstrosity or something else that goes beyond the confines of naturalness is a forgery or imitation, unless ... the picture represents Hell or a part of it.[77]

Quite how 'natural' some of his motifs actually were is debatable. And his use of them was not confined to scenes of Hell or Purgatory. The trials and tortures undergone by saints and martyrs also contain them, such as his *Temptation of St Anthony* scenes.

More recent study of Bosch's use of fantastical imagery has led to a wide range of both plausible and implausible interpretations. The idea that he was a member of a small heretical sect – the naturist, free-spirited Adamites – largely on the basis of the erotic nudity and sexually explicit scenes in his *Garden of Earthly Delights* (Figure 40) has been shown to be unfounded. The notion that he was a heretic of any kind was countermanded by the fact that the hyper-pious Philip II of Spain kept a number of his works in his palace-monastery of the Escorial. And the desire of ever-hopeful iconographers to seek profound psychological meaning in his more bizarre imagery has been treated with the scepticism which it probably deserves. Some early, near-contemporary commentators and critics may have pointed to a more helpful approach by speaking of this kind of painting as

> comical and macaronic (on the outside), yet mixing with such jests many things that are beautiful and extraordinary with regard to imagination as well as execution ... now and then revealing how skilful he was.[78]

The Spanish Hieronimite monk Jose de Siguenza (1544–1606) was attempting to show that Bosch painted 'man as he is on the inside' by representing the inner self in an outward form, making the individual 'realize what is inside him and ... to become ... aware of the passions and vices which keep him transformed into a beast, or rather so many beasts'. To Siguenza, Bosch's purpose was an essentially didactic and moralizing one. It was to show that even though the 'arch-fiend' (the Devil) creates 'endless fantasies and monsters ... to confuse, worry and disturb the pious soul', these can be overcome by the grace of God. To illustrate them in this way was to show that the pious soul

> cannot at all be dislodged or diverted from its goal, even though, in the imagination and to the outer and inner eye, the devil depicts that which can excite laughter or vain delight, or anger and other inordinate passions.[79]

The allusion to 'laughter or vain delight' refers back to the notion of Bosch's paintings as 'comical and macaronic'. The (macaronic) mixing of incompatible elements, animal and human; the giving of animate features and qualities to inanimate and unrelated objects, such as the Tree and Egg Man (*Hell* panel from the *Garden of Earthly Delights*); or the attribution of eyes to fields and ears to trees all point to a bizarre fusion of themes and motifs, some of which stem from verbal puns, proverbs and popular sayings of the time. His *Ship of Fools* (c. 1494–1500) and *The Stone Operation* (c. 1505–15)[80] may both have taken some of their subject matter from carnival and festival plays (Figures 42, 43). The one shows a ship full of clerical and lay fools, including a jester, the other a gullible and stupid patient ('*Lubbert Das*' or 'Stupid Das') in the hands of a rapacious surgeon-quack who removes the 'stone of folly' from his head. Bosch's strange creatures, moreover, may not be so far removed from the mass-produced sexual and scatological badges, pressed or cast from lead or tin, which proliferated, especially in the Low Countries and England, at this time.[81] Their origins and purpose have been much debated. They showed phalluses with legs and wings, vulvas transmuted

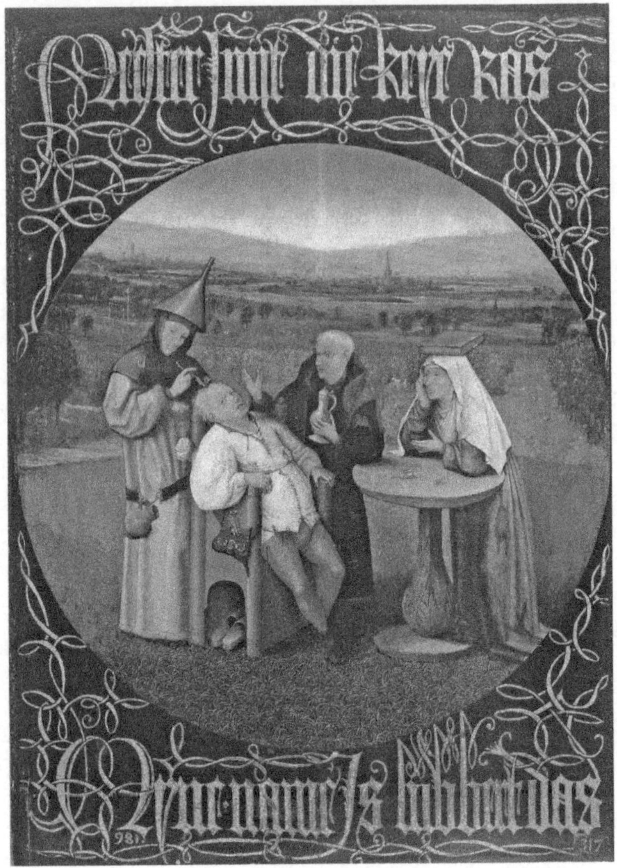

Figure 42 Hieronymus Bosch: *The Stone Operation* (Madrid, Prado).
(Photo by DeAgostini/Getty Images.)

into pilgrims' badges, or borne in procession, as statues of the Virgin Mary or a patron saint might be carried, but by walking phalluses. One interpretation sees these as apotropaic talismans, as antidotes to ward off and disarm evil spirits and forces by diverting them, as Roman *fascina* or *tintinabula* did, towards the genital icon. Another interpretation would see them as being rather like devotional pilgrims' badges, on which they were clearly directly modelled, acquired by pilgrims on visits to saints' shrines. It is possible, if unlikely, on that argument, that they might have represented souvenirs or tokens of visits to brothels, sometimes

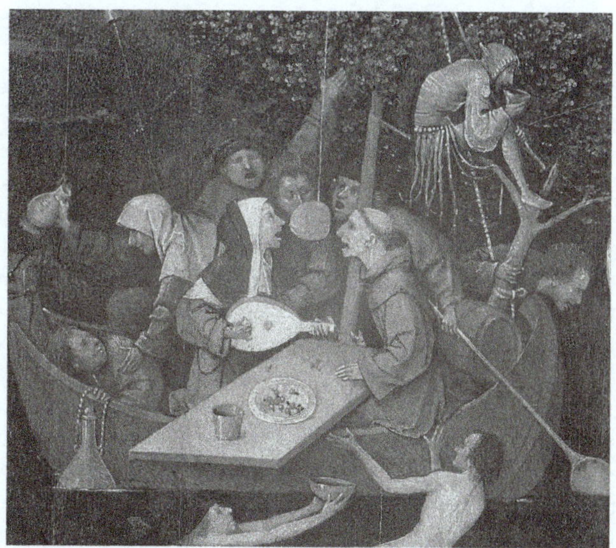

Figure 43 Hieronymus Bosch: *The Ship of Fools* (detail).
(Photo by Francis G. Mayer/Corbis/VCG/Getty Images.)

euphemistically described as 'Shrines' or 'Temples of Venus'. But they may also have served as charms or amulets to bring good luck, especially in sexual matters. A later fourteenth-century badge from the Netherlands shows a legged phallus approaching a similarly legged vulva, with the inscription 'Pintel-in'. 'Pintel' derives from Middle Low German 'pin' (penis) and 'pintel' or 'pintle' (Middle English) was its diminutive, although that is hardly apparent from the apparatus on the badge.[82] But there is surely room for an interpretation which puts more emphasis on the simple fact that such objects can evoke spontaneous laughter. Bosch's bizarre creatures, combining human heads with animal, insect or reptile body parts, though never quite so explicitly sexual, may inhabit a similar world. Again, another interpretation could see his use of such images as evidence of a robust, earthy, often anal and excremental sense of humour, also found in the carnival plays and *Fastnachtspielen*, which were simply meant to elicit laughter, whether they were the work of the devil or, more plausibly, simply the fertile human imagination.

Nor were the high-status Burgundian courtiers who contributed to the *Cent Nouvelles*, with its satirical, mocking tales of both clerical and lay sexual misadventure, its bawdy (and entertaining) allusions full of double entendre and sexual metaphor, unfamiliar with such images. The hundred 'new' *nouvelles* (*novellas*), or tales, were intended to act as a supplement to Boccaccio's *Decameron* (*c.* 1349–53), but surpassed it in their broader, more explicit, sexual humour. And the fact that Bosch's *Garden of Earthly Delights* was seen in the early sixteenth century in the Nassau family palace on the Coudenberg in Brussels, at the very centre of Burgundian-Habsburg power, must raise questions about the nature of high-status patronage and its motives. The Book of Hours of Engelbert II of Nassau (made in Ghent, *c.* 1470–90) contains an image of such *drolleries* as a helmeted, jousting lion, mounted on a unicorn, with a monkey riding pillion. Many other manuscripts feature border decorations (as they had done in the past) which include grotesque figures and beasts, and other clearly humorous fusions of the human and the animal. What had previously occupied the margins of written texts now began to occupy the centre stage. These images were intended to distract and divert. But there is sometimes little time for the study of fun as a category in the repertoire of either art historians or historians. And it was, after all, in the same Nassau family's Brussels palace that a huge

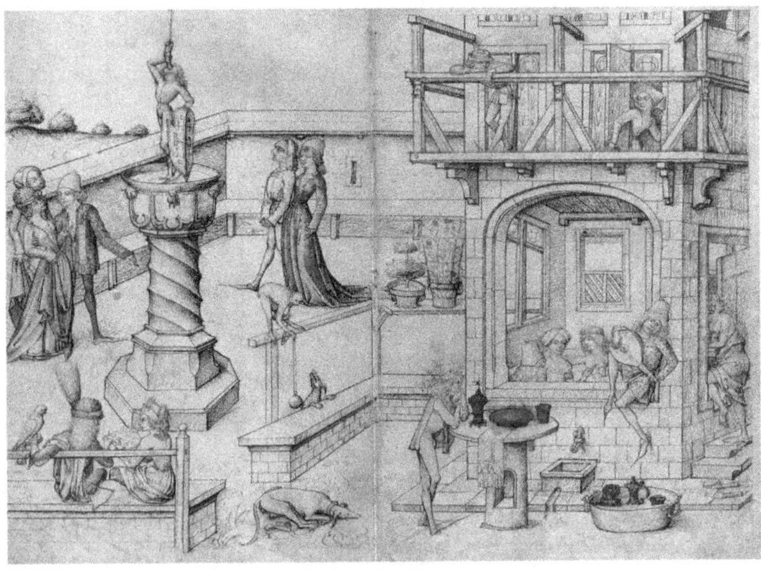

Figure 44 Master of the Housebook (attrib.): *A Bathhouse* (*c.* 1480): (Schloss Wolfegg).

198

bed was kept, into which drunken and incapable guests, experiencing the effects of legendary (but real) Burgundian hospitality, were thrown. The pursuit of earthly delights, reminiscent of the Land of Cockaigne, whatever its causes and consequences, did not exist only in fantastical images allegedly depicting man's sinfulness, but – in reality – in the bathhouses, brothels and taverns of every Northern European town (Figures 44, 20). The engravers, such as the Housebook Master and Master E. S., following the example of manuscript illuminators, appear to have rendered such scenes, despite the moralizing texts which they often illustrated, with a certain amount of relish. The po-faced godly were perhaps far less interesting to them than the communal mixed bathers and frequenters of houses of ill repute. But the latter had, perforce, often to adopt the features of the former. The sins of lust-driven folly and folly-driven lust had always to be expiated.

Conclusion

'This I drew, using a mirror; it is my own likeness, in the year 1484, when I was still a child.'[1] So wrote Albrecht Durer at the head of his supremely confident and already highly skilled early self-portrait, drawn when he was thirteen (Figure 45). Durer's words expressed one of the fundamental characteristics of the Renaissance in Northern Europe: the holding up of a mirror, both physically and metaphorically, to life and death in all its manifold forms. Sometimes that mirror was an intentionally distorting one, as illusionistic techniques became part of the artist's normal repertoire. The supreme example of the use of a mirror image in Western art emerged from the city of Bruges in 1434. Jan van Eyck had introduced a circular convex mirror into his double portrait of Giovanni Arnolfini and his wife into which we are invited to look[2] (Figure 19). In it we can see two figures representing the witnesses and spectators of the scene, including the artist and, therefore, ourselves. We are left in no doubt that we are in the presence not only of the Arnolfinis but also of Jan himself. The calligraphically flamboyant inscription painted on the rear wall of the room could not be clearer: 'Jan van Eyck was here. 1434' ('*Johannes de Eyck fuit hic. 1434*'). In the visual arts of the time, contemporaries could see themselves, either in their own portraits, as they were in life, or through identification with the participants in the dramas and scenarios now so realistically rendered by artists, sculptors and printmakers. The so-called Eyckian revolution meant that the face of Western art, in more senses than one, was changed for ever – or at least until the coming of impressionism and its non-representational successors in the twentieth century. Much of this art had a transcendental content and dimension. But it nonetheless depicted recognizable human beings, animals, objects, landscapes, townscapes and seascapes with a degree of apparent realism and verisimilitude which had rarely been seen since the fall of the Roman Empire in the West.

It has been said that in the visual arts of the Northern Renaissance 'curiosity about the individual and the natural world was *more* than a

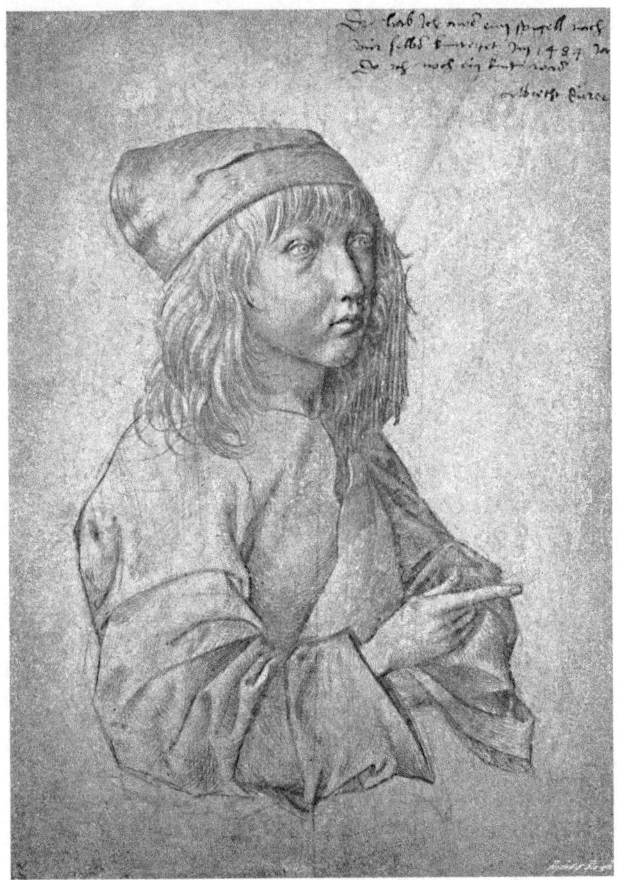

Figure 45 Albrecht Durer: *Self-Portrait at the Age of 13* (1484) (Vienna).
(Photo by Print Collector/Getty Images.)

renewed dialogue with antiquity' [emphasis mine].[3] The present book has largely endorsed that view and attempted to trace it beyond the visual arts. 'Dialogue with antiquity' there certainly was, but there was a great deal more in Northern European art and culture than, as was more prominently the case in Italy, the retrieval, reception and reshaping of the classical Hellenic and Roman tradition. The Renaissance was not an exclusively Italian phenomenon. The idea that there was an essentially 'Northern' Renaissance was first mooted in the late nineteenth century. The term itself was first used in 1905, as *La Renaissance Septentrionale*

(*The Northern Renaissance*). Its outstanding characteristic was deemed to be a new concept and rendering of pictorial space, in which closely observed and realistic depiction was paramount. But the Northern Renaissance embraced many cultural forms. They can be summed up as: the rise of representational realism, however illusionistically produced; the evolution of the 'likeness', that is the portrait and self-portrait; the close observation of the natural world; the discovery, introduction and exploitation of new techniques of disseminating ideas and images; the creation and evolution of musical forms which has led to their being described as an *ars nova* ('new art'); and the vivid immediacy with which scenes and events were both described in literature and depicted in the visual arts. All of these 'Renaissance' characteristics were, or became, present in Northern Europe between the later fourteenth and mid-sixteenth centuries. And there was, running in parallel – and often intersecting – with these tendencies, what might be called a 'Christian Renaissance', which was far less visible in Italy. The problems of the contemporary institutional Church led to the emergence of many forms of personal religion. These were often expressed by tendencies towards devotional individualism, which could be seen as analogous to more secular forms of self-awareness and self-representation. Foremost among them, in Northern Europe, was the 'new' or 'modern' devotion (*devotio moderna*) originating in the Netherlands, but soon spreading more widely. This was not an exclusively clerical tendency, for lay people were also closely involved in it, and influenced by it. 'Christian humanism' also had its converts and exponents, seeking to humanize the Christian story and to apply and adapt the lessons of Italian humanistic scholarship to a Northern setting. And the desire for a simpler, more sincere, more Christo-centric form of piety and religious observance contributed a large share to the first stirrings of the Protestant Reformation.

The differences between Northern and Italian civilization during the Renaissance can of course be overdrawn and exaggerated. The notion, for example, that the 'Renaissance in Northern Europe' was essentially an Italian import or transplant held sway for a long time. So did the idea that the North saw a period of cultural decadence and decay before its reception of Italian humanism and the arts, followed by the onset of the Protestant Reformation which changed the world for ever. But differences there certainly were between Italy and the North, in religious observance and, not least, in the structures and preoccupations of the intellectual world. The rise and development of humanism was certainly an important element in both Italy and the North. Yet, even there, there were cultural and institutional differences. Universities in Northern Europe had always tended to privilege the study of theology and canon law over the liberal arts, civil law and medicine. This began to change at this time, but the collegiate Northern European universities (most of them new foundations) that introduced the critical techniques of humanist scholarship applied them as much to the Bible and other sacred writings as to the works of pagan and pre-Christian authors. The skills of rhetoric and persuasion were taught, as they were in Italy, but the social range of the student population in the North was, it seems, wider than that in Italian universities. Young nobles and members of the gentry, as well as commoners of humble origin, were instructed in the skills thought desirable to govern and administer both Church and state. The education of Northern aristocracies in the Renaissance was well provided for, and it produced a number of nobly born and gentlemen thinkers, writers and scholars. Humanism in the North, unlike Italy, was also closely bound up with movements towards the reform and reformation of the Church. Erasmus was perhaps the archetypal Christian humanist, representative of a type of clerical intellectual no longer caught, as he himself claimed, in the traps and snares of scholasticism. Novelty and innovation began to characterize Northern universities, both long-standing and newly created. Although Italy had, for example, led the way in the reception and dissemination in the West of Greek studies, as worthy of study in their own right, the movement was soon taken up in the North. It did not lag far behind the Italians in that respect.

In the dissemination of knowledge and ideas, a new medium of transmission – printing with movable type – played a significant part. The precise nature and extent of that part has been the subject of controversy. Gutenberg's mid-fifteenth-century invention was an entirely Northern European phenomenon, although it was soon to have a very marked effect on Europe as a whole, not least upon Italy. The volume of written material in circulation between 1450 and 1530 expanded to an unprecedented degree. The increased availability of the printed written word, in vernacular as well as classical languages, could hardly have been without effect in a society in which levels of literacy, especially among lay people, were rising. Without printing, Renaissance humanism, Catholic reform movements and the Protestant Reformation might have taken very different forms. And the development of techniques for the multiple reproduction of images on paper also created new artistic forms – the woodcut, the engraving and the etching. Printmakers now found a place besides painters as respected creative artists supplying their products to an expanding market.

That market, as did that for the painted and sculpted image, demanded both religious and secular representations. A substantial increase in the availability of devotional imagery was one product of the mass production of relatively cheap woodcuts and engravings. It added to an existing abundance of religious images which one great cultural historian – Johan Huizinga – thought had reached a saturation point. But the worldly and profane was also well represented. The independent landscape, for example, was a creation of this period. Much of the secular literature and drama of the time was satirical and keen to point to the folly of mankind. Debates about wisdom and folly were commonplace. Works such as Erasmus's *Praise of Folly* and Sebastian Brant's *Ship of Fools*, as well as more 'popular' creations such as the Shrovetide and carnival plays (*Fastnachtspielen*) of the German and Netherlandish towns, offered plenty of opportunities for lively and robustly profane ideas and for their dramatic performance. They also provided themes for artists and engravers. There was a direct link connecting Hieronymus Bosch (d. 1516) with Pieter Bruegel the Elder (d. 1569) giving rise to a new genre of Netherlandish and German painting. And there was a darker side to the Northern Renaissance. This expressed itself both in 'real' life and in the arts and literature. It saw the production of the most influential manual of witchcraft prosecution – the *Malleus maleficarum* or *Hammer of Witches* (1487) – and the nightmarish visions of Hell now rendered so vividly and realistically in the visual arts. But representations of man's natural state tended, in some quarters, to change over the period from an emphasis on the brutishness of 'primitive' people and their lives to a perception that their simplicity gave them an advantage over 'civilized' beings. The idea of the noble savage and the Golden Age had its Northern European versions. The mythical satyrs and fauns of antiquity, celebrated by the Italian Renaissance, had their Northern equivalents in the mythical wild men and wild women of the Germanic forests. And the discoveries of 'primitive' peoples in Africa, India and the New World were to give rise to visions of the 'other' based more on observed and reported reality than, as previously, on fantasy.

The Northern Renaissance, and its forms of life, art and thought, left a legacy to succeeding ages. What has been called 'the unflinching realism of early Flemish painting'[4] made a profound impression on subsequent generations of artists, not least upon the British Pre-Raphaelites, the German Guild of St Luke and the Nazarenes. Many of the works of Dante Gabriel Rossetti, Holman Hunt and Ford Madox Brown owed as much to the Netherlandish 'Primitives' as to the Italians who preceded

Raphael[5] (Figures 46, 14). William Morris adopted Jan van Eyck's motto and incorporated it into some of his designs for the furnishing of his own house. Van Eyck's *Arnolfini* panel has exerted its enigmatic appeal over both artists and the viewing public since its acquisition by the London National Gallery in 1842. The personality and works of Albrecht Durer have played a similarly significant role, resting in part upon a constructed legacy devised in his own time and subsequently developed, expressive of self-cultivation and of both civic (Nuremberg) and national (German) identity. In the world of thought, the influence of Erasmus on the

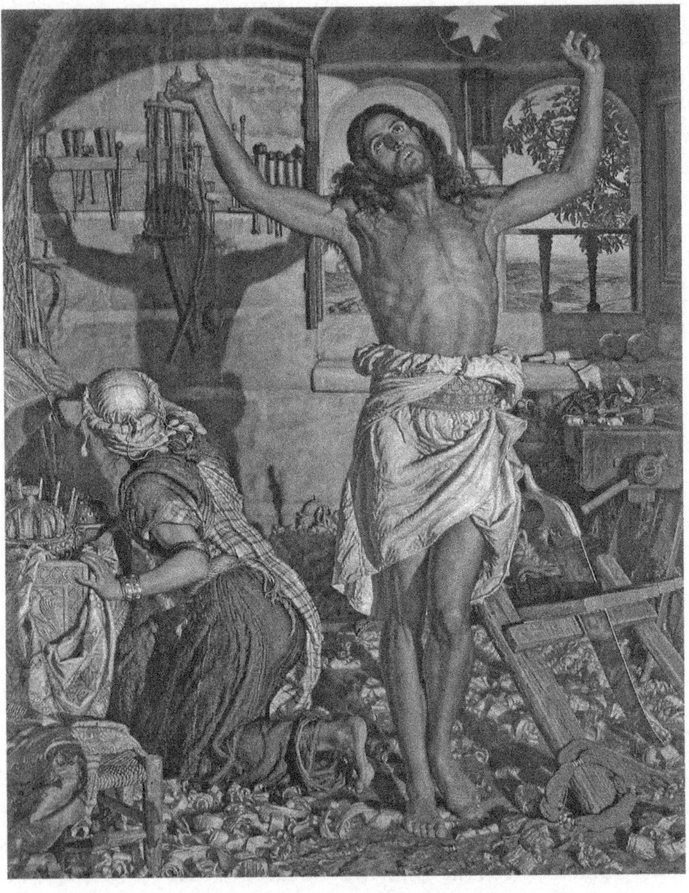

Figure 46 Holman Hunt: *The Shadow of Death* (Manchester). (Photo by Picturenow/Universal Images Group/Getty Images.)

community of scholars and the Republic of Letters has been marked. The introduction and evolution of classical studies, so prominent a feature of educated Europeans in the past, owed much to Northern Renaissance initiatives and innovations. Perhaps most significant of all was the invention and development of the printing press which, arguably, has played a truly transformative role in Western culture.

Durer was a master of the printed image. His engraving and etching techniques brought the print to its highest levels of refinement and expressiveness. He was also, like his Netherlandish precursors, a consummate portraitist, and created some of the earliest independent self-portraits in Western art. Five self-portraits survive, including one remarkably frank, if not alarming, example of him completely in the

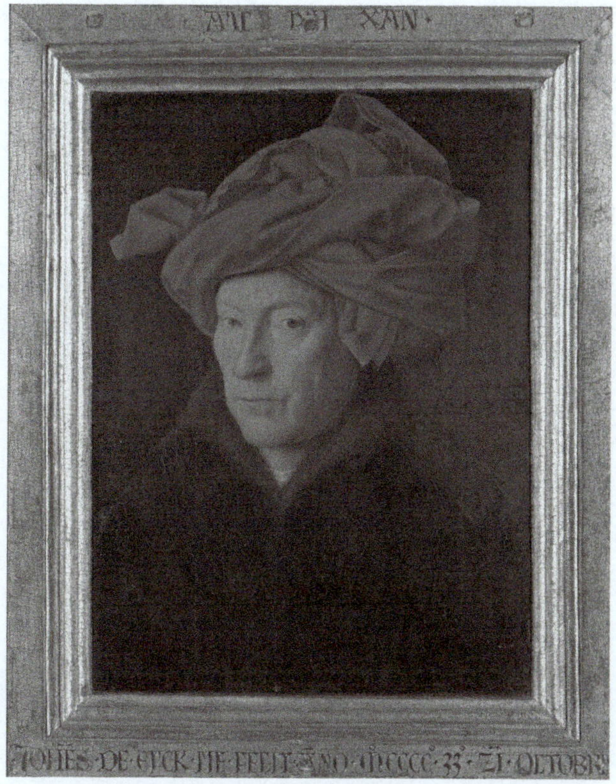

Figure 47 Jan van Eyck: *Portrait of a Man (Self-Portrait?)* (London, NG). (Photo by VCG Wilson/Corbis/Getty Images.)

nude. On the (fashionably clothed) painted image of himself aged twenty-two, in 1493, he inscribed the words 'Things with me fare as ordained from above'[6] (Figure 13). Resignation to God's will and acceptance of life's realities, whatever they might bring, was a profession of faith by a Renaissance artist living in an essentially Christian world. The last word can perhaps be left to Jan van Eyck. A realistic sense of self-awareness could, in his case, go hand in hand with the striking veracity and realism of his portraiture. His punning motto 'Als ik kan' ('As well as I [Eyck] can') is inscribed on the frame of his suggested self-portrait, dated 1433[7] (Figure 47). The phrase may be derived from a Flemish proverb: 'As well as I can, but not as I would wish.' The realistic appraisal of possibilities, the implied aspiration to do even better and the acknowledgement of inevitable limitations were perhaps hallmarks of Northern Renaissance self-awareness, self-representation and self-knowledge.

Notes

INTRODUCTION

1 Some recent art-historical opinion has inclined in this direction. See, for example, J. Chipps Smith, *The Northern Renaissance. Art and Ideas* (New York and London, 2004). The chronological span of the Northern Renaissance is, however, there extended to *c.* 1580.
2 *The Guardian*, 24 March 1992.
3 Neil McGregor, *Pisanello: Painter to the Renaissance Court*, ed. L. Syson and D. Gordon (London, 2001), p. 2.
4 This, and the following figures, is set out in J. de Vries, *European Urbanization, 1500-1800* (New York, 1984), pp. 125–40.

CHAPTER 1

1 Quoted in E. H. Gombrich, *Aby Warburg: An Intellectual Biography* (London, 1970), p. 137.
2 G. Vasari, *The Lives of the Artists*, trans. J. C. and P. Bondanella (Oxford, 2018), pp. 5–6.
3 J. Huizinga, *The Waning of the Middle Ages*, trans. F. Hopman (London, 1996), p. ix.
4 For a discussion of conflicting views, see H. Wijsman, 'Northern Renaissance? Burgundy and Netherlandish Art in Fifteenth-Century Europe', in *Perceptions of Continuity and Discontinuity in Europe, c. 1300-c. 1500*, ed. A. Lee, P. Peporte and H. Schnitker (Leiden, 2010), pp. 269–88.
5 E. L. Eisenstein, *The Printing Revolution in Early Modern Europe* (2nd edn, Cambridge, 2013), pp. 127–8.
6 Eisenstein, *Printing Revolution*, p. 127.

7 In 1974, discussing religious and spiritual issues, W. J. Bouwsma was of
   the opinion that 'the time has come to … abandon the traditional contrast
   between Italy and the North, which seems … to have been in some measure
   the result of a failure to get beneath surface differences'. See W. J. Bouwsma,
   'Renaissance and Reformation', in *A Usable Past: Essays in European Cultural
   History* (Bekeley, Los Angeles, and Oxford, 1990), p. 233.

8 G. Leff, *The Dissolution of the Medieval Outlook: An Essay on Intellectual
   and Spiritual Change in the Fourteenth Century* (New York, 1976), p. 147.

9 E. H. Gombrich, *In Search of Cultural History* (London, 1969), p. 34.

10 Gombrich, *Aby Warburg*, p. 313.

11 Leff, *Dissolution*, p. 4.

12 See J. B. Bullen, *The Myth of the Renaissance in Nineteenth-Century Writings*
   (Oxford, 1994), p. 59.

13 See Bullen, *The Myth of the Renaissance*, pp. 59–60.

14 J. Huizinga, 'The Problem of the Renaissance', in *Men and Ideas: History, the
   Middle Ages, the Renaissance*, trans. J. S. Holmes and H. van Marle (London,
   1960), pp. 243, 252.

15 H. de Balzac, *Le Bal de Sceaux* in *Oeuvres Completes de H. de Balzac*, i (Paris,
   1855), p. 105.

16 Quoted in Bullen, *The Myth of the Renaissance*, p. 139.

17 Huizinga, 'Problem of the Renaissance', p. 271.

18 See L. Courajod, *Lecons professes a l'Ecole du Louvre (1887–1896)*, ed.
   H. Lemonnier and A. Michel, 3 vols (Paris, 1899, 1901, 1903) and H. Fierens-
   Gevaert, *Etudes sur l'Art Flamand. La Renaissance Septentrionale et les
   premiers maitres des Flandres* (Brussels, 1905).

19 See Huizinga, 'Problem of the Renaissance', p. 265.

20 Fierens-Gevaert, *Etudes sur l'Art Flamand*, p. 25.

21 Quoted in Gombrich, *Aby Warburg*, p. 117: 'dabei kommt die Religion und
   Kunst schlecht, die Familie aber sehr gut ab'.

22 Quoted in Gombrich, *Aby Warburg*, p. 137.

23 Gombrich, *Aby Warburg*, p. 27.

24 E. B. Tylor, *Primitive Culture: Researches into the Development of Mythology,
   Philosophy, Religion, Language, Art and Custom*, 2 vols (London, 1871), p. 1.

25 See below, pp. 107–8, 182–5.

26 For an assessment of Huizinga's place in historical writing and his use
   of evidence from the visual arts see F. Haskell, *History and Its Images*
   (New Haven/London, 1993), pp. 431–95 ('Huizinga and the "Flemish
   Renaissance"').

27 For a detailed account, see L. Dearn, 'Flemish v. Netherlandish: A Discourse
   of Nationalism', *Renaissance Quarterly*, 51:1 (1998), pp. 1–33; also S.
   Sulzberger, *La rehabilitation des primitifs flamands, 1802–67* (Brussels, 1961).

28 Huizinga, 'Problem of the Renaissance', p. 263.

29 See the summary of his lectures in *Jaarboek van de Litterarische Faculteitsvereeniging te Groningen, 1907–8*, p. 14.

30 See below, pp. 94–97.

31 J. Huizinga, *Homo Ludens* (London, 1970), p. 206.

32 Quoted in W. Krul, 'In the Mirror of Van Eyck: Johan Huizinga's *Autumn of the Middle Ages*', *Journal of Medieval and Renaissance Studies*, 27:3 (1997), p. 362.

33 P. Verlaine, *Sagesse*, Poem IX.

34 J. Huizinga, *Herfsttij der Middeleeuwen*, ed. A. van der Lem (Amsterdam, 1997), p. 10. A blood-red sky also featured in Edvard Munch's famous Symbolist painting *The Scream*.

35 Verlaine, *Sagesse*, Poem VII.

36 Quoted in J.-K. Huysmans, *Against Nature (A Rebours)*, trans. R. Baldick (London, 2003), Introduction (by P. McGuiness), p. 12.

37 Huysmans, *Against Nature*, p. 30.

38 See below, pp. 183–5.

39 See below, pp. 159–72.

40 See below, pp. 151–2, 157.

41 M. Bass, *Jan Gossart and the Invention of Netherlandish Antiquity* (Princeton, 2016), p. 2.

42 See below, pp. 98–103.

43 See, for a good example, J. Chipps Smith, *The Northern Renaissance: Art and Ideas* (New York and London, 2004). His periodization extends, however, to *c.* 1580.

CHAPTER 2

1 J.-K. Huysmans, *The Damned (La-Bas)*, trans. T. Hale (London, 2001), p. 34.

2 M. Levy, *Early Renaissance* (London, 1991), pp. 33–4.

3 J. R. Hale, *The Civilisations of Europe in the Renaissance* (London, 1995), p. 215.

4 See B. Nauert, 'The Clash of Humanists and Scholastics: An Approach to Pre-reformation Controversies', *Sixteenth-Century Journal*, 4 (1973), pp. 1–18.

5 See E. Panofsky, *Gothic Architecture and Scholasticism* (London, 2005), esp. pp. 5–8, 25–30.

6 See Leff, 'Conclusion', *Dissolution*, pp. 144–7.

7 Leff, *Dissolution*, p. 92.

8 See below, pp. 118–20, 135, 136.

9 Krul, 'In the Mirror of Van Eyck', p. 354.

10 See below, pp. 121–2, 123–4.

11 J. Malpas, *Realism* (London, 1997), p. 7.

12 G. Braque, *Illustrated Notebooks, 1917–1955* (New York, 1971), p. 31.

13 Braque, *Nord-Sud* (1917), p. 4.

14 See below, pp. 156–7, 173–6.

15 See W. Sauerlander, 'Die Naumburger Stiftfiguren: Ruckblick und Fragen', in *Die Zeit der Staufer*, ed. R. Hausherr and C. Vaterlein (Stuttgart, 1997), vol. 5 (Suppl.), pp. 169–245.

16 A. Martindale, *Heroes, Ancestors, Relatives and the Birth of the Portrait* (The Hague, 1988), p. 19.

17 For a comprehensive survey of the origins and development of the portrait at this time, see L. Campbell, *Renaissance Portraits: European Portrait-Painting in the 14ᵗʰ, 15ᵗʰ and 16ᵗʰ Centuries* (New Haven and London, 1990).

18 For a recent, lavishly illustrated account of the essentially personal nature of Books of Hours, see E. Duffy, *Marking the Hours: English People and Their Prayers, 1240–1570* (New Haven and London, 2004), esp. Chapter 2. For the More family group portrait, see pp. 57–8 and Pl. 43.

19 Martindale, *Heroes, Heroes, Ancestors, Relatives and the Birth of the Portrait*, p. 20.

20 See below, pp. 62–3.

21 See H. Langdon, *Holbein* (London, 1993), p. 5.

22 T. Kempis, *The Imitation of Christ*, ed. and trans. R. Jeffery and M. von Habsburg (London, 2013), p. 105.

23 Langdon, *Holbein*, p. 5.

24 See below, pp. 128–9.

25 See below, pp. 129–31.

26 See A. Schultz, 'Der Weisskunig', *Jahrbuch der kunsthistorischen Sammlungen des allerhochsten Kaiserhauses*, 6 (1888), p. 66. For Maximilian's cult of commemoration and memory (*Gedachtnis*), see J. D. Muller, *Gedechtnus: Literatur und Hofgeseelschaft um Maximilian I* (Munich, 1982).

27 C. S. Wood, *Albrecht Altdorfer and the Origins of Landscape* (London, 2014), p. 14.

28 A. Durer, *Schriftlicher Nachlass*, ed. H. Rupprich, 3 vols (Berlin, 1956–69), 2, p. 100; 3, p. 295.

29 Wood, *Altdorfer*, p. 74.

30 See below, pp. 185–9.

31 See below, pp. 201, 208.

32 See below, pp. 154–7.

CHAPTER 3

1 See above, pp. 43–4, 54–5.

2 See below, pp. 82, 94–6, 109–10.

3 *Concise Encyclopedia of the Italian Renaissance*, ed. J. R. Hale (Oxford, 1981), p. 171.

4 N. Mann, 'The Origins of Humanism', in *The Cambridge Companion to Humanism*, ed. J. Kraye (Cambridge, 1996), p. 2.

5 See below, pp. 93–6.

6 A. Cobban, 'The Role of Colleges in the Medieval Universities of Northern Europe, with special reference to England and France', *BJRL*, 71:1 (1989), p. 70.

7 R. Walsh, 'The Coming of Humanism to the Low Countries: Some Italian Influences at the Court of Charles the Bold', *Humanistica Lovaniensia. Journal of Neo-Latin Studies*, xxv (1976), p. 162.

8 Quoted in J. H. Hexter, 'The Education of the Aristocracy in the Renaissance', *Journal of Modern History*, 22:1 (1950), p. 14 where *'thioise'* is rendered as 'German'.

9 Hexter, 'Education of the Aristocracy', p. 14.

10 See P. S, Allen, *The Age of Erasmus* (Oxford, 1914), pp. 14 and 13–20 for a biography of Agricola.

11 Mann, 'Origins of Humanism', p. 16.

12 E. Nuti, 'Reconsidering Renaissance Greek Grammars through the Case of Chrysoloras's *Erotemata*', *Greek, Roman and Byzantine Studies*, 52 (2012), p. 262.

13 J. Huizinga, *Erasmus and the Age of Reformation*, trans. F. Hopman (1st edn, New York, 1924; repr. 1957), p. 35.

14 A. Hiatt, *The Making of Medieval Forgeries* (Toronto, 2004), p. 156.

15 *The Catholic Concordance*, ed. P. E. Sigmund (Cambridge, 1991), Bk III, Ch. II, p. 217.

16 Leff, *Dissolution*, p. 21.

17 Huizinga, *Erasmus*, p. 41.

18 See below, pp. 97, 159–60, 165–6.

19 *Epistles of Erasmus*, ed. F. M. Nichols, 3 vols (New York, 1962), iii, p. 71.

20 See C. Celenza, 'Renaissance Humanism and the New Testament: Lorenzo Valla's Annotations to the Vulgate', *Journal of Medieval and Renaissance Studies*, 24 (1994), pp. 33–52.

21 See below, pp. 116–17, 124.

22 Huizinga, *Erasmus*, pp. 103, 110.

23 See below, pp. 123–4, 127–8.

24 Erasmus, *Praise of Folly*, trans. B. Radice, ed. A. H. T. Levi (London, 1971), p. 150.

25 *Praise of Folly*, Introduction, pp. viii–ix.

26 Bass, *Jan Gossart and the Invention of Netherlandish Antiquity*, p. 2.

27 Bass, *Jan Gossart and the Invention of Netherlandish Antiquity*, p. 2.

28 See below, pp. 186–8, 199.

29 Bass, *Jan Gossart and the Invention of Netherlandish Antiquity*, p. 45.

30 Bass, *Jan Gossart and the Invention of Netherlandish Antiquity*, p. 40.

31 See also below, p. 90.

32 C. H. Clough, 'The Relations between the English and Urbino Courts, 1474–1508', *Studies in the Renaissance*, 14 (1967), p. 203.

33 Clough, 'The Relations between the English and Urbino Courts', pp. 214–5.

34 A. P. Darr, *New Oxford DNB* (2008) under 'Torrigiano' and 'The Sculpture of Torrigiano: Westminster Abbey Tombs', *The Connoisseur*, 200 (1979), pp. 177–84.

35 R. Weiss, 'The Castle of Gaillon in 1509–10', *JWCI*, 16 (1953), p. 1.

36 See also below pp. 106–7, 171–2.

37 Gombrich, *Aby Warburg*, p. 181.

38 A. Warburg, 'Durer and Italian Antiquity', in *The Renewal of Pagan Antiquity: Contributions to the Cultural History of the European Renaissance*, ed. K. W. Forster, trans. D. Britt (Los Angeles, 1999), p. 556.

39 Quoted in D. van Maelsaeke, 'Durer and Leonardo: A Comparative Study', *Theoria: A Journal of Social and Political Theory*, 33 (1969), p. 48.

40 Warburg, 'Durer and Italian Antiquity', p. 558.

41 See also below, p. 182.

42 See below, pp. 182–4.

CHAPTER 4

1 Quoted in V. Reinsburg, '*Liturgy and the Laity in Late Medieval and Reformation France*', *Sixteenth-Century Journal*, 23 (1992), p. 545.

2 See N. L. Brann, *The Abbot Trithemius (1462–1516): The Renaissance of Monastic Humanism* (Leiden, 1981).

3 The problem of the relationship between private devotion and public worship is discussed, in relation to the ownership and use of Books of Hours by the laity, in E. Duffy, 'Devotional Isolation?', *Marking the Hours*, Chap. 3, pp. 53–64.

4 *Antequam essent clerici* in *Three Royalsi Tracts*, ed. R. W. Dyson (Bristol, 1999), p. 4. My translation.

5 The two demands – personal devotion and collective worship – are not seen to be in any way incompatible by Duffy, *Marking the Hours*, pp. 56–60. Devotional 'idiosyncracy and individualism' are, on this argument, therefore rejected (p. 59). For Netherlandish vernacular translations of some of the 'Hours' See below, pp. 127, 133–4.

6 See J. van Engen, 'Multiple Options: The World of the Fifteenth-Century Church', *Church History,* 77:2 (2008), pp. 257–84 for a good introduction to the range of beliefs, styles and observances within the Church.

7 R. R. Post, *The Modern Devotion* (Leiden, 1968), p. 680.

8 See J. van Engen, *Sisters and Brothers of the Common Life* (Philadelphia, 2008) and *Devotio Moderna: Basic Writings* (New York, 1988).

9 For a recent survey of this important period in the history of music, see R. Strohm, *The Rise of European Music, 1380–1500* (Cambridge, 2008).

10 For an excellent study of musical life and culture in one city, see R. Strohm, *Music in Late Medieval Bruges* (Oxford, 1990).

11 R. van Dijk, 'Het Kapittel van Windesheim', in *Windesheim, 1395–1995: Kloosters, teksten, invloeden …,* ed, A. J. Hendrikmann et al. (Nijmegen, 1996), p. 5.

12 JRL, Incunable 19648.2: *Gemmula vocabulorum cum additio* under '*devotio*', '*devotarius*' and '*modernus*' (printed at Antwerp by Gerard Leeuw, 19 May 1488).

13 See R. van Dijk, '*Geert Grote en de modern Devotie: een beweging vom vernieuwde innerlijkheid in de late middeleeuwen*', in *Moderne Devotie: Figuren en Facetten,* ed. C. C. Bruin (Nijmegen, 1984).

14 See 'Introduction: Music and the Devotio Moderna', in *Music in the Spiritual Culture of the Devotio Moderna,* ed. U. Hascher-Burger and H. Joldersma (Leiden, 2008), pp. 313–4.

15 N. R. Rice, 'Walter Hilton's *Mixed Life* and the Transformation of Clerical Discipline', *Leeds Studies in English,* n.s. 38 (2007), p. 148.

16 See below, p. 146.

17 D. MacCullough, *Reformation: Europe's House Divided, 1490–1700* (London, 2004), p. 22.

18 Hascher-Burger and Joldersma, *Music in the Spiritual Culture of the Devotio MOderna,* p. 313.

19 M. von Habsburg, *Catholic and Protestant Translations of the Imitatio Christi, 1425–1650: From Late Medieval Classic to Early Modern Bestseller* (London, 2016), p. 1.

20 Kempis, *Imitation,* p. 55.

21 Kempis, *Imitation,* p. 76.

22 Kempis, *Imitation* p. 38.

23 Kempis, *Imitation,* p. 71.

24 Kempis, *Imitation,* p. 149.

25 Kempis, *Imitation,* p. 7.

26 Kempis, *Imitation,* p. 192.

27 Kempis, *Imitation,* p. 17.

28 Kempis, *Imitation,* p. 27.

29 Kempis, *Imitation,* p. 29.

30 Kempis, *Imitation,* p. 31.

31 Kempis, *Imitation,* p. 54.

32 Kempis, *Imitation,* p. 63.

33 Kempis, *Imitation,* p. 117.

34 Kempis, *Imitation,* p. 106.

35 Kempis, *Imitation,* p. 59.

36 Kempis, *Imitation,* p. 215.

37 *Chronicle of the Canons Regular of Mount St Agnes,* trans. P. Arthur (London, 1906), p. 86.

38 *Chronicle,* p. 109.

39 *Chronicle,* pp. 111, 119.

40 *Chronicle,* p. 131.

41 *Chronicle,* pp. 182–3.

42 *Chronicle,* p. 175.

43 Kempis, *Imitation* p. 175.

44 V. Reinsburg, 'Litany and the Laity in Late Medieval and Reformation France', pp. 527, 542.

45 E. H. Gombrich, 'The Early Medici as Patrons of Art', in *Italian Renaissance Studies,* ed. E. F. Jacob (London, 1960), pp. 284–5, 289.

46 MacCullough, *Reformation,* p. 15.

47 MacCullough, *Reformation,* p. 14.

48 See Van Engen, 'Multiple Options', pp. 257–60.

49 For another view, see Duffy, *Marking the Hours,* esp. pp. 55–62.

50 See above, p. 52.

51 Kempis, *Imitation,* pp. 93–6.

52 *Chronicle,* p. 162.

53 See the epigraph above, p. 109.

54 Johann Ulrich Surgant, *Manuale curatorum predicandi prebens modum* … (Basel, 1506), fo, xl, quoted in *Worship: Adoration and Action,* ed. D. A. Carson (London, 2002), p. 99.

55 See below, pp. 145–7. This conclusion appears, on the basis of extensive statistical analysis of the sheer volume, speed of production and geographical spread of printed material between 1450 and 1500, to be endorsed by the Oxford research project the 15cBOOKTRADE. See below, p. 152.

56 MacCullough, *Reformation,* p. 97.

57 See above, pp. 135–6.

58 MacCullough, *Reformation,* p. 102.

59 See above, pp. 148, 150–2.

60 J. F. White, *Protestant Worship: Traditions in Transition* (London, 1989), p. 61.

CHAPTER 5

1 Quoted in Brann, *The Abbot Trithemius (1462–1516)*, p. 145.

2 Quoted in Eisenstein, *The Printing Revolution*, p. 357.

3 The art of printing and the discoveries came together in Hans Burgkmair's woodcut frieze (1508) of the *King of Cochin,* showing people from distant lands, illustrating a report on expeditions to Arabia, India and Africa commissioned by the Welser Company of Augsburg. See A. G. Stewart, 'The Birth of Mass Media: Printmaking in Early Modern Europe', in *A Companion to Renaissance and Baroque Art,* ed. B. Bohn and J. M. Saslow (Chichester, 2013), p. 267.

4 For a useful survey of relatively recent work, see C. Dondi, 'The European Printing Revolution', in *The Oxford Companion to the Book*, ed. M. F. Suarez and H. R. Woudhuysen, 2 vols (Oxford, 2010), pp. 53–61.

5 See the epigraph above, p. 135.

6 H. J. Chaytor, *From Script to Print* (Cambridge, 1945), p. 1.

7 See, for attacks on the fundamental, (if flawed) pioneering work of the late Elizabeth L. Eisenstein, A. Johns, *The Nature of the Book: Print and Knowledge in the Making* (Chicago, 1998) and J. A. Dane, *The Myth of Print Culture* (Toronto, 2003). The criticism of Eisenstein's work began with a hostile review by P. Needham, 'Review: Elizabeth L. Eisenstein, *The Printing Press as an Agent of Change*', *Fine Print*, 6:1 (1980), pp. 23–5, 32–5. For a more moderate assessment see the review by D. Shaw in *The Library*, 6th ser. 3 (1981), pp. 261–3.

8 Objections to the thesis are set out in E. L. Eisenstein, 'An Unacknowledged Revolution Revisited', *American Historical Review*, 107 (2002), p. 87.

9 A. Grafton, 'How Revolutionary Was the Print Revolution?', *American Historical Review*, 107 (2002), p. 84.

10 See Eisenstein, 'An Unacknowledged Revolution', pp. 87, 104.

11 See below, pp. 155–6, 176–7.

12 E. L. Eisenstein, *Divine Art, Infernal Machine: The Reception of Printing in the West from First Impressions to a Sense of Ending* (Philadelphia, 2011), p. 28.

13 Eisenstein, 'Unacknowledged Revolution', p. 128.

14 See, for an uncompromising expression of this view, E. L. Eisenstein, *The Printing Revolution in Early Modern Europe* (2nd edn, Cambridge, 2013).

15 D. Landau and P. W. Parshall, *The Renaissance Print, 1470–1550* (New Haven, 1994), p. 1. See also below pp. 154–5, 157.

16 For an excellent and accessible account, see the website: www.library. manchester.ac.uk/firstimpressions/ The collection with essays by L. Hellinga, largely illustrated by incunabula from the collection of the John Rylands Library.

17 Eisenstein, *The Printing Revolution*, p. 14.

18 See the Oxford University 15cBOOKTRADE project's website on http://15cbooktrade.ox.ac.uk for this and much other information.

19 See Eisenstein, *Divine Art*, p. 13.

20 See Eisenstein, *Printing Revolution*, p. 322.

21 See www.library.manchester.ac.uk/firstimpressions, Essay 2: 'Early printing at Cologne and Caxton's first printed books': 'So kun wir all auch nit Latein'.

22 Quoted in Eisenstein, *Divine Art*, p. 16.

23 See above, pp. 117, 123.

24 K. Goudmann, 'The Devotio Moderna and the Printing Press (c.1475–1500)', *CHRC*, 94 (4) (2013), pp. 578–606.

25 P. Needham, 'Haec Sancta Ars: Gutenberg's Invention as Divine Gift', *Gazette of the Grolier Club*, 42 (1990), p. 106.

26 Eisenstein, 'Divine Art', p. 14.

27 See, for example, John Rylands Library (JRL), Incunable 5676: Valerius Maximus's *Facta et Dicta memorabilia* in the French translation by Simon de Hesdin and Nicolas de Gonesse (1401), printed in the Southern Netherlands, 1475–7.

28 JRL, Incunabule Spencer 10863, fo iiir.

29 JRL, Incunabule Spencer 10863, fo. 346r.

30 Ibid., fo. 346r.

31 For a recent, accessible account of early printing in Italy, see the oddly entitled *Printing [R]evolution, 1450–1500: Fifty Years That Changed Europe*, ed. C. Dondi (Venice, 2018), serving as a catalogue and guide to an exhibition of incunables from the Correr Museum's collection in Venice.

32 Figures such as these may be modified by the results of the Oxford 15cBOOKTRADE project in due course.

33 See N. L. Brann, *The Abbot Trithemius*, p. 138.

34 See J. T. McQuillen, *In Manuscript and Print: The Fifteenth-Century Library of Scheyern Abbey* (PhD Toronto, 2012), p. 303.

35 McQuillen, *In Manuscript and Print*, p. 303.

36 Eisenstein, *Printing Revolution*, pp. 47–8.

37 A. Monro, *The Paper Trail* (London, 2014), p. 232.

38 Monro, *The Paper Trail*, p. 239.

39 See D. Landau and P. W. Parshall, *The Renaissance Print, 1470–1550* (New Haven, 1994), pp. 11–12.

40 For a discussion of the contribution of printmakers to secular, vernacular culture, see below, pp. 156, 184.

41 Landau and Parshall, p. 38.

42 Landau and Parshall, p. 38.

43 See G. S. Williams, 'The Arthurian Model in the Emperor Maximilian's Autobiographic Writings', *Sixteenth-Century Journal*, 11:4 (1980), pp. 3–22.
44 See Chap. 6, pp. 159–200.
45 See Landau and Parshall, *The Renaissance Print*, p. 52.
46 Landau and Parshall, *The Renaissance Print*, pp. 7–8.
47 Quoted in Eisenstein, *Divine Art*, p. 24.
48 Eisenstein, Printing Revolution, p. 309.

CHAPTER 6

1 Erasmus, *Praise of Folly*, trans. B. Radice, ed. A. H. T. Levi (London, 1993), p. 29.
2 For a good survey of visual evidence, see C. Grossinger, *Humor and Folly in Secular and Profane Prints in Northern Europe, 1430–1540* (London, 2002).
3 Erasmus, *Letter to Maarten van Dorp* (1515) in *Praise of Folly*, p. 144.
4 Sebastian Brant, *The Ship of Fools*, ed. E. H. Zeydel (New York, 1962), p. 363.
5 Brant, *Ship of Fools*, p. 348.
6 Brant, *Ship of Fools*, p. 347.
7 See below, pp. 167–9.
8 See below, pp. 167–9, 172–6, 178–80.
9 For a comprehensive catalogue, see *Livelier than Life: The Master of the Amsterdam Cabinet or the Housebook Master, c. 1470–1500*, ed. J. P. F. Kok. (Amsterdam, 1985).
10 See H. Pleij, *Dreaming of Cockaigne: Medieval Fantasies of the Perfect Life* (New York, 2001) and J. Verberckmoes, 'Land of Cockaigne', in *Laughter, Jestbooks and Society in the Spanish Netherlands* (London, 1999), Chapter 1.
11 BL, MS Harley 913, fos. 3r–6v. See www.soton.ac.uk/-wpwt/trans/cockaygn for the Middle English text of the *Land of Cockaigne* in modern English translation.
12 See K. Ridder, B. von Lupke and R Nocker, 'From Festival to Revolt: Carnival Theater during the Late Middle Ages and Early Reformation as Threat to Urban Order', in *Power and Violence in Medieval and Early Modern Theatre*, ed. C. Dietl, C. Schanze and G. Ehrstine (Gottingen, 2014), pp. 153–68.
13 See J. D. Martin, 'The Depiction of Jews in the Carnival Plays of Hans Folz and Hans Sachs in Early Modern Nuremberg', *Baylor Journal*, 3:2 (2006), pp. 43–65; K. A. Zaenker, 'The Bedevilled Beckmesser: Another Look at Anti-semitic Stereotypes in *Die Meistersinger von Nurnberg*', *German Studies Review*, 22:1 (1999), pp. 1–20. For another view, see D. B. Dennis, '"The Most German of All Operas": *Die Meistersinger* through the Lens of the Third Reich', *Loyola eCommons* (2002), pp. 98–119.

14 Martin, 'The Depiction of Jews', p. 43.

15 *Praise of Folly*, p. 146.

16 See *Ship of Fools*, Introduction, pp. 13, 32.

17 Quoted in U. Gaier, 'Sebastian Brant's *Narrenschiff* and the Humanists', *PMLA*, 83 (1968), p. 283. Also *Ship of Fools*, p. 13. For connections between humanism and the German theatre, see C. Dietl, 'Neo-Latin Humanist and Protestant Drama in Germany', in *Neo-Latin Drama and Theatre in Early Modern Europe*, ed. J. Bloemendal and H. B. Norland (Leiden, 2013), pp. 103–83.

18 See Gaier, 'Sebastian Brant's *Narrenschiff* and the Humanists', p. 282.

19 *Praise of Folly*, p. 57.

20 *Praise of Folly*, p. 57.

21 *Praise of Folly*, pp. 129, 132–3.

22 *Praise of Folly*, p. 133. The constant use by Erasmus of the term 'man' for humankind is a reminder not only of its biblical usage but of the misogyny which underlies much of his thought. See p. 134 for his final taunt about the garrulous folly of women.

23 *Praise of Folly*, pp. 133–4.

24 See M. L. Fuehrer, 'Wisdom and Eloquence in Nicholas of Cusa's "Idiota de sapientia et de mente"', *Vivarium*, 16 (1978), pp. 142–55.

25 J. Hutchinson, 'The Housebook Master and the Folly of Wise Men', *Art Bulletin*, 48 (1966), pp. 77–8.

26 Hutchinson, 'The Housebook Master', p. 76.

27 Quoted in C. J. Nedermann, 'The Union of Wisdom and Eloquence before the Renaissance: The Ciceronian Orator in Medieval Thought', *Journal of Medieval History*, 18 (1992), p. 79.

28 See E. F. Rice, Jr., *The Renaissance Idea of Wisdom* (Cambridge, MA, 1958).

29 H. Baron, 'The Secularization of Wisdom and Political Humanism in the Renaissance', *Journal of the History of Ideas*, 21 (1960), p. 133.

30 For an excellent recent survey, see M. Kempshall, *Rhetoric and the Writing of History* (Manchester, 2012).

31 See Kempshall, *Rhetoric and the Writing of History*, pp. 453–8.

32 See above, pp. 91–3.

33 See W. J. Bouwsma, 'The Politics of Commynes', in *A Usable Past: Essays in European Cultural History* (Berkeley, Los Angeles and Oxford, 1990), pp. 194–5, 204.

34 See above, pp. 105–7.

35 See above, pp. 106–7.

36 See above, pp. 161–2.

37 *Ship of Fools*, p. 323.

38 See J. Elord, 'Spotlight: The Ballock Dagger'; http://myarmoury.com and C. Blair, *European and American Arms, c. 1100–1850* (London, 1962), Plate 183.

39 See above, pp. 177, 195.

40 See A. Minnis, *Magister Amoris. The Roman de la Rose and Vernacular Hermeneutics* (Oxford, 2001).

41 T. van Hemelryck, 'Le *Debat de Mars et du Cul*: contrepoint erotico-guerrier et fricassee linguistique', in *'Pour acquerir honneur et pris'. Melanges de Moyen Francaise offerts a Guiseppe di Stefano*, ed. M. C. Timelli and C. Galderisi (Montreal, 2004), p. 315.

42 See K. Baldinger, 'Six dessins dialogues a double sens (flandr. Vers 1470)', *Travaux de linguistique et literature*, 31 (1993), pp. 7–36; Jones, *The Secret Middle Ages*, colour plates 22, 23, 24 and pp. 257–8.

43 Jones, *The Secret Middle Ages*, pp. 257–8 for the texts. The translations, however, are mine.

44 See below, pp. 193, 197.

45 See K. P. F. Moxey, 'Master E.S and the Folly of Love', *Simiolus*, 11 (1980), p. 139.

46 See Moxey, 'Master E.S and the Folly of Love', p. 147.

47 *Ship of Fools*, p. 111.

48 *Ship of Fools*, pp. 349–50.

49 See U. Gaier, 'Sebastian Brant's *Narrenschiff* and the Humanists', *PMLA*, 83 (1968), pp. 266–70, esp. pp. 267–8.

50 *Praise of Folly*, Preface, p. xi.

51 *Ship of Fools*, p. 268.

52 *Ship of Fools*, pp. 242–3.

53 See M. R. Jones, *Radical Pastoral, 1381–1594: Appropriation and the Writing of Religious Controversy* (London, 2016), esp. pp. 85–7.

54 Quoted in K. B. McFarlane, *Memling* (Oxford, 1971), p. 70.

55 Gombrich, *Aby Warburg: An Intellectual Biography*, p. 57.

56 See K. Harloe, *Winckelmann and the Invention of Antiquity* (Oxford, 2013).

57 See M. Hurtig, *Antiquity Unleashed: Aby Warburg, Durer and Mantegna* (London: Courtauld Gallery, 2013), p. 14.

58 Warburg, 'Durer and Italian Antiquity', p. 553.

59 See above pp. 67–76, 155–6 and below pp. 186–8.

60 H. C. E. Midelfort, *A History of Madness in Sixteenth-Century Germany* (Stanford, 1999), p. 26.

61 See above, pp. 53, 182–4.

62 T. Husband, *The Wild Man: Medieval Myth and Symbolism* (New York, 1980), p. 5.

63 See M. Mosely-Christian, 'From Page to Print: The Transformation of the "Wild Woman" in Early Modern Northern Engravings', *Word and Image*, 27:4 (2011), pp. 429–42.

64 See above pp. 87, 176.

65 See *The Darker Vision of the Renaissance*, ed. R. S. Kinsman (Berkeley, LA and London, 1974). More recently, see *A Companion to the Worlds of the Renaissance*, ed. G. Ruggiero (Oxford, 2002, 2007), esp. the 'Introduction: Renaissance Dreaming: In Search of a Paradigm' & Part V: 'Anti-Worlds'.

66 See J. Destree, *Hugo van der Goes* (Brussels, Paris, 1914), pp. 214–8.

67 See *The Darker Vision*, ed. Kinsman, p. 17.

68 Midelfort. *History of Madness*, p. 30; Kinsman, *Darker Vision*, p. 18, quoting Ofhuys.

69 See Lynn White, Jr., 'Death and the Devil', in Kinsman, *Darker Vision*, p. 26.

70 See also below, p. 205.

71 Lynn White, Jr., 'Death and the Devil', p. 25.

72 See above, pp. 38, 115–16.

73 See above, p. 164.

74 M. Foucault, *Madness and Civilisation: A History of Insanity in the Age of Reason* (New York, 1967), p. 39.

75 Recent interest in Bosch has been stimulated by the exhibition of his works in s'-Hertogenbosch (2016–17). See M. Ilsink and J. Joldewij, *Hieronymus Bosch: Visions of Genius* (Brussels/s'-Hertogenbosch, 2016). Also, for a recent up-to-date survey, see W. Bosing, *Hieronymus Bosch: Between Heaven and Hell* (Cologne, 2015).

76 M. J. Friedlander, *Die Altniederlandische Malerei*, v (Berlin, 1927), p. 123.

77 W. Stechow, *Northern Renaissance Art, 1400–1600* (New York, 1966, repr. 1989), pp. 19–20.

78 Fra Jose de Siguenza, *History of the Order of St Jerome* (1605) cited in Stechow, *Northern Renaissance Art*, p. 23.

79 Stechow, p. 24.

80 See L. Dixon, 'Bosch's Stone Operation: Meaning, Medicine and Morality', *Hektoen International: A Journal of Medical Humanities*, 11:1 (2019).

81 For a comprehensive survey of both pilgrimage and secular badges, see H. J. E. van Beuningen and A. M. Koldeweij, *Heilig en Profan. 1000 Laatmiddeleeuwse Insignes. Rotterdam Papers VIII: A Contribution to Medieval Archaeology* (Cothen, 1993). The secular badges are described (in English) by M. Jones, *The Secret Middle Ages* (Stroud, 2004), pp. 99–109.

82 See M. Jones, *The Secret Middle Ages*, p. 248; A. M. Koldeweij, *Foi et bonne fortune: parure et devotion en Flandre medieval* (Arnhem, 2006), cat. 7:27.

CONCLUSION

1 Graphische Sammlung Albertina, Vienna.

2 London, National Gallery.

3 J. Chipps Smith, *The Northern Renaissance*, p. 15.
4 *The Cambridge Companion to the Pre-Raphaelites*, ed. E. Prettejohn (Cambridge, 2012), p. 39.
5 See the exhibition catalogue *Reflections: Van Eyck and the Pre-Raphaelites*, ed. A. Smith, A. Koopstra, C. Bugler and S. Foister (London: National Gallery, 2017).
6 Paris, Musee du Louvre.
7 London, National Gallery.

Further reading

A guide to further reading on the Renaissance in Northern Europe or the 'Northern Renaissance' must take account of fundamental questions concerning its definition and scope. Works have to be included which describe and assess not only the impact of the Italian Renaissance on the North but also the extent to which an indigenous 'Renaissance' emerged in the lands on the other side of the Alps. The two categories are not, of course, mutually exclusive. But there are at least two historiographical streams to tap there and this bibliographical note attempts to reflect both. Some of the sources are visual, and the main printed works which contain these images are listed here. But most galleries and museums now have online sites which offer images of, and helpful information about, many of their Northern Renaissance holdings.

INTRODUCTION

There is now no lack of general surveys covering the period *c. 1350–c. 1540* in European history. Among the most useful are the volumes in the *New Cambridge Medieval History, 6, c. 1300–c. 1415*, ed. M. Jones (Cambridge, 2000) and *7, c. 1415–c. 1500*, ed. C. Allmand (Cambridge, 1998) [both available online, 2008]. See also D. Nicholas, *The Transformation of Europe, 1300–1600* (London, 1999); and J. Watts, *The Making of Polities: Europe, 1300–1500* (Cambridge, 2009). A useful introduction to the later period, not least for its excellent subject-specific Bibliographies, is *The Routledge Companion to Early Modern Europe, 1453–1763*, ed. C. Cook and P. Broadhead (London, 2012).

Towns and cities are well covered in recent works, but a good starting point still remains J. Le Goff, 'The Town as an Agent of Civilisation', in

The Fontana Economic History of Europe: The Middle Ages, ed. C. M. Cipolla (London, 1971), i, part 2. A good general survey is D. Nicholas, *The Later Medieval City, 1300–1500* (New York, 1997). Contrasts and comparisons between the towns and cities of Italy and Northern Europe were first addressed in J. Lestocquoy, *Aux Origines de la Bourgeoisie: les villes de Flandres et d'Italie sous le gouvernement des patriciens* (Paris, 1952) and much more recently by *Villes de Flandres et d'Italie: relectures d'une comparaison traditionelle*, ed. E. Crouzet-Pavan and E. Lecuppre-Desjardin (Turnhout, 2007). See also P. Lantschner, *The Logic of Political Conflict: Cities in Italy and the Low Countries, c. 1370–1440* (Oxford, 2015). The degrees of 'urbanization' and its definition are discussed in J. de Vries, *European Urbanization, 1500–1800* (Harvard, 1984).

Courts and court culture are treated in M. Vale, *The Princely Court: Medieval Courts and Culture in North-West Europe, 1270–1380* (Oxford, 2004); *The Court as a Stage: England and the Low Countries in the Late Middle Ages*, ed. S. Gunn and A. Janse (Woodbridge, 2006); and *Princes, Patronage and the Nobility: The Court at the Beginning of the Modern Age, c. 1450–1650*, ed. R. G. Asch and A. M. Birke (London, 1991). For the court of Burgundy and its European counterparts, see *La Cour de Bourgogne et l'Europe: le rayonnement et les limites d'un modele culturel*, ed. W. Paravicini (Ostfilden, 2013). There is a useful volume of texts, with commentary, on the relationship between the court and the city in *Court and Civic Society in the Burgundian Low Countries, c. 1420–1530*, ed. G. Small and A. Brown (Manchester, 2007). A good study of civic culture in one major city is J. Chipps Smith, *Nuremberg: A Renaissance City, 1500–1618* (Austin, TX, 1983), while a broader canvas is broached in *Medieval Urban Culture*, ed. A. Brown and J. Dumolyn (Turnhout, 2017).

A fundamental work which stresses continuities between medieval and Renaissance attitudes to classical antiquity is E. Curtius, *European Literature and the Latin Middle Ages* (Princeton, 1973); see also, for another view, R. Weiss, *The Renaissance Discovery of Classical Antiquity* (2nd edn, Oxford, 1988). A useful study of early humanist thought is M. McLaughlin, 'Humanist Concepts of the Renaissance and Middle Ages in the Tre- and Quattrocento', *Renaissance Studies*, 2 (1988), pp. 131–42.

CHAPTER 1: WHAT WAS THE 'NORTHERN RENAISSANCE'?

A good recent starting point is H. Wijsman, 'Northern Renaissance? Burgundy and Netherlandish Art in Fifteenth-Century Europe', in

Perceptions of Continuity and Discontinuity in Europe, c. 1300–c. 1500, ed. A. Lee, H. Schnitker and P. Peporte (Leiden, 2010), pp. 269–88. The first published work to use the term 'Northern Renaissance' in its title was H. Fierens-Gevaert, *Etudes sur l'Art Flamand. La Renaissance Septentrionale et les premiers maitres des Flandres* (Brussels, 1905). A useful sourcebook of texts and documents is *The Renaissance and Reformation in Northern Europe*, ed. K. R. Bartlett and M. McGlynn (Toronto, 2014). For the concept of a Renaissance, a classic study is E. Panofsky, *Renaissance and Renascences in Western Art* (New York and London, 1972); more recent discussions are to be found in F. Haskell, *History and Its Images: Art and the Interpretation of the Past* (New Haven and London, 1993), esp. 'Huizinga and the "Flemish Renaissance"', pp. 431–95; W. Krul, 'Realism, Renaissance and Nationalism', in *Early Netherlandish Paintings: Rediscovery, Reception and Research*, ed. B. Ridderbos, A. van Buren and H. van Veen (Amsterdam, 2005), pp. 252–89; M. Belozerskaya, *Rethinking the Renaissance: Burgundian Arts across Europe* (Cambridge, 2002). In the study of the visual arts, the influence of G. Vasari, *The Lives of the Artists*, trans. J. C. Bondarella and P. Bondarella (Oxford, 2008) was felt for perhaps too long a time but its importance cannot be dismissed.

Further treatments of the historiography of the subject are E. H. Gombrich, *In Search of Cultural History* (London, 1969); J. Huizinga, 'The Problem of the Renaissance', in *Men and Ideas: History, the Middle Ages, the Renaissance*, ed. and trans., J. S. Holmes and H. van Marle (London, 1960), pp. 243–87; W. Krul, 'In the Mirror of Van Eyck: Johan Huizinga's *Autumn of the Middle Ages*', *Journal of Medieval and Early Modern Studies*, 27:3 (1997), pp. 353–84; J. Tollebeek, '"Renaissance" and "Fossilization": Michelet, Burckhardt and Huizinga', *Renaissance Studies*, 15 (2001), pp. 354–66; W. J. Bouwsma, *A Usable Past: Essays in European Cultural History* (Berkeley, Los Angeles, Oxford, 1990); J. B. Bullen, *The Myth of the Renaissance in Nineteenth-Century Writings* (Oxford, 1994); and two articles by L. Silver, 'The State of Research: Northern European Art of the Renaissance Era', *Art Bulletin*, 68 (1986), pp. 518–35; and 'Arts and Minds: Scholarship on Early Modern Art History (Northern Europe)', *Renaissance Quarterly*, 59 (2006), pp. 351–73.

Fundamental texts remain J. Burckhardt, *The Civilisation of the Renaissance in Italy*, ed. P. Burke, trans. S. Middlemore (London, 1990); and J. Huizinga, *The Waning of the Middle Ages: A Study of the Forms of Life, Thought and Art in France and the Burgundian Lands in the Fourteenth and Fifteenth Centuries*, trans. F. Hopman (London, 1924 and many subsequent editions). A more recent translation is entitled *The Autumn of the Middle Ages,* trans. R. J. Payton and U. Mammitzsch (Chicago, 1997) discussed and subjected to criticism in W. P. Simons, 'About *The Autumn of the Middle Ages* by J. Huizinga, R. J. Payton and U. Mammitzsch', *Speculum,* 72 (1997), pp. 488–91 and in more general terms in E. Peters and W. P. Simons, 'The New Huizinga and the Old Middle Ages', *Speculum,* 74 (1999), pp. 587–620.

CHAPTER 2: REALISM AND THE VISUAL ARTS

The work of Aby Warburg, idiosyncratic though it was, is fundamental: see E. H. Gombrich, *Aby Warburg: An Intellectual Biography* (London, 1986) and A. Warburg, *The Renewal of Pagan Antiquity: Contributions to the Cultural History of the European Renaissance,* ed. K. W. Forster, trans. D. Britt (Los Angeles, 1999). A good general survey of the arts is J. R. Hale, *The Civilisation of Europe in the Renaissance* (London, 2008). The concept of artistic Realism, in its more modern sense, is studied in J. Malpas, *Realism* (Cambridge, 1997). An essential sourcebook of texts and documents is W. Stechow, *Northern Renaissance Art, 1400–1600: Sources and Documents* (New York, 1966, repr. 1989).

Among many art-historical studies, especially important are E. Panofsky, *Early Netherlandish Painting: Its Origins and Character*, 2 vols (Cambridge, MA, 1953 and subsequent editions); more recently, C. Harbison, *The Art of the Northern Renaissance* (London, 1995); essential reading is the excellent Introduction to L. Campbell, *National Gallery Catalogues. The Fifteenth-Century Netherlandish Schools* (London: National Gallery, 1998); J. Chipps Smith, *The Art of the Northern Renaissance* (London, 2004); P. Nuttall, *From Flanders to Florence: The Impact of Netherlandish Painting, 1400–1500* (New Haven and London, 2004) covers an important theme, as does *Cultural Exchange between the Low Countries and Italy, 1400–1600,* ed. I. Alexander-Skipnes (Turnhout, 2007); S. Nash, *Northern Renaissance Art* (Oxford, 2008) is a comprehensive survey, and has a very useful Bibliography. Religious art is surveyed in H. van Os, *The Art of Devotion in the Late Middle Ages in Europe, 1300–1500* (Princeton, 1994). German art is treated in B. Corley, *Painting and Patronage in Cologne, 1300–1500* (London, 2000) and *Gothic and Renaissance Art in Nuremberg, 1300–1550* (New York, 1986); for individual German artists, see M. Bailey, *Durer* (London, 1995); H. Langdon, *Holbein* (London, 1993);

C. S. Wood, *Albrecht Altdorfer and the Origins of Landscape* (London, 2014).

For portraiture see L. Campbell, *Renaissance Portraits: European Portrait-Painting in the 14th, 15th and 16th Centuries* (New Haven and London, 1990); and A. Martindale, *Heroes, Ancestors, Relatives and the Birth of the Portrait* (The Hague, 1988).

CHAPTER 3: HUMANISM IN THE NORTH

The role of humanism and humanists in Renaissance thought and culture has attracted a very large literature, but a good place at which to start is N. Mann, 'The Origins of Humanism', in *The Cambridge Companion to Renaissance Humanism,* ed. J. Kraye (Cambridge, 1996), pp. 1–19. The later stages of medieval scholasticism are analysed in G. Leff, *The Dissolution of the Medieval Outlook: An Essay on Intellectual and Spiritual Change in the Fourteenth Century* (New York, 1976). Humanist positions on scholastic thought are discussed in B. Nauert, 'The Clash of Humanists and Scholastics: An Approach to Pre-Reformation Controversies', *Sixteenth-Century Journal*, 4 (1973), pp. 1–18 and *Humanism and the Culture of Renaissance Europe* (Cambridge, 1995). For a fundamental humanist critical text, highly influential in Northern Europe, see L. Valla, *On the Donation of Constantine*, ed. G. W. Bowersock (Cambridge, MA, 2007); also, on this subject, see A. Hiatt, *The Making of Medieval Forgeries* (Toronto, 2004).

Recent work has tended to take issue with the notion that Renaissance humanism was a uniquely Italian product, exported elsewhere, as argued in the classic study by R. Weiss, *Humanism in England during the Fifteenth Century* (Oxford, 1941) now edited with a new Introduction by D. Rundle and A. J. Lappin (4th edn, London, 2010). Recent approaches and interpretations are well set out in *Humanism in Fifteenth-Century Europe*, ed. D. Rundle (Oxford, 2012) although the Burgundian Netherlands are there omitted. For the latter see A. Vanderjagt 'Expropriating the Past: Tradition and Innovation in the Use of Texts in Fifteenth-Century Burgundy', in *Tradition and Innovation in an Era of Change*, ed. R. Suntrup and J. R. Veenstra (Leiden, 2001), pp. 177–201 and his 'Classical Learning and the Building of Power at the Fifteenth-Century Burgundian Court', in *Centres of Learning: Learning and Location in Pre-modern Europe and the Near East*, ed. J. W. Drijvers and A. MacDonald (Leiden, 1995); and R. Walsh, 'The

Coming of Humanism in the Low Countries: Some Italian Influences at the Court of Charles the Bold', *Humanistica Lovaniensia*, 25 (1976), pp. 146–97. For cultural relations and humanist contacts between an Italian court and the English court, see C. H. Clough, 'The Relations between the English and Urbino Courts, 1474–1508', *Studies in the Renaissance*, 14 (1967), pp. 202–18.

For humanism in the universities, see the comprehensive series of essays in *A History of the University in Europe*, ed. H. de Ridder-Symoens, *Volume I, Universities in the Middle Ages* and *Volume 2. Universities in Early Modern Europe (1500–1800)* (both Cambridge, 2003); also J. H. Hexter, 'The Education of the Aristocracy in the Renaissance', in *Reappraisals in History* (London, 1961), pp. 45–70; A. Cobban, 'The Role of Colleges in the Medieval Universities of Northern Europe with Special Reference to England and France', *BJRL*, 71:1 (1989), pp. 49–70; A. Grafton and L. Jardine, *From Humanism to the Humanities: Education and the Liberal Arts in Fifteenth- and Sixteenth-Century Europe* (Cambridge, MA, 1986).

For Erasmus, a lively and stimulating introduction is L. Jardine, *Erasmus, Man of Letters: The Construction of Charisma in Print* (Princeton, 1993); also see J. D. Tracy, *Erasmus: The Growth of a Mind* (Geneva, 1972); for his writings see M. M. Philips, *The Adages of Erasmus* (Cambridge, 1964); *Praise of Folly and Letter to Maarten van Dorp, 1515*, ed. A. H. T. Levi, trans. B. Radice (London, 1993). His letters can be sampled in English translation in the ongoing series of volumes of *The Collected Works of Erasmus: The Correspondence of Erasmus* (Toronto, 1974–). The study by P. S. Allen, *The Age of Erasmus* (Oxford, 1913) has useful biographies of leading Northern humanists and is still worth consulting, as is J. Huizinga, *Erasmus and the Age of Reformation*, trans. F. Hopman (1924, repr. New York, 2001). The magisterial study by E. van Gulik, *Erasmus and His Books*, trans. J. C. Grayson, ed. J. McConica and J. Trapman (Toronto, 2018) reconstitutes the contents of his library and discusses his acquisition of books and his working habits in fascinating detail.

CHAPTER 4: THE OLD AND THE NEW DEVOTION

The history of later medieval and pre-Reformation religion has attracted a very large volume of recent historical writing. The following list is very selective indeed. Devotional religion is treated in general surveys by R. N. Swanson, *Religion and Devotion in Europe, 1215–1515* (Cambridge, 1995); A. Vauchez, *The Laity in the Middle Ages: Beliefs and Practices* (Notre Dame, 1993); more specifically focussed are J. van Engen, *Sisters and Brothers of the Common Life: The Devotio Moderna and the Late Medieval World* (Philadelphia, 2008); and *Devotio Moderna: Basic Writings* (New York, 1988). The context of the 'new' or 'modern' devotion is well set out in J. van Engen, 'Multiple Options: The World of the Fifteenth-Century Church', *Church History*, 77:2 (2008), pp. 257–84. The essential text for the *devotio* is Thomas Kempis, *The Imitation of Christ*, ed. and trans. R. Jeffery and M. von Habsburg (London, 2013); for differing assessments of the *devotio* and its impact, see R. R. Post, *The Modern Devotion* (Leiden, 1968), now balanced by Van Engen (above), and M. von Habsburg, *Catholic and Protestant Translations of the Imitation of Christ, 1425–1650* (Farnham, 2011). See also the chapter in R. W. Southern, *Western Society and the Church in the Middle Ages* (London, 1990), Chap. 7: II 'The Religious Brethren of Deventer and Its Neighbourhood'. H. van Os, *The Art of Devotion in the Late Middle Ages in Europe, 1300–1500* (Princeton, 1994) is a useful survey of devotional imagery, and E. Duffy, *Marking the Hours: English People and Their Prayers* (New Haven and London, 2004) discusses and illustrates the functions and significance of devotional Books of Hours. Women's devotional lives are examined in M. Clanchy, 'Images of Ladies with Prayer Books: What Do They Signify?', *Studies in Church History*, 38 (2004), pp. 106–22; H. M. Colvin, *Architecture and the After-Life* (New Haven and London, 1992) discusses the provision of prayers for the dead and their architectural and material settings.

For excellent accounts of the rise of Protestantism and, among many other topics, its relationship to humanism, see D. MacCullough, *Reformation. Europe's House Divided, 1490–1700* (London, 2004) and E. Cameron, *The European Reformation* (Oxford, 1991). W. J. Bouwsma's 'Renaissance and Reformation: An Essay on Their Affinities and Connections', in *A Usable Past: Essays in European Cultural History* (Berkeley, Los Angeles and Oxford, 1990), pp. 225–46 is also stimulating. For both Catholic and Protestant reform movements, and much else, see N. L. Brann, *The Abbot Trithemius (1462–1516): The Renaissance of Monastic Humanism* (Leiden, 1981); and L. Spitz, *The Religious Renaissance of the German Humanists* (Cambridge, MA, 1963).

Old and new devotional practices and observances are described and discussed in V. Reinsburg, 'Liturgy and the Laity in Late Medieval and Reformation France', *Sixteenth-Century Journal*, 23 (1992), pp. 527–42;

A. T. Thayer, 'Judge and Doctor: Images of the Confessor in Printed Model Sermon Collections', in *Penitence in the Age of Reformations*, ed. K. J. Luddi and A. T. Thayer (Aldershot, 2000), pp. 10–29; *Worship: Adoration and Action*, ed. D. A. Carson (London, 2002); and J. F. White, *Protestant Worship: Traditions in Transition* (London, 1989).

The music of devotion (and its secular counterparts) has received a great deal of attention from musicologists and other scholars in recent years, exemplified by R. Strohm, *The Rise of European Music, 1380–1500* (Cambridge, 2008), preceded by his earlier excellent study *Music in Late Medieval Bruges* (Oxford, 1990); see also E. E. Leach's *Guillaume de Machaut: Secretary, Poet, Musician* (New York, 2014); while *Music in the Spiritual Culture of the Devotio Moderna*, ed. U. Hascher-Burger and H. Joldersma (Leiden, 2008) also breaks new ground.

CHAPTER 5: THE IMPACT OF PRINT

The early history of printing has been the subject of much scholarly and popular interest, as well as of considerable academic controversy. The issues are briefly summarized in A. Grafton, 'How Revolutionary was the Print Revolution?', *AHR*, 107 (2002), pp. 84–6. The best introduction remains E. L. Eisenstein, *The Printing Revolution in Early Modern Europe* (Cambridge, 1983, 2nd edn, 2013). Also see her *The Printing Press as an Agent of Change* (Cambridge, 1979); 'An Unacknowledged Revolution Revisited', *AHR*, 107 (2002), pp. 87–105; and *Divine Art, Infernal Machine: The Reception of Printing in the West from First Impressions to the Sense of an Ending* (Philadelphia, 2011). There are useful essays in *Agent of Change: Print Culture Studies after Elizabeth L. Eisenstein*, ed. S. Baron, E. Lindquist and E. Shevlin (Amherst, MA, 2007). Eisenstein's pioneering work is heavily criticized in, among other sources, A. Johns, *The Nature of the Book: Print and Knowledge in the Making* (Chicago, 1998) and J. A. Dare, *The Myth of Print Culture* (Toronto, 2003). Most recently, studies of the 'printing revolution' have now to take account of the results of the research resulting from the Oxford University Fifteenth–Century Book Trade project, set out for a general audience in *Printing R-Evolution, 1450–1500: Fifty Years that Changed Europe*, ed. C. Dondi (exhib. cat., Correr Museum, Venice, 2018).

Studies of the relationship between manuscript and print culture are included in *The Uses of Script and Print, 1300–1700*, ed. J. Crick and A. Walsham (Cambridge, 2004) and see also D. McKitterick, *Print, Manuscript and the Search for Order, 1450–1830* (Cambridge, 2003);

also J. Boffey, *Manuscript and Print in London, c. 1475–1530* (London, 2012). There is much interesting material on early printing in L. Holborn, 'Printing and the Growth of a Protestant Movement in Germany from 1517–1524', *Church History*, 2 (1942), pp. 1–15; N. L. Brann, *The Abbot Trithemius (1462–1516): The Renaissance of Monastic Humanism* (Leiden, 1981); and L. Spitz, *The Religious Renaissance of the German Humanists* (Cambridge, MA, 1963). A classic work on the transition from manuscript to print is L. Febvre and H. Martin, *The Coming of the Book: The Impact of Printing, 1450–1800* (3rd edn, New York, 2010). For the significance of the introduction and development of paper in the history of printing, see the popular work by A. Monro, *The Paper Trail: An Unexpected History of a Revolutionary Invention* (New York, 2017). K. Goudmann, 'The Devotio Moderna and the Printing Press (c. 1475–1500)', *CHRC*, 93:4 (2013), pp. 578–606 casts some new light on the printing of religious texts. The essays by L. Hellinga in www.library.manchester.ac .uk/firstimpressions/The-Collection discuss incunables in the John Rylands collection but also provide a very good introduction to early printing.

The emergence of the printed image through woodblock printing and engraving is comprehensively treated in D. Landau and P. W. Parshall, *The Renaissance Print, 1470–1550* (New Haven, 1994) and a good introduction is to be found in A. G. Stewart, 'The Birth of Mass Media: Printmaking in Early Modern Europe', in *A Companion to Renaissance and Baroque Art*, ed. B. Bohn and J. M. Saslow (Chichester, 2013), pp. 253–73. Interesting material on the Emperor Maximilian I's use of the printed book and the printed image is presented in S. Fussel, *Emperor Maximilian and the Media of His Day. The Theuerdank of 1517* (Cologne, 2003); and G. S. Williams, 'The Arthurian Model in the Emperor Maximilian's Autobiographical Writings', *Sixteenth-Century Journal*, 11:4 (1980), pp. 3–22.

CHAPTER 6: WISDOM, FOLLY AND THE DARKER VISION

Wisdom and Folly are the subject of two fundamental texts: Desiderius Erasmus, *Praise of Folly and Letter to Maarten van Dorp*, trans. B. Radice, ed. A. H. T. Levi (London, 1993) and Sebastian Brant, *The Ship of Fools*, trans. and ed. E. H. Zeydel (New York, 1962). H. Pleij, *Dreaming of Cockaigne: Medieval Fantasies of the Perfect Life* (New York, 2001) has plenty of stimulating ideas, some relating to the early modern rather than medieval period. See also J. Verberckmoes, 'The Land of Cockaigne', *Laughter, Jestbooks and Society in the Spanish Netherlands* (London,

1999), esp. Chap. 1. Brant's satire is put into a more general context in U. Gaier, 'Sebastian Brant's *Narrenschiff* and the Humanists', *PMLA*, 83 (1968), pp. 266–84. The intellectual background to the debates on wisdom and folly is analysed in E. F. Rice, *The Renaissance Idea of Wisdom* (Cambridge, MA, 1958); H. Baron, 'The Secularization of Wisdom and Political Humanism in the Renaissance', *Journal of the History of Ideas*, 21 (1960), pp. 131–50; and C. J. Nedermann, 'The Union of Wisdom and Eloquence before the Renaissance: The Ciceronian Orator in Medieval Thought', *Journal of Medieval History*, 18 (1992), pp. 75–95. Historical writing and its relation to rhetoric is explored in M. Kempshall, *Rhetoric and the Writing of History, 400–1500* (Manchester, 2012), while the rise of the *Memoir* as a vehicle for the dissemination of ideas about wisdom and folly is discussed in W. J. Bouwsma, 'The Politics of Commynes', in *A Usable Past: Essays in European Cultural History* (Berkeley, Los Angeles and Oxford, 1990), pp. 190–208.

The theatre of satire and dissent is discussed in K. Ridder, B. von Lupke and R. Nocker, 'From Festival to Revolt: Carnival Theater during the Late Middle Ages and Early Reformation as Threat to Urban Order', in *Power and Violence in Medieval and Early Modern Theatre*, ed. C. Dietl, C. Schanze and G. Ehrstine (Gottingen, 2014), pp. 153–68; and C. Dietl, 'Neo-Latin Humanist and Protestant Drama in Germany', in *Neo-Latin Drama and Theatre in Europe*, ed. J. Bloemendal and H. B. Norland (Leiden, 2013), pp. 103–33. See also M. de Roos, 'Misogynie et matriacat: le role de la femme dans les jeux de carnaval (xve-xvie siecles)', in *Theatre et Spectacles hier et aujourd'hui: Moyen Age et Renaissance* (Paris, CTHS, 1991), pp. 213–26; and 'Battles and Bottles: Shrovetide Performances in the Low Countries (c. 1350–c. 1550)', in *Festive Drama*, ed. M. Twycross (Woodbridge, 1996), pp. 167–78.

The 'darker' side of the Renaissance has recently become a more frequently visited subject of study but an earlier and still valuable example is *The Darker Vision of the Renaissance*, ed. R. S. Kinsman (Berkeley, Los Angeles and London, 1974). More recently, see *A Companion to the Worlds of the Renaissance*, ed. G. Ruggiero (Oxford, 2nd edn, 2007). The artistic representation of folly and visual satire are treated and illustrated in C. Grossinger, *Humor and Folly in Secular and Profane Prints in Northern Europe, 1430–1540* (London, 2002); *Livelier than Life: The Master of the Amsterdam Cabinet or the Housebook Master, c. 1470–1500*, ed. J. P. F. Kok (Amsterdam, 1985); J. C. Hutchinson, 'The Housebook Master and the Folly of Wise Men', *Art Bulletin*, 48 (1966), pp. 73–78; and K. P. F. Moxey, 'Master E.S. and the Folly of Love', *Simiolus*, 11 (1980), pp. 125–

4. There is much fascinating material in M. Jones, *The Secret Middle Ages: Discovering the Real Medieval World* (Stroud, 2002); for secular and profane metal badges and their meaning, see *Heilig en profaan. 1000 laat-middeleuwse insignes uit de collectie H.J.E. van Beuningen* (Rotterdam, 1993) and *Heilig en profaan 2* (Rotterdam, 2001) (both with some contributions, and a summary, in English); and S. Ostkamp, 'The World Upside Down. Secular Badges and the Iconography of the Late Medieval Period: Ordinary Pins with Multiple Meanings', *Journal of Archaeology in the Low Countries*, 1–2 (2009), pp. 108–25.

Passion and violence in Northern Renaissance art is discussed in A. Warburg, 'Durer and Italian Antiquity (1905)', in *The Renewal of Pagan Antiquity: Contributions to the Cultural History of the European Renaissance*, ed. K. W. Forster, trans. D. Britt (Los Angeles, 1999), pp. 553–60 and more recently in M. A. Hurtig, *Antiquity Unleashed: Aby Warburg, Durer and Mantegna* (London: Courtauld Gallery, 2013). Insanity and mental disturbance is covered in H. C. E. Middelfort, *A History of Madness in Sixteenth-Century Germany* (Stanford, 1999). Primitivism is well documented in T. Husband, *The Wild Man: Medieval Myth and Symbolism* (New York, 1980); R. Bernheimer, *Wildmen in the Middle Ages: A Study in Art, Sentiment and Demonology* (Cambridge, MA, 1952); and M. Mosely-Christian, 'From Page to Print: The Transformation of the "Wild Woman" in Early Modern Northern Engravings', *Word and Image*, 27:4 (2011), pp. 429–42. The works of Hieronymus Bosch are described and analysed in W. Bosing, *Hieronymus Bosch: Between Heaven and Hell* (Cologne, 2015) and *Hieronymus Bosch: Visions of Genius,* ed. M. Ilsink and J. Koldeweij (Brussels/s'-Hertogenbosch, 2016). For a recent, lavishly illustrated survey of another important theme, covering both Northern and Southern Europe, see *The Renaissance Nude*, ed. T. Kren, J. Burke, S. J. Campbell (Los Angeles, 2018).

CONCLUSION

For Durer's self-portraits, see M. Bailey, *Durer* (London, 1995); and for Van Eyck, L. Campbell, *National Gallery Catalogues: The Fifteenth-Century Netherlandish Schools* (London, 1998), esp. pp. 174–217; for Northern Renaissance painting and the Pre-Raphaelites, see *Reflections: Van Eyck and the Pre-Raphaelites,* ed. A. Smith, C. Bugler, S. Foister and A. Koopstra (London: National Gallery, 2017); and J. Trewherz, *Pre-Raphaelite Paintings from Manchester City Art Galleries* (Manchester, 1993).

Index